THE NATURE OF CREATION

Biblical Challenges in the Contemporary World

Editors: J.W. Rogerson, University of Sheffield,
and Mark Harris, University of Edinburgh

Current uses of the Bible in debates about issues such as human sexuality, war and wealth and poverty often amount to either a literalist concentration on a few selected texts, or an accommodation of the Bible to secular trends. The "Biblical Challenges" series aims to acquaint readers with the biblical material pertinent to particular issues, including that which causes difficulty or embarrassment in today's world, together with suggestions about how the Bible can nonetheless present a challenge in the contemporary age. The series seeks to open up a critical dialogue between the Bible and the chosen issue, which will lead to a dialogue between the biblical text and readers, challenging them to reflection and praxis. Each volume is designed with the needs of undergraduate and college students in mind, and can serve as a course book either for a complete unit or a component.

Published

The Nature of Creation: Examining the Bible and Science
Mark Harris

The Bible and the Environment: Towards a Critical Ecological Biblical Theology
David G. Horrell

Justice: The Biblical Challenge
Walter J. Houston

The City in Biblical Perspective
J. W. Rogerson and John Vincent

*According to the Scriptures? The Challenge of Using the Bible
in Social, Moral and Political Questions*
J. W. Rogerson

The Nature of Creation

Examining the Bible and Science

Mark Harris

ACUMEN

First published in 2013 by Acumen

Acumen Publishing Limited
4 Saddler Street
Durham
DH1 3NP

ISD, 70 Enterprise Drive
Bristol, CT 06010, USA

www.acumenpublishing.com

ISBN: 978-1-84465-724-7 (hardcover)
ISBN: 978-1-84465-725-4 (paperback)

British Library Cataloguing-in-Publication Data
A catalogue record for this book is available from the British Library.

Designed and typeset in Warnock Pro by JS Typesetting Ltd.
Printed and bound in the UK by CPI Group (UK) Ltd, Croydon, CR0 4YY.

CONTENTS

CONTENTS

PREFACE

Science has not done the Bible many favours lately: it is all too common to hear that it has disproved the Bible. In my opinion this misrepresents both. This book, which explores the relationship between the Bible and science by focusing on the theological theme of "creation", is my first attempt to suggest how the Bible might retain its normative status in a scientific world.

Like many who work in the science–religion field, I have come to it by a not altogether straightforward path, and I am sure that this colours my presentation of it. But then the subject is not altogether straightforward either. After a background of many years' research experience in experimental physics, I followed a calling to ordained ministry in the Church of England by undergoing theological training. Discovering that it was every bit as enlivening as physics, I followed this with a number of years' teaching biblical studies in universities. If this has left me with a somewhat Jekyll and Hyde personality – I sometimes approach science as if it were a religious epiphany (Chapter 10), and the Bible as though it were experimental data (Chapter 1) – I hope that I am no more eccentric or eclectic than many of my peers in the science–religion field. What is unusual, I know, is my interest in the Bible. But it is my conviction that it has been neglected for too long in this field, and left to the attention of those who have shown little interest in revealing its riches to mainstream science and critical theology. I speak, of course, of Creationism and Christian fundamentalism, which have so successfully claimed the Bible as their sovereign territory when science is in view, that the rest of us often judge it prudent to leave well enough alone. This book is the beginning of my attempt to regain for those who stand outside the fundamentalist camp the scriptural territory which has been so fundamental for two thousand years, namely the Bible's texts of creation.

I owe many favours to many people for the time and space it has taken to write this book. I received valuable inspiration from my fellow members in the Bible and Society Group, especially John Rogerson, Walter Houston, Dagmar Winter, John Vincent and Stephen Barton, the latter of whom encouraged me robustly to take a much more unashamedly theological view than I was originally willing to take. The book is hopefully more honest for his input, even if it does thereby stray from the conventional paths of biblical scholarship even more than would otherwise have been the case. Thanks go to John Rogerson, for invaluable comments on an early draft, to my wife Harriet, who similarly read the entire manuscript in various rough drafts, and to Tristan Palmer, who has been a supportive and encouraging editor. But it is to my children, Ben, Isaac, Reuben and Susanna, that I owe my greatest thanks, for their forbearance. I wrote the first few thousand words just days before the birth of my daughter Susanna. She was two years old before I was able to write the next few thousand, and now she is six. I can think of no better reason to delay the writing of a book, and it is to her and her three brothers that I dedicate it in the hope that, by the time they are old enough to understand it, we will have moved on to a clearer understanding of the Bible's role in providing the data of faith.

Bible quotations are taken from the NRSV. I have substituted my own translations in some sections for particular emphasis; these are shown in italics.

ABBREVIATIONS

ANE   Ancient Near East(ern)
ET   English translation
J   The second Genesis creation account (Genesis 2:4b–3:24)
KJB   King James Bible (Authorized Version)
NJB   New Jerusalem Bible
NRSV New Revised Standard Version
P   The first Genesis creation account (Genesis 1:1–2:4a)

Chapter 1

INTRODUCTION

SCIENCE AND RELIGION: A CONFLICT OR A NEGLECT?

The relationship between modern science and religious belief has become one of the most debated matters of our time. It is impossible not to hold an opinion on it. While there are many who claim that science has made religious belief redundant, there are at least as many who insist that faith is alive and well.

At the same time, a flourishing academic discipline has grown up which has attempted to find a way forward by building bridges. This field – "science and religion", or "theology and science" – has tended to concentrate on *historical* discussions of how the two areas have interacted in the past, and on *philosophical* investigations which seek understanding of how they might mutually benefit each other now. In this, history and philosophy have taken mediatorial roles between science and theology. But this has meant that the dialogue between science and religion has operated at a "meta" level, at least one remove from the basic data and core observations which underlie them. Discussion has therefore largely been about how to relate higher-level scientific and religious interpretations to each other, not about the core data and *their* interpretation. Much of the science–religion dialogue has taken place in the Western world, where the "religion" half of the pairing has been Christianity. In this case, the core data are defined to a large extent by a set of scriptures, the Bible. It is this foundational book above all which has suffered from a general lack of engagement in the science–religion dialogue.

Ironically, part of the reason for this relative neglect of the Bible stems from Creationism, which has tended to insist that the Bible's creation texts – those most relevant to much of the science–religion dialogue – should be read in the light of a literalist hermeneutic. For those who adhere to its most rigid form – "young earth" Creationism – this has meant the rejection (or revision) of large swathes of modern science in order to maintain

1

belief that the earth was created over six literal days some scant thousands of years ago. As a result, the debate has tended to take place on scientific grounds, focusing on the interpretation of scientific data and theories rather than the interpretation of Scripture. In this, the real agenda has been missed: namely the fundamentalist conviction that the Bible is "inerrant", and transcends all considerations of science and history (McCalla 2006: 199). And such has been the ferocity of the debate, especially in North America, that the science–religion dialogue has tended largely to avoid the key scriptural areas of contention, and to engage with creation at a more philosophical level instead, where, it is believed by many mainstream scholars, the real issues of interest lie in any case. This has meant that the many subtle and complex depths in the texts unearthed by critical biblical scholarship have gone largely unnoticed, or have been obscured by endless debates over questions such as whether Adam and Eve really existed (Chapter 7).

It is the aim of this book to engage with the apparent conflict between science and religion by addressing the very real neglect of the Bible by the science–religion field. Some recent studies by biblical scholars have paved the way. There has been a considerable broadening in our understanding of Old Testament theologies of creation (Fretheim 2005), and in the ways in which Old Testament creation texts may be appropriated imaginatively in the modern scientific worldview (W. P. Brown 2010). This present book brings two new perspectives. First, it considers the impact of science on critical interpretation of the *whole* Christian Bible, so that important discussions in the science–religion field are brought into view, such as the role of Christ in creation. Second, it takes an overarching *theological* perspective: God as Trinity is seen ultimately to provide the bridge between critical biblical scholarship and science. This does, of course, mean covering a lot of ground in terms of both biblical scholarship and Christian theology, not to mention science. The scope of this project therefore means that we will at times pass all too quickly over some tortuous issues, especially in biblical interpretation. This is not so much because we are attempting to provide an overview of an already existing field of scholarship, but are instead seeking to set up the parameters for a new one.

It is not to be expected that this approach will single-handedly change the popular perception that science and religion are at war with each other. And neither will it resolve the Creationist debate. What is to be hoped rather is that it will reveal something of the deeper levels underlying the debates, demonstrating at a more fundamental level what it is that science and religion can share through their views of creation, and how they differ and *ought* to differ.

THE QUESTION OF REALITY

Much of the perceived conflict between science and religion arises over competing claims regarding what is said to constitute reality. Biblical criticism has traditionally seen itself as "scientific" in its methodology, seeking to uncover something of the *historical* reality underlying biblical texts, without necessarily making live religious claims. Such claims are the task of theology instead, which, in its aim to uncover *divine* realities and their role in creation, impinges more directly on the natural sciences. Biblical study does not escape though, since theology has a particular interest in the historical realities underlying biblical texts, and the extent to which these realities informed the testimonies of the original communities of faith. Their testimonies – part of the *Holy* Bible – are believed by the Christian Church to be sanctified: vehicles of divine revelation. Their testimonies are foundational and authoritative; above all they point to the one reality which Christian theology wishes to uncover and apprehend.

Walter Brueggemann has put this provocatively: "The God of the Bible is not 'somewhere else', but is given only in, with, and under the text itself" (Brueggemann 1997: 19). This is not to say that there is no divine reality outside of the text, nor that the text is a "sacrament". And neither is it a statement of the Reformation principle that salvific knowledge can only be found in the pages of Scripture (*sola scriptura*). Rather, our "objective" access to the God of the Bible is through the hermeneutical process of interpreting and re-interpreting the text in the light of the Church's tradition, namely theological interpretation. A sceptic might construe this as making God out to be a psychological or rhetorical construct, but religious claims have always been vulnerable to such reductionism, by their very nature.

This is no mere academic point. Our understanding of who God is will affect our understanding of what creation is, as the sphere of God's creative activity. The same is true in reverse. And in Christianity the Bible has always been one of the principal points of access to the Creator–creation relationship. As we investigate the various biblical creation texts we shall see repeatedly that to speak of "creation" is immediately to suggest a point of origin – a Creator – and a relationship between creation and Creator. We shall also see that the biblical texts provide many different perspectives on that relationship.

THE CHRISTIAN DOCTRINE OF CREATION

Before the development of modern science there had been a long-standing consensus in Western Christian culture on the way the natural world was to be viewed, based in the main upon the Bible's creation texts. God was seen as central to the natural world, both in its original making and in its ongoing existence. The consensus doctrine of creation can be summarized in a number of simple statements:

- When God created the world, God made it *ex nihilo*; that is, God made the world "from nothing": God is therefore not dependent upon the world, nor is God necessarily a part of it.
- On the other hand, since the world was made from nothing by God, it is *wholly* dependent (contingent) upon God and not upon any other being or thing.
- God is therefore both the initial creator of the world, and also its continuing sustainer.
- God created the world as good; it reflects God's nature as its maker.
- Nevertheless, evil came to be present in the world, although it did not derive from God.
- In creating and sustaining the world, God has also made provision for its end, when there will be a "new heaven and a new earth".
- In the meantime, God supports and cares for the life of the created world through "providence": special divine actions of guidance and miracles performed in historical time.

This brief summary represents the widespread Christian view of the natural world which held roughly up until the last few centuries. But since then, many of the cultural, aesthetic and intellectual values that characterized pre-modern times have been questioned and steadily eroded. More to the point, advances in understanding the natural world scientifically have been immense, steadily pushing theology out of territory over which it had once ruled supreme. Many features of the world which once could only be explained by invoking God now have a scientific explanation.

THE RISE OF SCIENCE AND THE FALL OF RELIGION

The change in intellectual perspective is usually traced back to the seventeenth century, and the Enlightenment of the eighteenth century. This is said to be the beginning of the "modern" era, when a new confidence gradually emerged in the power of rational thought and scientific procedure to derive objective, universal truth. We might associate this revolution with such thinkers as Descartes and Kant, but these largely philosophical figures were at least partly building on foundations laid by experimental scientists. The astronomical discoveries of Copernicus (1473–1543), Kepler (1571–1630) and Galileo (1564–1642) were largely ignored or suppressed in their lifetimes, but their significance gradually gathered momentum, and widely called into question the common logic that the earth (and therefore humankind) was at the centre of the known universe, and that the heavens were the stairway to God.

The religious consequences of the scientific discoveries set out in Newton's *Principia* (1687) were especially profound. As they were gradually debated and assimilated into culture, these discoveries changed the way the creator God was viewed in relation to creation. Although Newton had understood his work as being fully consonant with theology, the completeness of his system had the inevitable effect of forcing God to the margins. If the natural world could be explained rationally without calling on divine intervention, then perhaps God was not so closely involved after all. Certainly, by the time of Laplace, a century after Newton, the natural world could be seen to exist without the need to invoke God as an explanation or cause (Brooke 1996: 18).

As well as affecting how God's relationship with the world was construed, these developments had a profound influence upon Christian doctrine. The doctrine of the incarnation – that in Jesus of Nazareth, both fully human and fully divine natures co-exist – was correspondingly weakened for many, and likewise the doctrine of the Trinity – that God consists and co-exists in three persons – Father, Son and Holy Spirit. Unitarianism (the idea that only the Father is fully divine) emerged as a recognized religious option, as did deism – the belief that God does not intervene in the world after its creation, and therefore that reason (rather than belief in revelation or miracle) should be the basis for faith (McGrath [2002] 2006a: 181–4). Deism arose in Britain in the seventeenth and eighteenth centuries, influenced strongly by the burgeoning belief that the universe was governed and determined by physical "laws". Although deism has fared less well historically since the eighteenth century, the ideas behind it have been influential in modern religious thought, as we shall discuss at various stages throughout this book.

These religious developments have led to the logical conclusion for many that, not only is God's involvement in the world to be doubted, but also God's basic existence. And so atheism has gone from being viewed as intellectually and morally reprehensible in previous centuries to a viewpoint which receives widespread interest and acceptance, especially in the guise of the "New Atheism".

It is highly relevant that many people in the Western world today cite natural disasters, famine and disease as strong reasons for not believing in God. The suggestion is that, ironically, God ought to be a strongly interventionist God of the traditional Judaeo-Christian variety in order to be believed – one who works salvation directly in the world. But occurrences of disaster and suffering, which once would have been interpreted in the traditional Judaeo-Christian paradigm as signs of divine judgement, are now taken as evidence of God's lack of existence. In such instances, atheism is implicitly seen to occupy the moral high ground, while traditional theistic belief must defend itself.

And yet, there have always been those who have pointed to the beauty and order of the natural world as evidence of a divine Creator: the "argument from design". For many who work in the physical sciences especially, there is deep appeal in the symmetry and elegance of the mathematical laws which appear to underpin the universe. As the physicist John Barrow explained in an interview:

> The laws [of nature] are highly mathematical but very mysterious. You cannot see or touch them. There are mysterious symmetries in the universe. It is no coincidence that biologists like [Richard] Dawkins feel very uncomfortable with religion and unanswered questions because they are dealing with the messy complexities of nature ... There is a real cultural difference between biologists and physicists.   (Garner 2009: 33)

This speaks of a difference in outlook between the physical and biological sciences which should not be brushed aside. Science is by no means a united enterprise in its attitude towards religion, and it is often noted that biologists appear to be more sceptical than physicists. As the biochemist Arthur Peacocke (1996a: 4) puts it, "To this day it is still not regarded as quite professionally respectable for a biologist to admit to being a Christian."

However, there are further complexities, and it is too glib to say that physicists have one approach to religion and biologists another. For one thing, many physicists are persuaded by the beauty and order of the natural world to make exactly the *opposite* point of the argument from design, feeling that science has been so successful in explaining the natural world that there is no point in calling upon a Creator. This stance was stated eloquently in Carl Sagan's introduction to Stephen Hawking's bestseller *A Brief History of Time*:

> This is also a book about God ... or perhaps about the absence of God. The word God fills these pages. Hawking embarks on a quest to answer Einstein's famous question about whether God had any choice in creating the universe. Hawking is attempting, as he explicitly states, to understand the mind of God. And this makes all the more unexpected the conclusion of the effort, at least so far: a universe with no edge in space, no beginning or end in time, and nothing for a Creator to do. (Hawking 1988: x)

Radical statements such as this have caught the popular imagination, reinforcing the (already widespread) perception that science has superseded religion, or, at best, is at odds with it. However, many scientists and theologians have argued that this is a misunderstanding, and that actually the picture is considerably more complex – that science and theology are not necessarily in conflict with one another because there are other valid ways of looking at their relationship. Ian Barbour sees four, each of which puts the relationship in a progressively more positive light (Barbour 1997: 77–105). First, there is the widespread and popular notion that they are said to be in *conflict* with each other. However, second, they may instead be said to operate in entirely *independent* ways to each other: they use contrasting methods and differing languages to speak of different kinds of reality. Third, science and religion may be said to be in *dialogue* with each other: they may benefit from both their differences and their similarities, so that each informs the other. The fourth approach sees an even more optimistic relationship between science and religion, suggesting that they might *integrate* with each other, perhaps even converging to each other's mutual advantage. The holistic studies of Teilhard de Chardin are a case in point of this approach, seeing the risen Christ as the goal of biological evolution (Chapter 8).

However, many scholars believe that the relationship between science and religion is considerably more complex than any one of these four models might indicate, and that it is too simplistic to isolate any one of them as the "answer". The relationship is highly dependent (for one thing) on which scientific questions and which religious questions are being asked. As a result, not only has the relationship between science and religion changed dramatically through history, it is of such complexity that we do not even find consistency in individual thinkers (Brooke 1991: 42).

THE BIBLE AND HISTORY

And what of the Bible? Before the Enlightenment, and the world-shattering developments of geology and evolutionary biology in the nineteenth century, the Bible's status as an unimpeachable record of religious truths was matched by its authority as a reliable source of *historical* truths. The dates of creation and the flood published by James Ussher in 1648 are often cited as prime examples of this way of thinking. By comparing various genealogical lists and dates given in the Bible, and comparing them with other ANE records, Ussher calculated that creation occurred in the evening of Saturday 22 October 4004 BCE, and the flood on Sunday 7 December 2349 BCE (Cohn 1996: 95–6).

Ussher's confidence in the precision of the biblical record is often treated with astonishment these days (although note that his dates are still held with respect by many young-earth Creationists). But in his day, Ussher's approach was typical of the high degree of authority which was accorded to the Bible as an accurate source of history, and others before him had attempted to calculate the age of the world from biblical data in a similar way. The singular attention given to Ussher's calculation came about largely because his dates were printed in editions of the King James Bible in the eighteenth century, effectively "setting them in stone". But by the beginning of the nineteenth century, with the birth of the new science of geology, serious doubts were being cast on Ussher's dates, and it was becoming clear that the earth was vastly older.

At the same time, new kinds of historical questions were being asked of much of the biblical text. The idea that we might need a specialized way of reading the Bible, a "critical" method, with its own conventions, aims and objectives, is not new; Philo and Origen, to name but two, pioneered one particular methodology (allegorical exegesis) in the first centuries CE. But to many biblical scholars of these past few hundred years, the idea of "biblical criticism" has been virtually synonymous with "historical criticism", an intellectually rigorous method of studying the biblical text which highlights historical enquiry as the most appropriate lens through which to view and understand it. In this, the historical-critical method makes the straightforward assertion that, since the text arose in particular historical contexts very different from our own, interpretation must be informed by as full an understanding as possible of these contexts. In its most confident formulations, the method goes beyond this, contending that before we can begin to grasp the theological meaning of the text, we must first appreciate its historical setting and its author's original intentions. Biblical scholarship in the modern era has, therefore, been dominated by historical questions.

One of its most famous examples (and with special relevance for this book) is the "Documentary Hypothesis". Both Witter in 1711 and Astruc in 1753 noticed independently that the Pentateuch appeared to consist of several parallel sources ("documents") woven together. In Genesis and Exodus especially, there are many repetitions and double accounts of substantially the same material, but often contradicting each other. For instance, the Flood story of Genesis 6–9 appears to be made up of two sources edited together, which disagree on a number of details, such as the number of animals taken into the ark. These sources also use different terminology. Perhaps the most obvious instance comes in the two creation accounts in Genesis 1–2: in addition to many differences in style and content, the first creation account (Gen. 1–2:4a) uses the Hebrew name *Elohim* exclusively for God, while the second (Gen. 2:4b-25) uses *YHWH Elohim*. Scholars therefore attributed these to two different sources, known as the "Priestly" and "Yahwist" sources, respectively. In time, four sources came to be detected within the text of the Pentateuch: J (the "Yahwist" source), E ("Elohist"), D ("Deuteronomist") and P ("Priestly"). The definitive history behind these four sources was reconstructed by Wellhausen in 1878, and still informs many modern historical studies of the Pentateuch, although it has been endlessly debated and revised, and even rejected outright by some.

But the field of biblical studies has come a long way since Wellhausen. In addition to source criticism, other forms of historical criticism have grown up, which focus on the *form* (i.e. genre) of the literature which makes up the Bible, the *redaction* (i.e. editorial) tendencies of the scribes and editors who put it together, as well as their *social* and *political* contexts. All of these seek to uncover something of what the texts *originally* meant to say when they first came into being, working on the premise that *the original histori-cal meaning is the most authentic meaning*, which should set the bounda-ries for further interpretations. However, the rise of postmodernism since the 1970s has led to some disillusionment with the quest for the original meaning – a "crisis of objectivity" – and many alternative kinds of criticism have proliferated instead, which do not have a primarily historical inten-tion. A number are drawn from literary theory, such as reader-response criticism, rhetorical criticism and narrative criticism. But at the same time, more explicitly theological forms have developed (e.g. canonical criticism), together with types of criticism motivated by political and social concerns, especially those drawn from feminist and liberation perspectives. While this change of focus has inevitably moderated some of the more confident claims for the historical method made by scholars in the past, it has also had the effect that many fresh riches and new perspectives are being dis-covered in the Bible's texts. The historical perspective still remains central though, if more cautious than it once was. And it performs a highly valu-able task in maintaining the historical witness of this foundational docu-ment to a world which has often bent and shaped it to its own end:

> the Church needs on occasion to hear the biblical message in all its strangeness, its cutting edge not blunted by the familiarity of hallowed religious expectations. A historical scholarship that stands at one remove from the Church's daily converse with its scripture fulfils a valuable function.
> (Morgan with Barton 1988: 179)

This is a point of prime importance for this book. If the science–reli-gion dialogue has proceeded with little engagement so far with Scripture then that is perhaps because Scripture's cutting edge has not been brought to bear with sufficient accuracy (Hebrews 4:12). This is why this book attempts a sustained historical investigation of what the creation texts of the Bible have to say, and how this relates to modern science, in the hope that it might help to re-inform and to re-align.

CREATION IN THE BIBLE

The first few chapters of the Bible (Genesis 1–3) are justifiably memorable, telling the story of the creation of the world in resonant prose, from the beginnings of time ("In the beginning") to the story of the first humans and their shortcomings. When we speak of creation and the Bible, it is invariably these chapters which come to mind. However, there is a great wealth of additional creation material spread throughout the Bible, much of which does not show awareness of this initial section. For instance, some of the psalms and prophets speak about creation in terms of a mythological battle between God and the sea, while the book of Proverbs speaks of creation through the personified divine figure of Wisdom. Therefore, one of the first points that should be made in approaching the Bible's creation texts is that there is no single theological understanding but a diversity, and it is not clear that this diversity can (or should) be collapsed into a single, harmonized unity. In any case, it is not even as if Genesis 1–3 presents a uniform picture. As we pointed out in the previous section, Genesis 1–3 contains at least two distinct creation traditions, probably from different stages in Israel's history, and representing different theological presuppositions. In short, the Bible holds several understandings of creation in tension.

A second, related, point to make about the Bible's creation material is that, while it is theological, it cannot be seen as a series of easily digestible metaphysical propositions like the Christian doctrine of creation (see § "The Christian doctrine of creation", above). Rather, it is a diverse variety of narrative and poetic themes which do not always relate closely to each other. Moreover, while some of these creation themes crop up repeatedly in the Bible, others appear very seldom. Somewhat counter-intuitively, much of the material in the celebrated creation stories of Genesis falls into the latter category.

A third, equally important point is that this diverse body of material (what we will refer to as "the creation motif"; see § "Creation and narrative", in Chapter 4) is central to everything the Bible has to say about who God is. It is not easily separable from other theological issues such as redemption, and neither should it be. We can see this from the simple fact that the Bible opens with an account of one creation (Gen. 1) and closes with another, which is only a view of redemption because it is of the *new* creation (Rev. 21–22). In terms of the Christian Bible's canonical shape, then, creation is the first and the last theological statement to be made, and it is theologically foundational; it opens and closes all other statements about God which can be made. It is upon this foundational image of God as Creator that the Bible's theologies of redemption, ethics and eschatology are built. Therefore, as we look at the creation material in this book, and at the ways in which it has been construed scientifically, we shall see again and again that it is best interpreted in terms of what we learn about God rather than in terms of what we learn about the world.

But having said this, modern science has made all the difference to reading the creation texts. While the Bible's creation material shows evidence of what we might call scientific thinking (a cosmology, together with mentions of structures and mechanisms in nature), it is mostly worlds away from the scientific thinking of our time. Young-earth Creationists resolve this dilemma by rejecting modern science and using a literal reading of Genesis 1–3 to inform their view of the origins of the world. And this is a popular approach to origins, especially in the United States. According to Lamoureux (2008: 22), perhaps as many as sixty per cent of American adults believe that the world was created in six days and that Genesis 1 is "literally true, meaning that it happened that way word-for-word". Of course, many other Christians take a looser, more metaphorical view of Genesis 1–3, preferring to let modern science inform their view of the physical origins of the world. But the sensitivity of this issue has meant that it has become the central interpretative question in Genesis 1–3 for millions of Christians and millions of Atheists alike, and so is argued endlessly. If there are notable apologies written from a conservative Christian perspective which attempt to resolve the issue, then there are also ridiculing attacks by New Atheists who are mystified that anyone would take an ancient religious text so seriously that they might question the findings of modern science on its basis. Barton and Wilkinson have highlighted the problems well:

> From six-day creationism to Richard Dawkins's *The God Delusion*, the public dialogue on science and religion either uses the early chapters of Genesis in a naïve and simplistic way or rejects their relevance to contemporary questions. This is reinforced by the myth that Darwin undermined any possibility of an intelligent reading of Genesis 1, and, from that point on, most Christian theology lost confidence in these texts.
> (Barton & Wilkinson 2009: xi)

Lost confidence indeed: those Christians who prefer to steer clear of this debate usually resort to a more poetic/metaphorical reading of Genesis 1–3, which avoids thinking of the text in scientific/concrete terms at all. But we shall see that this overlooks important points about what the author was trying to achieve. In other words, although the Creationist debate has achieved little but a polarization of opinions, we will find that we do indeed need to engage with both modern and ancient scientific ideas in order to appreciate these biblical texts. But we shall also find that we quickly move beyond scientific ideas. For instance, Genesis 1 appears to describe something like a developmental picture of beginnings, which has been compared with modern evolutionary ideas, yet the text is concerned with illustrating how creation is *ordered* by God in moral and aesthetic terms. God frequently sees that what has been made is "good" (Gen. 1:4, 10, 12, 18, 21, 25, 31). This is a statement of approval and satisfaction, a value judgement more than a scientific statement. And if we look at the creation imagery more widely in the Bible, we find that it points repeatedly to moral, aesthetic and spiritual values over anything we might construe as "scientific". We find that it demonstrates God's fruitfulness, constancy and faithfulness to the world. Similar qualities are therefore enjoined upon humankind's relationship to the world. Humans are set in the widest possible environment, and are instructed to work and to care for it. In this way they will reap its rewards and take delight in it in something of the way that God does. Seen from this angle, the Bible made an important ecological challenge to humankind long before our modern over-exploitation of the natural world made its re-discovery necessary.

"CREATION" IN THE LIGHT OF "SCIENCE"

It is common in religious circles to refer to the whole of the world – not just the earth but the whole universe – as "creation", implying the existence of a "creator". But scientists, even those of a religious persuasion, tend to avoid using such terminology in scientific contexts. The modern natural sciences, by definition, can say nothing one way or another about the possibility of a creator, a *super*-natural being. They assume that there are other, mundane ways of explaining the world. And in this they have been enormously successful, which has given the New Atheists an argument against God's existence: if the world can be explained without the need for God, then that might suggest there is no God. It is not often acknowledged, or perhaps even realized, but this argument is logically fallacious – the natural sciences cannot discern the possibility or impossibility of the supernatural by definition; they have no means to do so. This instead is the task of theology, of what has in past times been referred to as "the queen of the sciences".

No longer, though. Westermann (1974) has made some important criticisms of theology, suggesting that it has suffered in relation to science because it put forward an inadequate understanding of the biblical creation material at the Reformation. This was because the key theological issues under debate concerned *salvation* rather than creation, leaving the way open for science to encroach steadily upon theology's territory while its back was, as it were, turned. Pre-occupied with the salvific relationship between God and humankind, theology has neglected its foundational biblical texts which cast a much wider sweep, seeing the relationship in terms of the Creator and all of creation. Hence, if God's dealings with the world are seen myopically, in terms of forgiveness of human sin or justification, then it is only in this context that God deals with the world, and vice versa. "This means that God is not concerned with a worm being trodden to the earth or with the appearance of a new star in the Milky Way" (*ibid.*: 3–4).

It is the primary aim of this book to present a theological analysis of the Bible's creation material in terms which take the wider perspective, and therefore engage with modern science. In that sense, this book is part of a wider trend in contemporary theological publishing to develop modern theologies of creation, partly motivated by our increased sensitivity to environmental and ecological issues. It is perhaps too much to hope that Westermann's complaints might be redressed by this exercise, but it is worth considering what might be achieved by it. Certainly, one of the most frequent objections to religious belief in a creator is that the biblical stories of creation are implausible, because they have been superseded by science. And young-earth Creationism serves to drive the wedge between theology and science even deeper. An attempt like this one, then, which looks at the creation texts at a deeper level than the extent to which they agree with modern science, might help to pull the wedge back out.

Indeed, it might do more. Modern science has become so specialized and so fragmented that, although it is common to speak of "science" as a unified entity, and one which has overtaken theology to boot, yet no scientist is capable of apprehending the *entire* scientific reality of the world on anything but a superficial level. In other words, we might become experts in one branch of science, but we will never master it in its entirety. If "science" has become the intellectual framework by which we understand the world, then it is becoming an ever more bewildering and incomprehensible framework. But consider this: if it was the case for the ancient biblical authors that the religious concept of "creation" gave meaning and understanding to an otherwise bewildering and incomprehensible reality, then it was also the case that it provided a graspable, overarching and unified framework in which to apprehend that reality. Westermann (1974: 36–7) makes the point that it might do so again: the religious concept of "creation" might once again provide the most appropriate framework for situating the vast complexities of the natural sciences. But we must begin with the Bible's creation texts, and work towards a theology of science, for which this book provides a possible starting point (Chapter 10).

This is not to make theology queen of the sciences once again in any kind of pre-modern sense. Clearly, the creation material of the Bible cannot regain its central place by turning the clock back. Rather, creation must be seen through the insights of modern science and modern biblical scholarship together, and it must be seen theologically. In this way, we argue, science and biblical studies can be brought together to allow the living God to speak into our critical and modernist framework.

In this book, after looking briefly at some of the relevant scientific ideas (Chapter 2), we shall turn to the Genesis creation texts (Chapter 3), and other elements in the Bible's creation motif (Chapter 4), making sure that the New Testament is thoroughly represented. We shall then construct a scientific framework in which to understand this material, emphasizing distinctions and parallels between ancient and modern ways of thinking (Chapter 5). This will be used to explore how the biblical creation motif sets up the relationship between Creator and creation (Chapter 6), before we examine biblical perspectives on some of the most difficult areas of controversy between science and theology, especially evolution (Chapter 7), the problem of evil (Chapter 8) and the far future (Chapter 9). Chapter 10 will not summarize so much as draw the various elements of the argument together, to present a biblical model for the nature of creation.

Chapter 2

CREATION ACCORDING TO MODERN SCIENCE

Space, time and matter

Our attitudes towards space and time are deeply ingrained, and we rarely question them. St Augustine famously noted in his *Confessions* that, in our everyday conversation, no word is more familiar or more readily understood than that of "time". But if we ask ourselves what is "time", we quickly find ourselves baffled. "I know well enough what it is, provided that nobody asks me", says Augustine (*Confessions* XI: 14). And when he tries to define time, he does so in terms of events and happenings relative to himself: "I can confidently say that I know that if nothing passed, there would be no past time; if nothing were going to happen, there would be no future time; and if nothing were, there would be no present time." This is significant, because Augustine has little of the sense of *absolute* time as a universal entity, an idea which is perhaps more familiar to us as a result of Newton.

For Newton, both space and time were absolute and independent of any local frame of reference. They were universal, and in this way Newton was able to define motion as the movement of an object relative to a fixed frame of reference, of both space and time. Space and time effectively became a fixed matrix in which all events and beings could be seen to exist, move and operate. Newton did not, however, go so far as to think of space and time as inseparably connected into one entity, "spacetime". That came later with Einstein, whose general theory of relativity revolutionized the physics of space and time. But for Newton, the over-arching universality of his reference frames of space and time could not but take on almost divine attributes. This was the criticism of one of Newton's contemporaries: Bishop Berkeley (1685–1753) complained that Newton had conceived of space as unchangeable, infinite and eternal; what then is there to stop it from being God? Either God is reduced to space, or space is exalted to God

(Buckley 1987: 118). Newton's response pointed out that space is not a thing as such, and does not exist by itself, but is a consequence of God, emanating from God's existence everywhere. For a being to exist, there must be space, and so if God is said to be present at all times and all places in the world, then there must be everlasting space everywhere (*ibid.*: 137–8). This means that time and space are not *things* as such in Newton's thinking – either things to be created or divine with their own existence – but rather they are *effects*, outflowings of God's own existence. This has important implications for Newton's understanding of God, who is seen as the being whose own existence and omnipresence makes all existence and movement possible. Indeed, Newton saw his famous development of the law of gravitation as a description of divine power: objects are not attracted to each other by any innate force of their own, but by God's will.

One further consequence of Newton's understanding of space and time is that they are linear. In other words, they progress in ways which are steady, continuous and regular, and will always do so; there are no jumps, lumps, cycles or local irregularities. Theologically, such a picture reflects a dependable and predictable God, a God of law and regularity. It is perhaps no surprise that within this worldview the idea that there are fixed and universal "laws of nature" might take hold so firmly, as we shall discuss shortly.

Einstein's development of relativity in the early part of the twentieth century, on the other hand, put forward a completely different perspective. For Einstein, space and time are no longer absolute, because it is the speed of light which becomes the new absolute reference point. Measurements of space and time become relative to the observer making the measurement, and there is no sense in which they are experienced alike universally. What is more, space and time become related to each other in a four-dimensional entity called "spacetime", but they are also related to matter itself. Space and time can therefore hardly be said to be independent reference frames. And neither are they linear, since matter causes spacetime to curve, which in turn causes the trajectories of moving objects to curve. This is how Einstein incorporated gravity into his general theory of relativity – gravity is no longer a force like others, but a consequence of the fact that spacetime is curved according to the distribution of matter and energy in it. Furthermore, not only does spacetime curve, but it possesses singularities under certain conditions, such as in the initial singularity of the Big Bang, beyond which we are unable to see. Spacetime is clearly no longer fixed and absolute in the way it was for Newton.

Relativity brings many challenges to our "common sense" view of the world, not least our understanding of time. In particular, our concept of "now", such an important part of our common human experience on earth, is not a true scientific property of the world, because it is dependent on the frame of reference of the observer. Effectively, our experience of the present becomes illusory in the relativistic worldview. For this reason, it has been suggested that the concept of "block time" offers a more useful view, where all of time from beginning to end is seen as existing together "all at once". This arises from the proposition that if there were no minds such as ours to distinguish past, present and future, there would simply be the four-dimensional spacetime universe existing as a single entity. If so, our more familiar concept of "flowing time", where there is a past which grows linearly as we move into the open future, is a subjective illusion of our human consciousness (Copan & Craig 2004: 160–61; Ward 2008: 120).

All of this is theologically relevant, and it has been argued that God's experience of the universe is essentially a "block" view, perceiving it all simultaneously. Such an approach has some merit (Polkinghorne 2011: 62–5), because it resolves paradoxes that arise in our talk of God and time (Chapter 5).

As well as relativistic physics, the early twentieth century saw the development of another new scientific paradigm which shook accepted ideas of reality: quantum mechanics. The quantum view of the world arose from the realization that basic physical entities at the atomic and sub-atomic level, such as electrons or photons, can be described mathematically either as waves or as particles, depending on the kind of experiment being done. For example, electrons can be diffracted very much as ocean waves passing through a narrow harbour mouth are diffracted to fan out and fill the whole harbour. But they can also be scattered, like billiard balls bouncing off each other. It all depends on the type of measurement which you perform. If you look at an electron as if it is a wave, you will see wave properties; if you look at it as if it is a particle, you will see particle properties. But both of these categories – wave and particle – ought to be mutually exclusive according to the classical physics of Newton and his successors. This realization that matter on its most basic level does not behave classically led to the development of the quantum view of the world, summarized succinctly by Heisenberg's uncertainty principle – if we try to measure certain properties of a quantum object (such as an electron) ever more precisely we find that other properties become ever more uncertain. In short, the electron defies precise description in classical terms. This has led physicists to speak sometimes of the "fuzzy" and imprecise nature of the quantum world. It is unclear whether such language is fair, given that the quantum world can be described well mathematically. But the problems come when we try to understand it in the simple conceptual pictures of classical physics of our everyday world (e.g. waves or particles, but not both). This difficulty has led to many philosophical discussions and unanswered questions about the nature of reality, and about our ability to understand it in terms which make conceptual sense to us. Even now, a century since the first development of quantum mechanics, it is still unclear whether we can even speak of such a thing as "objective reality" when we are considering quantum entities such as electrons. One of the best-known attempts to answer this question – the "Copenhagen" interpretation – has highlighted the observer's role in affecting the outcome of an observation at the quantum level, and so has denied our ability even to speak of an independent reality as such:

> In the experiments about atomic events we have to do with things and facts, with phenomena that are just as real as any phenomena in daily life. But the atoms or the elementary particles themselves are not as real; they form a world of potentialities or possibilities rather than one of things or facts.
>
> (Heisenberg 1989: 174)

Quite simply, in this view of the quantum world we have observations and measurements, and we have interpretations of them, but it is not clear that we have concrete and objective "things" as such.

There are, however, other interpretations of quantum mechanics besides the Copenhagen interpretation. Perhaps the best-known is the many-worlds interpretation. Rather than suggesting that the underlying quantum reality is elusive, and perhaps not even a concrete objective "reality" as such, the many-worlds interpretation attempts to explain the puzzles by postulating the existence of many worlds, rather like the idea of parallel universes. When a quantum event occurs, say the observation of an electron behaving like a wave, then there exists another universe where it behaves as a particle. The upshot is that in this interpretation of quantum mechanics there is a rapidly proliferating tree of universes as each quantum eventuality unfolds. It hardly needs pointing out the extreme speculation involved in such an idea. And yet such is the strangeness of the quantum world that many scientists are willing to countenance such ideas in an attempt to make some sense of it. If the Copenhagen interpretation calls into doubt basic scientific notions like reality, causality and determinism, the many-worlds interpretation and others like it are able to rescue them, albeit at the price of introducing many more unknowns in the shape of multiple universes. Indeed, the many-worlds interpretation is related to an important interpretative option in modern cosmological research into the origins of our universe, where additional universes are postulated as existing alongside our own, a grand ensemble known as the "multiverse". It has not escaped the attention of theologians that such ideas are every bit as speculative and experimentally untestable as anything in theology, and it is not clear how they might even count as scientific propositions as such; in other words, they require a great deal of faith (e.g. Ellis 2008). There is more in common with modern physics and theology than is often realized.

The idea of the multiverse has also been one of the main answers to the challenge posed by the so-called "anthropic principle". As thinking on the

evolution of the universe has developed it has been noticed that, if fundamental physical constants such as the speed of light and the charge of the
electron were slightly different, then the kind of universe we exist in, with
a planet like ours – fertile and inhabitable – could not have existed. In
other words, the physical constants appear to be just right for us to exist –
"finely tuned". To theists this "anthropic principle" suggests the existence of
a Creator who tuned the physical constants so that this kind of planet and
this kind of life would be precisely the outcome. Those who are unwilling to
accept such an explanation must find another that does not involve a divine
Creator. The main alternative is to say that there are many universes, with
different values of the physical constants, and we just happen to be in the
one where they are just right for life. There has been extensive debate about
the anthropic principle and the idea of the multiverse, and these issues are
still wide open, not least because they get to the roots of what constitutes
reality, both physical and theological, and how far our human rationality is
able to perceive it (Ward 2008: 120–23, 233–9).

If we are now moving way beyond the scope of what is needed for interpretation of the biblical narratives, it has at least highlighted the speculative state to which modern cosmological research has attained. This is the
same cosmological research which is so-often called upon in modern readings of Genesis 1 and other creation passages in the Bible, sometimes to
refute those readings, sometimes to support them, but rarely with an eye
to the deeper metaphysical questions which undergird them.

The laws of nature

One of the outcomes of the birth of the natural sciences in the seventeenth
century was the strong notion that the universe follows mathematical or
conceptual principles which might be uncovered by scientific research –
"the laws of nature". When first articulated, this idea was undergirded by
the deeper notion of a Creator God, who had made the world to reflect the
divine nature; the world was therefore intelligible, dependable and consistent (Harrison 2008). The irony is that it was the very consistency of
these laws which, in time, made God increasingly irrelevant to science. But
although science no longer relies on its original theological foundations in
order to go about its daily business, yet the language of divine law remains
in much of its understanding of the world, with all that implies. For many
scientists, especially in the biological sciences, a "law" might be a statistical observation of observed regularities concerning life on earth, but it
does not necessarily claim deep truths about the wider universe (Lucas
[1989] 2005: 38). For many physical scientists, though, talk of "law" has a
deeper meaning, something more akin to a fixed and unalterable framework which governs how the universe *must* behave, not simply a heuristic

approximation to the world's regularities (McGrath [2002] 2006a: 227–8). In such cases, talk of law begins to point to a deeper principle, a reason behind why the world is regulated as it is. So when we begin to ask questions such as "Why are there laws at all?", "Why are they so often mathematical in form?", "Why should they be universal and exceptionless?" or "Why this law rather than that?", we find that we have come either to the limits of science, to its most basic presuppositions beyond which we cannot go, or to the point at which theology must take over (Harrison 2008: 27–8). Those who argue that the laws of nature are a sufficient explanation in themselves for all there is (e.g. Hawking & Mlodinow 2010: 180) are unwittingly making a theological (not scientific) claim about the status of those laws. This is particularly clear in the rhetoric used in theoretical physics of the search for a "theory of everything", which study of hypothetical "superstrings" (also known as "M-theory") is hoped to provide by some theoreticians. The details are less important for our purposes than the claims, because there is a danger in exalting law to such a high status that it effectively becomes more "real" in an ontological sense than the reality which it attempts to describe. As Ward puts it:

> This is the ultimate irony of some modern science, that it begins by trying to explain and understand the rich, particular, concrete world as experienced by humans, and ends by seeing that phenomenal world as an illusion ... This fallacy has snared philosophers from Plato to Leibniz and beyond, and it still snares many major physicists.   (Ward 1996a: 28)

Ward is hinting at the philosophical approach known as Platonism. It has often been noticed that mathematics has an uncanny ability to mirror the patterns of nature, and to provide a way into modelling nature's regularities which would be impossible in any other way. Its success suggests that there is a deeply rational heart to the world, to the extent that it is often wondered if mathematics is less a human invention than a scientific discovery. Physicists such as Roger Penrose and Paul Davies have been taken with the approach of Platonism, which suggests that mathematical truth is not a human construct but is rather a deep, absolute and eternal fact of the world. In this view, mathematics forms a kind of reality in its own right, a sort of external fact of the world which is nevertheless not dependent on physical objects for its existence (McGrath [2002] 2006a: 212–14). In that case, mathematicians are seen to *discover* rather than *invent* mathematical theorems. It suggests that mathematics represents an organizational reality behind the world which is deeper than that accessible to science. Not surprisingly, this understanding of mathematics is attractive to theists, because it can be seen to flow directly from the idea of the Creator God, as reflecting the divine mind. The uniformity, regularity and intelligibility of nature, whether seen through laws or through mathematics, are key features of the Christian doctrine of creation (McGrath [2002] 2006b: 154).

We have already hinted that scientists working in the biological sciences may have a different view of the status of the laws of nature from those working in the physical sciences. By and large, those in the physical sciences are probably more likely to see the laws as reflective of a deep, objective truth about the universe, whether or not they interpret that in terms of a Creator God. Physics in particular can be guilty of a kind of cultural imperialism, assuming that since physics is the most fundamental science (in that it deals with matter at its most basic level, and with its most fundamental physical properties) then all of science eventually collapses into physics. In other words, all laws of nature, whether concerning complex or simple, living or inanimate matter, eventually reduce to the laws of physics.

Mathematicians sometimes take this one step further, arguing that physics ultimately reduces to mathematics. On the other hand, biologists argue that such reductionism is simply not helpful – physics may describe matter at its most basic level, but that does not mean that we need to reduce all higher-order entities to their most basic components before we can understand them. We may one day be able to describe the properties of every fundamental sub-atomic particle in a bird such as a swallow, for instance, but this does not mean that we will be able to *understand* its patterns of migration or feeding habits more easily. In higher-order sciences, when complex phenomena are in view it is often simply irrelevant to point out that all of nature reduces to the laws of physics.

This leads into an important distinction, which becomes especially important when we compare a science like evolutionary biology (which emphasizes the importance of accidental and contingent details) with a science like physics (which, by contrast, tends to look for regular and law-like behaviour). Not to put too fine a point on it, the former is preoccupied with chance, the latter with law. It is not that these approaches contradict each other, but they are complementary. Evolutionary biology may indeed reduce to the laws of physics ultimately, but it is the chance occurrences which provide the interest in trying to understand the paths chosen in the development of life. As the evolutionary biologist Stephen Jay Gould explains, "The law of gravity tells us how an apple falls, but not why that apple fell at that moment, and why Newton happened to be sitting there, ripe for inspiration" (Gould [1990] 2000: 278).

It is a question of focus. Biological life is as much in thrall to the laws of physics as are colliding galaxies (at one end of the scale of size in physics) or colliding sub-atomic particles (at the other), both of which are of perennial interest to physicists. Now the physicist would tend to see past the myriad chance events involved in both types of collisions, whether of galaxies or sub-atomic particles, and would attempt to extract law-like behaviour by thinking in terms of statistical averages of perhaps many such events. But it is precisely the individual chance events which are important to the biologist, because it is these which tell us the story of life and how it adapts to its environment. Perhaps the best-known example is the dramatic extinction of the dinosaurs at the end of the Cretaceous period, about sixty-five million years ago. It is widely thought that the collision of a very large meteorite with the earth led to a sharp change in climate, to which the dinosaurs were unable to adapt. As a consequence, mammals dominate the earth today rather than reptiles. The meteorite collision can be explained entirely within the laws of physics, but it was a chance event which completely affected the path of life on earth. Of course, the evolution of life on earth must follow physical laws in a very broad sense, in the same sense that meteors follow physical laws, and it may be that we need to look on an even wider scale than the last sixty-five million years, and of our planet, to see past the chance events and to build up a picture of the law-like regularities. But to the biologist the chance details are at least as important as the regularities. The same can be said even more emphatically of subjects such as history – the contingent and unexpected events provide some of the greatest interest, not so much the search for general and unshakeable principles.

We shall look at the interplay of chance and law again, because it is an important motif which runs through much of the dialogue between science and theology. This interplay is nowhere more evident than in the two scientific models of development and evolution which have come to dominate all interactions between science and theology: the Big Bang model and biological evolution. We shall describe these briefly here, paying special attention to issues that are relevant for interpretation of the Bible; more comprehensive presentations which highlight general issues of interest to the science–theology field can be found in Polkinghorne (1994, 1998), Dobson (2005) and Hodgson (2005).

MODERN SCIENTIFIC ACCOUNTS OF BEGINNINGS

The Big Bang model

One of the best-known – and most surprising – discoveries of observational astronomy of the last century is that the universe appears to be expanding. Indeed, it appears to be expanding at a phenomenal rate – the most distant galaxies are receding from us at speeds of more than 100,000 km/s, a third of the speed of light (Dobson 2005: 300). The consequence of this discovery for our understanding of the early history of the cosmos has been equally startling. Assuming that this expansion has been going on throughout the history of the universe, the best explanation is that it began approximately fourteen billion years or so before the present day, with all matter, energy and even space itself expanding out from a single point. This point, the "initial singularity", is a mathematical concept arising from Einstein's general theory of relativity. It describes an infinitely dense and infinitesimally tiny clump of matter or energy in an extremely unstable state. In this model, the universe would therefore have begun as a tremendously powerful explosion from this point, a "Big Bang", where energy and the most fundamental particles were flung outwards, slowly cooling as they did so, and condensing into more complex sub-atomic particles and basic atomic nuclei. As the universe – and with it space – expanded further, the force of gravity would have begun to make itself felt: matter would have begun to cluster, and stars and galaxies would have been formed, which in their turn began to generate atoms of increasing complexity, and finally planets.

Much of this broad picture is well understood by cosmologists, and has been verified by a number of experimental observations, most notably the discovery by Penzias and Wilson in 1964 of the "cosmic microwave background" – the realization that all of space is filled with relatively low-energy electromagnetic radiation from the early stages of the Big Bang when the first and simplest atoms came to be formed. Further study of this background radiation has been something of an experimental *tour de force* of recent decades, especially measurement of tiny irregularities in the distribution of the background across the sky. These irregularities have been interpreted as resounding confirmation of the Big Bang model, a snapshot of the fluctuations which the early universe was undergoing soon after the Big Bang; in time these fluctuations grew to become the galaxies we know today.

The Big Bang model appears such a fixed part of the scientific landscape now that it is surprising to learn that it was highly controversial in its early decades. Originally suggested in the 1920s by the priest–physicist Georges Lemaître (1894–1966), many cosmologists were sceptical of the Big Bang model because it was thought too "religious", too similar to Judeo-Christian ideas of creation where time has an absolute beginning (§ "Genesis 1 and modern science" in Chapter 3, below). The experimental evidence in its favour has made all the difference though, and the Big Bang model is now seen as such a success that we find the ironical reversal whereby some scientists (e.g. Stephen Hawking, Lawrence Krauss) use the Big Bang as evidence *against* religious ideas of creation: it is seen to explain the origins of the world so well as to undermine religious claims.

Despite its current wide acceptance, it is important to remember that many of the details of the Big Bang model are very sketchy, especially for the crucial earliest moments of the universe. Indeed, at the initial singularity, the laws of physics as we know them break down. On the other hand, the developments of a branch of research known as "quantum cosmology" suggest that there was never a true singularity in the sense of an

infinitesimally small and infinitely dense universe. The initial state may
have been minutely small, and hugely dense and hot, but for temperatures
exceeding the so-called Planck temperature (10^{32} K) the physics of general relativity (which provides this picture) no longer strictly applies, since
quantum effects take over (Stoeger 2010: 175–6).

The details of the initial quantum state are highly mysterious. Not only
is the physics of the "Planck era" beyond present experimental capabili-
ties, it is uncertain how to develop a quantum treatment of spacetime and
gravity into a consistent theory of the early universe. Many hopes are being
pinned on the hypothetical existence of superstrings as a way forward
("M-theory"), although it is not clear how or whether they can be verified
experimentally.

A measure of the intriguing thinking at play in the physics of the Planck
era is provided by one of its best-known models, the "Hartle–Hawking
no-boundary proposal". Here, time in the Planck era behaves like a spatial
dimension. This means that the universe has no initial boundary in time or
space – no point of "creation" – and it becomes as meaningless to speak of
time having a strict beginning as it does to say that the South Pole is the
spatial beginning of the earth (Stoeger 2010: 178; Hawking & Mlodinow
2010: 134–5). Although it has famously been argued that such explanations
dispense with the need for a Creator (e.g. Hawking 1988: 136), they are
unable to explain the ultimate origin of the quantum physics on which they
rely. This means that one basic contingency at least remains unexplained,
and the theological idea of *creatio ex nihilo* (Chapter 6) is left largely intact
as a still more fundamental explanation for why there is something rather
than nothing.

Unfortunately, the very earliest history of the universe can only be the
subject for poorly founded speculation, and many questions remain. It is
possible that, once physicists have learned fully how to integrate all four
forces of nature into a single consistent theory, and have made significant
advances in experimental techniques, the situation will become clearer. On
the other hand, it is possible that other intriguing possibilities might turn
up. But at the moment, the Big Bang model is the consensus among cosmologists for understanding the physical evolution of our universe.

Darwin and biological evolution

Darwin's model of evolution by natural selection is arguably even more
ground-breaking than the Big Bang model. Darwin's achievement has been
at the forefront of popular consciousness for considerably longer, and has
been more consistently fought over in the vociferous clashes between
science and religion. Darwin's idea is well known – that life developed
(evolved) over the course of millions of years from the simplest unicellular

forms, through simple plants and soft-bodied animals living in the sea, through the first land plants and insects, bony fish, amphibians, land animals, the great dinosaurs, to the modern birds, fish and mammals of our contemporary world. Increasing complexity and diversity are important features of this model.

In retrospect, it is possible to argue that the evolutionary picture was inevitable to some degree. Once science began to take the place of religion in explaining the world, it became very hard to sustain the view where species sprang forth miraculously and fully formed, so a developmental perspective was more or less the only option (Farrer [1966] 2009 : 42–3). The new science of geology had already begun to develop such ideas, from the work of Hutton in the eighteenth century to Lyell's monumental *Principles of Geology* in the nineteenth. They are largely responsible for the idea known as uniformitarianism, that the earth has been shaped throughout its history by the same slow and gradual geological processes we see operating today. In this context, it is hardly surprising that gradual, evolutionary views such as those of Darwin might also develop in biology.

Darwin began his key work, *On the Origin of Species by Means of Natural Selection* (1859), by looking at the great variety of domesticated animals, and how they had been bred to possess certain key characteristics – "variation under domestication" he called it. He then went on to look at the wider natural world and described a comparable situation – "variation under nature". This led him to make his key arguments about the "struggle for existence" and "natural selection". As species struggle to survive in diverse and often harsh environments, and also in competition with each other, it is those that possess a biological advantage over their adversaries who win through and survive, those that are best adapted to the particular context who are effectively selected to continue. The great variety of contexts in the world is the reason for the great variety of species seen to exist today and in the geological record.

It is often pointed out that Darwin's idea is an interplay of *chance* and *necessity* (e.g. Dobson 2005: 342). *Chance* gives rise to a high level of variation among species, but only some of these are equipped with the *necessary* qualities for survival. This is why, of all of the species which have ever existed on earth, some 99.9 per cent are now extinct. The ability to survive in the face of intense competition is therefore a critical necessity which gives rise to the idea of natural selection. From that point of view, natural selection bears something of the quality of a law of nature, and the interplay of chance and law in evolution can be seen as related to our previous discussion of chance and law. There is a general law which governs the overall picture of the evolution of life, but the individual encounters and their outcomes appear to be governed by chance.

The interplay between chance and necessity, which enables evolution continually to provide fertile solutions to the problems of existence in changing environments, is held in a very delicate balance, "at the edge of chaos" (Polkinghorne 2011: 59). If the balance was shifted in the favour of chance over necessity, then there would be too many haphazard solutions for the important stable novelties to emerge, but if the balance shifted in the opposite direction then the dominating regularities would stifle the creativity necessary to survive new challenges (Peacocke 2001: 26).

The Big Bang model of the cosmos is also an evolutionary idea, since it describes the growth and fruition of the universe. And it also incorporates the interplay of chance and law. But these two models – the Big Bang and biological evolution – have been used in opposite theological directions to each other. The Big Bang model is often compared with the biblical narrative of creation in Genesis 1, and its success in terms of fundamental physics has meant that it is seen as imbuing the universe with an inherent beauty and intelligibility. This has been taken by some as support for *design* (i.e. a divine Creator), especially when combined with the anthropic principle. On the other hand, biological evolution has often been used to *discredit* the Christian picture of creation, especially as it is described in Genesis 2–3 with the story of Adam and Eve in the garden, who disobey God and introduce sin into the world. This particular biblical story can be made to cohere with the scientific idea of evolution, but only by introducing some imaginative interpretations (Chapter 7).

Biology has done more than any other branch of thought to bring humankind down to size, to remind us that the anthropocentrism of the pre-modern era was misleading, and had been fed to some extent by the traditional Christian views of creation and the incarnation, which appeared to place humankind at the universal pinnacle of existence. Instead, evolution introduces a sea-change in thinking not unlike that of the Copernican revolution – the earth is not at the centre of the universe and neither are humans. And the picture of struggle and competition which Darwinism paints is substantially harder to equate with the supposed purposes of a loving God. Chance, violence, suffering and death come to be placed squarely at the heart of existence, as does the principle of the survival of the fittest, rather than divine providence, peace and benevolence. This discovery has had an impact on Christian theology, although admittedly perhaps no more so than the need to account for purely *human* outrages in the twentieth century, such as the Holocaust, which pose a similar challenge to traditional views of God's loving purposes. And the New Atheism of recent decades makes explicit use of evolutionary arguments as a challenge to traditional religious belief.

All of this means that biological evolution is still, more than 150 years since the publication of Darwin's *Origin of Species*, a highly contentious issue in certain Christian circles, and much more so than is the Big Bang. This is largely down to the resistance of various forms of Creationism to biological evolution. And yet, the resistance owes less to the scientific credentials of evolution than to the view that it is seen to jeopardize the integrity of the Bible as the divinely inspired word of God. Major developments have been made in the biological sciences since Darwin's day, which have underscored heavily the basic correctness of the main sweep of his evolutionary view. Darwin's specific model of *natural selection* is still the subject of active debate though, and the importance of additional (or alternative) forces driving evolution has been proposed, notably self-organization (Kauffmann), and purely contingent chance (Gould). But the majority of scientists adhere to a new synthesis of evolutionary ideas based around Darwinism (often referred to as "neo-Darwinism"), which has cemented many of Darwin's ideas while expanding and adapting others. The modern science of genetics has been especially important, since it is able to explain the reason for the variations between species, through mutations in genes. Darwin could not have anticipated this, and neither did he have any inkling as to the existence of DNA, nor the huge revolution which the discovery of its double-helix structure has brought to our understanding of the biochemical processes which underlie both the chance and the necessity of evolution, together with the possible origins of life itself.

The modern biological sciences have assembled an impressive edifice of evidence to support Darwin's general idea that life on earth has evolved from simple to more complex life forms, and largely through the twin principles of chance and necessity. There is no reason to believe that the process has reached its culmination with us as human beings. We are, then, apparently not the product of a one-off creation in the beginning of the world, but rather one link in a long chain of life; a link which has appeared only very recently in the history of life, and is the result of myriads of other evolutionary developments before us. The Big Bang model also presents challenges for theology, but the challenges of the biological picture are more immediate.

CHANCE AND LAW, CONTINGENCY AND EMERGENCE

At this point, it is worth highlighting the idea of *contingency*. Not only does it help us to work through the issues involved in chance and law, but it is also an important general concept in philosophical and theological views of creation. Simply defined, an event is contingent if it is a possibility rather than a certainty or a necessity, if it need not turn out in one particular way. And there is a basic theological form of contingency which arises from the Christian doctrine of creation, since it insists that the world is contingent upon God for its very existence from the first moment of creation up to the present day. The world is utterly dependent upon God, but God, who is not contingent, is dependent upon nothing. God alone is the fixed and certain point.

There are other, scientific ways in which the world might be said to be contingent, one of which arises from the evolutionary models we have just seen. If it is true to say that the world exists in a state of continuous coming-into-being (which is the essence of the word "evolution"), then the exact form of the world may be said to be undetermined and contingent at every step. We have already highlighted the interplay of chance and necessity (law), and pointed out the importance of chance in biological evolution. It clearly presents a highly contingent view of life on earth. But what about the Big Bang model: to what extent is chance, and this type of contingency, important on a universal scale?

Let us think this through carefully. The Big Bang model is often said to be evolutionary, but if it describes the evolution of the universe in terms of precisely defined laws and principles at every stage, then the universe can hardly be said to evolve in a contingent fashion; it simply develops according to a pre-determined fixed plan. If this is the case, then knowledge of the beginning state of the universe would specify every subsequent stage, once the laws are fully known. And this is the view of the universe which held sway in classical physics following the development of Newtonian mechanics. It was in large part the reason why deism became an important form of belief in God shortly after Newton's time: once God had created the world, it was seen that there was no need for divine involvement in its further development and history. Such a universe is known as *deterministic*: every physical process and event is determined by what came before it.

This "clockwork" view of the universe is now widely questioned, although Newtonian physics still continues to be extremely valuable, and deistic tendencies remain in modern Christian beliefs. But as we have seen, an amazing revolution has taken place in many areas of science over the past century, which has proved the deficiency of determinism again and again; the developments of relativity, quantum mechanics and chaos theory are three prime examples in twentieth-century physics which have played a large part in the demise of deterministic ways of looking at the world. As a result of this revolution, the natural sciences are much more alive than previously to novel and fresh possibilities of nature which often defy precise prediction.

Many scientists suspect that, even if we were to understand fully the most basic laws of physics which have held sway since the Big Bang, those laws would probably not enable us to predict accurately how the world will evolve, except in the most general terms, and this is the key. If we were to understand the laws of physics completely we might be able to describe the evolution of the universe on very large scales, since statistical effects would probably be averaged out, but as we focus in on smaller and smaller scales at individual stars and planets, we would find that the roles of chance and subtle indeterminacies become ever more important. There is also the more basic question of whether we will ever be able to understand the laws of physics completely. In this light, Gödel's famous theorem has been used to argue that no complete mathematical system (such as the putative complete laws of physics) can ever contain its own proof of consistency. This means that there are always propositions within the system that can neither be proved nor disproved but must be taken for granted. If this way of thinking is correct (and it is debated), then a "theory of everything" would be a contradiction in terms, never fully capable of explaining exactly how the world is as it is (Hodgson 2005: 186). In any case, Barbour (1997: 212) is at least partially correct to say "The cosmos is a unique and irreversible sequence of events. Our account of it must take a historical form rather than consist of laws alone."

A good analogy is provided by the game of chess: the rules can be stated in just a handful of principles, yet it is said that more games of chess are possible than there are atoms in the universe (Sharpe & Walgate 2003: 422). Knowledge of the rules provides us with the framework for each game, but does not teach us how to become a grand master, nor does it tell us how each game will proceed except in the most general terms. Certain patterns of play are more likely or more favourable than others, and a skilled player will be able to recreate or utilize them, but this is moving onto a level of experience which transcends knowledge of the basic rules. And it is by no means clear what the outcome will be when the game is played by two well-matched players. In short, in the game of chess we see a non-deterministic (i.e. non-predictive) reality emerging which is far more complex than its rules might indicate. The same is undoubtedly true in the case of the evolution of the universe, and so it is unclear whether, even if a "theory of everything" turns out to be feasible, it will be able to predict and explain the form of the world satisfactorily. Reduction is not the same as explanation.

Moreover, it is unlikely that a "theory of everything" would have much to offer the life sciences. Biological life arises from complex properties of nature which are not easily reduced to the more basic principles of physics and chemistry. Knowledge of matter at its most basic level (such as subatomic particles) does not necessarily lead to full understanding of higher levels of reality (such as living organisms). This leads us into one final scientific principle that has become immensely important in modern scientific research, namely the idea of "emergence", which has become something of an emergent area itself in scientific research, connecting many previously disparate areas of thought in coherent patterns. Emergence works in exactly the opposite direction to reductionism: it emphasizes the appearance of complex properties which are not easily predicted by simple laws and principles.

Emergent properties of nature usually involve many entities acting co-operatively in such a way that the result is not obviously explained by the properties of the individual entities, even if they behave individually according to well understood laws. A higher-level structure becomes clear which might not be evident simply from knowledge of the lower-level science; there is a sense in which the result is "greater than the sum of the parts". In other words, the individual entities might be reasonably well understood up to a point, and even the nature of the local relationships and interactions between them, but their behaviour when combined might be strikingly novel, so that fundamentally and irreducibly new things occur. There are many examples of emergence in both the natural and the human worlds. The rings of Saturn, the shapes of clouds in the sky, structures in the earth's landscape and the co-operative behaviour of fish or birds when gathered together into shoals or flocks: these are all examples of structures which cannot easily be explained by (or reduced to) their individual components.

The simple fact of biological life offers one of the best examples of emergence. Life has emerged from inanimate matter, but relatively simple unicellular life forms are already so vastly complex that they cannot be explained neatly by the laws of physics and chemistry alone, which otherwise might describe many properties and features of inanimate matter well. But despite their complexity, these life forms operate as single, organized entities, and so are amenable to a scientific approach, albeit one that operates at a "higher" level than much of physics and chemistry: biology. This emergence from the lower levels of explanation to the higher can also be seen in a single biological subject – the human body. Individual cells in the body can be described, categorized and understood in biological terms, but this does not mean that the behaviour of the whole human being will necessarily be understood in the same way, not least because psychology and other higher-order disciplines come into play. The human body is an example of emergent behaviour which operates in ways that transcend those of its individual cells. And when we turn to the human world we find many more examples, such as the field of economics: understanding fundamental monetary principles does not provide for accurate prediction of global stock markets (especially during crashes), because they represent the kind of co-operative high-level behaviour which is not easily related to lower-level principles. These are all examples of how radically new coherent structures and forms of organization can appear in the world in ways which transcend basic laws; these are signs that the world is caught up in a process of continuous coming-into-being. The world is truly evolutionary.

Not just evolutionary biology, then, but many sciences point to emergent properties, and to the fact that there is a basic level of scientific contingency to the world, notwithstanding the even more basic theological contingency which underlies it. The implication is that the world need not have turned out the way it has. Other patterns could have occurred within the parameters of the scientific models, and within the physical constants of the universe and the laws of nature, and these could have resulted in different kinds of world to some degree.

But how different? There is a subtle argument going on at present, especially in evolutionary biology, about the balance between chance and law, contingency and inevitability. There is also a religious dimension to the debate, and those who advocate the anthropic principle as a contemporary version of the argument from design tend to place the balance in favour of law over chance, so that intelligent life was always inevitable, "designed" by divine purpose (*telos* in Greek).

Disregarding the religious dimension for the moment, the argument concerning the balance of chance against law in evolutionary biology is illustrated by a well-known disagreement between two evolutionary palaeontologists – Stephen Jay Gould and Simon Conway Morris. Both scientists have studied and written extensively on the Burgess Shale, a deposit of rock found in the Canadian Rockies which is rich in very unusual fossils showing bizarre forms of development. These fossils demonstrate that, at the beginning of the Cambrian Period (570 million years ago), nature was going through an unprecedented explosion of experimental life forms, many of which never appear again at a later stage. In the act of interpreting these observations both Gould and Conway Morris have access to the same experimental data, but they come to radically different conclusions. On the one hand, Gould concluded that the evolutionary process is entirely random. Nature equipped the Burgess fossils with many different characteristics, almost like a lottery, and it was simply down to the chance of their environment whether they survived or not. Many of them were failed experiments. And according to Gould this is true to some degree at every subsequent stage in the evolutionary process: it is "utterly unpredictable and quite unrepeatable". As Gould famously put it ([1990] 2000: 14), "Wind back the tape of life to the early days of the Burgess Shale; let it play again from an identical starting point, and the chance becomes vanishingly small that anything like human intelligence would grace the replay."

Conway Morris, on the other hand, draws quite the opposite conclusion: "Rerun the tape of life as often as you like, and the end result will be much the same" (Conway Morris 2003: 282). For Conway Morris, evolution may be driven by chance, but it is constrained to follow clear pathways. This is the principle of "evolutionary convergence", that there are only so many solutions to the problems of life which work well, and the evolutionary experiments of life will hit upon them again and again. Indeed, these solutions can be arrived at independently from different directions, which is why, as Conway Morris points out by way of example, the camera eye has evolved independently several different times in very different animals, not only in vertebrates such as humans, but also in types of squid, snail, jellyfish and even spiders. It is no accident that this type of eye is favoured by actively mobile and predatory animals, argues Conway Morris (*ibid.*: 157): it is the convergent solution for sight given such a lifestyle. There are many such convergences, and Conway Morris is sufficiently confident of the evolutionary inherence of certain characteristics, including intelligence, that he believes that we humans were almost inevitable as the outcome of the evolutionary process we find on earth (*ibid.*: xv–xvi).

So we find that Gould emphasizes the role of chance, while Conway Morris highlights necessity. They make their cases independently of any theological arguments, and they attempt to reason entirely from the scientific evidence (although Conway Morris is not averse to drawing theistic conclusions from his work). But in assessing their approaches, we inevitably find that higher-level philosophical ideas come into play. It is not dissimilar to the question of whether the universe is ultimately deterministic or not, and it has been pointed out that, even to speak of "determinism" (or its opposite, "indeterminism"), is to make a philosophical or perhaps even theological claim which lies beyond the scope of science (McGrath [2003] 2006c: 269).

There are, for instance, acutely difficult issues which arise around the concept of "chance". We have been considering chance as though it is a well-understood and clear concept in science. But this is not the case, since it draws on philosophical questions as much as scientific questions. When we speak of "chance" in biological evolution, do we mean pure, unalloyed chance such as in the proverbial throwing of dice, or is it simply a convenient umbrella term for the consequence of many complex factors that we cannot precisely pinpoint, such as changes in climate, food, or environment (Fergusson 1998: 57; Lucas [1989] 2005: 113–14)? It is often said that pure chance operates in quantum mechanics, and that this may somehow filter up to the level of natural selection. But even this is fraught with many layers of difficulty. Most fundamentally, we are not even sure if quantum mechanics entails pure chance, or whether "chance" in this case is largely a convenient name for deterministic effects that we currently do not understand (Hodgson 2005: 145–71). The Copenhagen interpretation against the many-worlds interpretation of quantum mechanics shows that there are completely different philosophical/theological answers to that question while the basic scientific observations remain the same. It is all too easy to put something down to "chance" which we do not currently understand (Watts 2008: 3).

The questions rapidly multiply, and it is not our intention here to muddy the waters further, simply to demonstrate that we can only go so far scientifically with issues such as chance and law before philosophical and theological considerations come into play.

"Chance" has become something of a bugbear in theological circles (Wilkins 2012). To many religious believers, the idea that the world has evolved randomly undermines some of the most abiding theological arguments for design, those which build on the regularity and harmony of the world to promote a God of law and order. For some, any suggestion that the development of human life was not inevitable causes supreme theological problems. So it is not uncommon to find that many Christian believers, even academic theologians, reject views of evolution such as Gould's, which place the role of chance foremost. And they reject such views not only because chance is seen to undermine the argument from design: at least as significant is the teleological belief that there is ultimate purpose in the world. Christianity is so habitually anthropocentric that any ideology that denies an ultimate purpose to the human world (especially a purpose ordained by God), is almost certain to be unpopular among Christians. Lamoureux (2008: xiv, 377), for instance, is so opposed to what he calls "dysteleological evolution" (i.e. evolution that does not have any kind of end or purpose in sight, but is governed entirely by chance) that he equates it with Atheism and argues that it is "anti-Christian", undemocratic and "insidious indoctrination".

Although chance seems to be regarded in many theological circles as largely inimical to the message of Christianity about a loving God who guides the world, this need not be the case. In Chapter 9 we will spend some time thinking about biblical eschatology and teleology, and especially the idea of a new creation. It will be argued that it is unlikely that this biblical material was ever intended to be read in an entirely literal way, as though it would have potential implications for our *scientific* view of the world. It was probably intended to be rather more suggestive, symbolic and open-ended than we often assume, with more pressing moral and spiritual implications than scientific. In any case, it is possible to see the scientific concept of chance in a positive theological light. There are theological approaches which marry with Gould's emphasis on chance in biological evolution just as there are theological approaches which agree with Conway Morris's more purposive understanding of evolution. In the former, an emphasis on the role of chance could be likened to a view of God working creatively in nature, continually creating it in the present, and always leading it into fresh possibilities which cannot be predicted by science in advance. This is a so-called *immanentist* view of God's relationship to the world. In the latter, Conway Morris's more directed and law-like view of evolution can be matched with the traditional view of God's transcendent guidance of creation from the beginning. It is not that either view is anti-Christian as such, but that both can be interpreted in terms of different views of God's relationship to the world. This is a theme which will come up again and again as we look at what the Bible says about creation, and how it may be interpreted with a view to science.

In this section we have done much to highlight the second level of contingency, which arises from the evolutionary nature of both the Big Bang model and Darwinism. This second level of contingency is not implicitly theological, as is that which arises from the doctrine of creation, but it does suggest a theological analogy, namely a creative and higher mind behind the perpetual novelty and freshness of the universe. It is such a mind that we find in many of the creation texts of the Bible.

Chapter 3

CREATION ACCORDING TO THE BIBLE I: GENESIS

THE FIRST GENESIS CREATION ACCOUNT: GENESIS 1:1–2:4a (P)

The "Priestly" author

The recognition that there are two distinct accounts of creation in the early chapters of Genesis is one of the foundation stones of the "documentary hypothesis" (Chapter 1). Although there have been many criticisms and revisions since Wellhausen's definitive formulation, the basic idea has stuck fast in biblical scholarship. Therefore, we will continue to use the terminology of the "Yahwist" and "Priestly" authors when looking at these first few crucial chapters of Genesis, without taking too firm a commitment on historical formulations behind them. Indeed, for the sake of convenience we will refer to the Genesis 1–2 creation story as P, and the Genesis 2–3 story as J. This is not meant to imply a firm commitment to any particular version of the documentary hypothesis so much as the general recognition that we are dealing here with at least two distinct creation traditions. But equally, it is worth bearing in mind that, from the point of view of the biblical canon which has been passed down to us, these creation stories are told together. And indeed, the relationship between them may be even more intimate. It is quite possible, for instance, that one (probably P) was composed at least in part as an introduction and complement to the other (Fretheim 2005: 33).

In Wellhausen's model P was composed in the sixth to fifth centuries BCE as part of the theological response to the Babylonian Exile. Opening the Bible, and written in a repetitive, rhythmic style suggestive of a liturgical text (one of the reasons for its attribution to the "Priestly" author), creation is described in terms of a regular step-like process starting from a "formless void" (one possible translation of the almost untranslatable Hebrew *tohu wabohu*; Gen. 1:2), and finally culminating in the creation of humankind, the only part of creation which is made in the "image" of

God (Gen. 1:26-27). The whole procedure takes six "days", with evening and morning defining each day; God rests on the seventh day.

It has often been wondered if P was based on an earlier creation text, perhaps from another ANE culture such as Babylon. In support, parallels have been drawn with the Babylonian creation myth, *Enuma elish*. However, it is thought unlikely that this represents direct borrowing so much as similarities in cosmology and worldview, because very stark differences also exist with *Enuma elish*, not least in the picture of God conveyed. For that reason, it has been suggested that P was written as a polemic against the Babylonian creation myth (Wenham 1987: 8–9).

Scholars have also noticed close parallels between Genesis 1 and Psalm 104, an extravagant hymn of praise to God for the act of creation. Such are the level of similarities that it is wondered whether one text is dependent upon the other. And since Psalm 104 contains more openly mythological traits (such as the personalization of the waters in vv. 6-9), as well as some tantalizing parallels with an Egyptian creation text, it has been suggested that Genesis 1 is a "demythologization" of Psalm 104, which is in turn dependent upon Egyptian myth (Day 1992: 41–2; 2000: 101). Of course, this thesis is equally as difficult to substantiate as the supposition that Genesis 1 was written as a polemic against the Babylonian creation myth; it is possible that both, or neither, ideas are true. Whatever the case, it seems safe to conclude that Genesis 1 shows close similarities with other ANE creation texts, and that, even if mythological motifs do not stand out clearly, they are nevertheless there in the background of the text. We will make more of this in the subsequent discussion and following chapters.

The sense of order, well-being and inherent satisfaction in the act of creation is evident in P. In connection, scholars have wondered whether there is a deeper literary symmetry underlying the text. Its repetitive style, with the frequent reiteration of phrases such as "And God said", "Let there be", "and it was so", and its methodical development, are all highly suggestive of a well-thought-out structure. Several suggestions of literary patterns have been made, and it is often noticed that the six days can be divided into two halves (days one to three, and days four to six), where each day is linked thematically with its equivalent in the other half (e.g. Wenham 1987: 6–7). So days one and four are joined by the creation of light and lights respectively, while days two and five are linked by the creation of the sky and birds. Days three and six are linked by the creation of land and the animals and humans who live on the land. But this is not the only pattern which has been seen in the text; and none of them is wholly conclusive as offering the "definitive" structure for the passage, so it is perhaps as well not to make too much of any one of them (Westermann 1984: 89). They do however support a vitally important point, that the Creator of the world is portrayed as a God of order and regularity who nevertheless delights in the work.

Genesis 1 and God

Whatever else we might say about Genesis 1, it is a story about God in the mode of creating, overseeing and making. God is the active agent in nearly every sentence; the world, by contrast, is entirely passive, entirely at the whim of God's (verbal) command. The rhythmic, repetitive nature of the narrative, and the orderly way in which God orders and constructs the world step-by-step, conjures up God as a master builder, taking pride in a job well done. God assesses every stage and pronounces it "good" (Hebrew *tov*, which can also have the sense of "beautiful"), and at the end the whole is "very good" (Gen. 1:31). As a skilled builder would do, the work is carefully appraised, and is pronounced fit for purpose: "The Creation account portrays a God who speaks, who evaluates, who deliberates, who forms, who animates, who regulates" (Hamilton 1990: 56). And, we might add, it portrays a God who *values* the work: in the repetition of the value judgement "good" there is the sense that an aesthetic judgement is being built up which is beyond the bounds of a purely factual or scientific account. Such a judgement elicits a comparable response from creation, namely praise of its Creator (Job 38:4-7).

Other metaphors are also appropriate for P's portrait of God, and as well as a skilled builder we might equally compare God with a human architect or an overseer, and with other possible roles such as speaker, evaluator, consultant, victor, and king (Fretheim 2005: 36–48). In fact, noticing that God does not so much fashion the universe directly in Genesis 1 as *exhort* it to come into being, we might even compare this God with a film director encouraging actors to interpret their roles and realize their potential through creativity of their own, within the limits God sets down. There is much that can be said of the God of Genesis 1, and no single human metaphor is exhaustive of all of the divine qualities portrayed.

The care and devotion of God the creator may be familiar from the human world, but the scale of the project is astronomical. The whole of creation is made sequentially and with the utmost care and satisfaction. The dimensions of time and space themselves are created and laid out systematically, almost as though God is following a cosmic blueprint and a meticulously planned schedule. It is easy to see the God of the physicist in such a picture, the God who carefully sets out universal law and order and follows the scheme to the letter, the God of the anthropic principle who creates humankind as the final crowning stage, and makes them in the divine image (Gen. 1:26-27), so that they might have dominion over it as God does.

And yet, humankind is not the final stage. There is one more thing to come, the seventh day, on which God rests. The text tells us that when God had finished from the work, God rested just as a professional builder might do. The special status of God's day off rings out clearly – "So God blessed the seventh day and hallowed it" (Gen. 2:3). God had already pronounced everything as "very good" (1:31), and in addition had blessed humankind (1:28), but this final creation, the seventh day, is now both blessed *and* "hallowed" (i.e. made holy, set apart). After having created time and space and the material world that fills it, God has now sanctified the week and especially the rest day.

And yet it is not the portrait of God, nor the status of the seventh day, which causes the controversy surrounding Genesis 1. Such has been the impact of the modern scientific consciousness on this passage that we might almost forget that its main subject matter is God, that the claims and pretensions of the passage are incontrovertibly theological, not scientific. To us, it is science which comes to the fore.

Genesis 1 and modern science

Putting to one side for the moment the fact that this narrative ostensibly describes creation of the material world taking place over six 24-hour periods, while modern science indicates that it took billions of years, a number of parallels have been seen between this story and modern Big Bang cosmology and evolutionary biology. For instance, the "formless void" (Gen. 1:2) is evocative of the initial quantum state in the Planck era, and the gigantic flash of energy at the beginning of the Big Bang has been linked with God's first act of creation in Genesis 1: "Let there be light" in Genesis 1:3 (Schroeder [1990] 1992: 84–9; Fatoorchi 2010: 101). Indeed, in the early years of the Big Bang model, its inference that there was an absolute beginning to time was regarded by some prominent scientists as too close to Genesis for comfort (Jastrow 1992: 104–5). Until scientific support was discovered in recent decades for the idea that the universe had an absolute beginning *on scientific grounds alone*, it seemed that the Genesis creation account might have been right about the theological origin of the universe after all, so that Jastrow's famous comment found a deep resonance:

> For the scientist who lived by his faith in the power of reason, the story ends like a bad dream. He has scaled the mountains of ignorance; he is about to conquer the highest peak; as he pulls himself over the final rock, he is greeted by a band of theologians who have been sitting there for centuries.   (*Ibid.*: 107)

And the resonances extend beyond the first few verses of Genesis 1. It has been noticed that the later order of creation, with the sea and dry land appearing first, followed by plants, sea creatures, land animals and then finally humans, is broadly similar to the pattern described by modern theories of biological evolution. But note that the appearance of the sun and stars (v. 16) *after* the creation of the earth (v. 10) and even after the Day and Night (v. 5) shows that there are also startling discrepancies between P and modern cosmology.

There has been enthusiastic discussion in some Christian (and Jewish) circles over how seriously one should take the parallels between P and science, and we find a number of complex questions arising (e.g. Hamilton 1990: 53–5; Lucas [1989] 2005). Are the parallels evidence that the author of P was privy to authentic divine revelation about the origins of the world, long before modern cosmologists came on the scene (e.g. Parker 2009; Lennox 2011: 142–4)? Or did the author make what amounts to a series of scientific guesses, influenced by the creation myths of neighbouring cultures, some of which turned out to bear happy coincidences with the discoveries of modern science, while other guesses (e.g. the six "days" of creation) show how completely uninformed he really was? Or is the situation helped if we argue that the author might not have meant "day" to be understood as a literal 24-hour period? If so, is it legitimate to interpret the "days" as metaphors for much longer episodes in time, such as geological periods? Or are the "six days" pointers to God's timescale, different from that of the earth's? Or it is better if we abandon all attempts to make scientific links and parallels with the text and say that it should simply be read as a parable?

These questions rapidly proliferate, and it soon becomes clear that the way in which we choose to answer them says a great deal about where we think theological "truth" resides. In other words, the text of Genesis 1–3 becomes quite a revealing litmus test of our understanding of Scripture. There are two common responses to the scientific questions raised:

1. Many conservative Christians take a "high" theological view of the literal authenticity of the text of Genesis 1–3 and affirm that it describes "what really happened". The six "days" are a notorious crux. Some interpreters find imaginative ways to make them cohere with science (e.g. Lennox 2011: 54–5, 60–63), while others simply reject mainstream science and assert that the world was made in six literal 24-hour days, believing this to be an important witness to Christian faith. As Whitcomb and Morris put it in their classic creationist text, *The Genesis Flood*: "Since God's revealed Word describes this Creation as taking place in six 'days' and since there apparently is no contextual basis for understanding these days in any sort of symbolic sense, it is an act of both faith and reason to accept them, literally, as real days" (Whitcomb & Morris 1961: 228).

2. Those who do not have such a strong theological investment in the text's literal authenticity are less likely to take an interest in how well it coheres with science and with the physical reality it purports to describe. In which case, the six days present no problems at all. Such readings may highlight the symbolic, theological and perhaps

even liturgical dimensions of the text, suggesting that it was never intended to be taken as a scientific description as we understand it, and that it is best read today as metaphor or perhaps even "poetry" on the idea of creation.

These two descriptions are caricatures to some degree, but they are representative of a debate which is not being resolved quickly. Although both responses are almost mutually exclusive, they are linked by their tendency to prioritize attitudes to *modern* science as their hermeneutical key: the first attempts to *cohere* the text with modern scientific claims (even if they are claims informed by "creation science" rather than mainstream science), while the second attempts to *isolate* the text from scientific claims. But neither response engages with the claims the text itself makes, which are informed by *ancient* science, and *ancient* functional and ontological categories. In effect, the text is placed in a framework which it was not constructed to inhabit, and judged according to criteria it could not possibly have anticipated (Briggs 2009: 66–7).

If response 1 reads too literally, then response 2 is not literal enough. The literal reading (1) does not take account of the fact that the text certainly contains multiple layers of meaning which refer to more realities than just the physical, while the metaphorical reading (2) is not careful enough about what those layers of reality might be. But it is not enough to refer to a text as metaphorical without being careful to explain what it is metaphorical of. A metaphor is a model, an image, constructed of concrete terms which we understand, of something else which we perhaps do not. If we feel that we cannot affirm the reality of the terms used in the model (e.g. the ancient science of Genesis 1), then the device is no longer acting as a metaphor but as a parable or fable. This is no mere semantic distinction, because we interpret a metaphor very differently from a parable. A metaphor entails a statement of identity between the image and its referent, while a parable is a simile at best, and is sometimes even more open-ended than that. We can see this by looking at some of the parables of Jesus. One of the most concise is that of the mustard seed, "The kingdom of heaven is like a mustard seed ..." (Mt. 13:31). Now if this were to be phrased as a metaphor rather than a parable then we would read, "The kingdom of heaven *is* a mustard seed", and we would no doubt draw much closer parallels between the kingdom and the reality of a mustard seed than a parable would either intend or justify.

Those who connect Genesis 1 closely with modern scientific views of origins are unwittingly illustrating precisely this point. They effectively read the text as a metaphor of our scientific worldview, and of our view of the material origins of the world, without attending to the alternative layers of reality contained in the metaphor, which are thereby lost. The following attempt to rewrite Genesis 1 in terms of modern science is a good example:

In the beginning, God said "Let there be ...," and he created the unified forces of physics, with perfect symmetry, and prescient precision. And out of nothing, God, by a free decision, set up the spontaneous production of particles, in newborn space and time, producing a silent, seething sphere, infinitesimally small, and unimaginably hot. *There was evolution and emergence the first stage of Creation.* During a tiny fraction of a second, an expansion took place, and the perfect symmetry of the forces was broken, step by step, as the temperature dropped, to produce the forces of nature we know today ... *There was evolution and emergence, the second stage of Creation.* (Burge 2005: 82–3)

Burge's paraphrase – echoing the highly resonant language of P – might offer us an attractive modern account of beginnings, but it does little or nothing to tell us about Genesis 1. There is therefore a need to be cautious about importing our scientific worldview: we should investigate carefully the different levels of reality to which the text points, on its own terms if possible, before applying ideas from modern science. This means careful engagement with the text in its historical context, seeing it as a product of its time before we unwittingly make it a product of our own. In which case, we may note that for all of the parallels adduced between Genesis 1 and modern scientific accounts of the origin of the world, we could point to an equal number of parallels between Genesis 1 and *ancient* scientific ideas, including cosmological and mythological ideas of neighbouring cultures. These are layers of reality which we need to explore before we can pronounce more confidently on the genre of the text, whether it is history, science, metaphor, fable or myth, or indeed whether these categories are even meaningful.

Cosmology

It is often said that the Bible presents a three-tiered cosmology; that is, a world arranged on three levels. There is (1) the earth which we inhabit, (2) the heavens above it and (3) the underworld below the earth. In Chapter 5 we will discuss this cosmological model in more detail, and question whether it was really seen as a literal representation of reality in ancient Hebrew thought. In fact, we will suggest that what scholars have described as the three-tiered Hebrew cosmology was more likely a metaphorical device to describe the divine transcendence and three entirely distinct realms of existence: (1) the living, (2) God and (3) the dead. In any case, P presents a picture which is at once both more complex and more ambiguously defined than the three-tiered model.

The initial state of the world appears to be a kind of watery wasteland (Gen. 1:2). Much that follows up to v.10 describes the process of *ordering* which God imposes on these pre-existent waters (not *making* from nothing, as those who read this text as if it prefigures a modern scientific account are wont to do). An important aspect to this cosmological view is that the primeval waters – a symbol of chaos in Hebrew thought – must be ordered and restrained by the imposition of boundaries, and that these boundaries constitute much of the structure on which the rest of creation can be placed.

After having made light, and day and night, God makes a solid surface, whose function it is to distinguish the waters above from those below it (Gen. 1:6-7). The Hebrew word for this surface, *raqia'*, conveys the sense of a sheet stretched out, or a lump of metal beaten out flat. Notable Bible translations render it as "dome" (NRSV), "vault" (NJB) or "firmament" (KJB). We will use "dome" for the time being, remembering that the text gives no indication that the surface actually has any kind of shape such as that of a dome or hemispherical shell except for the fact that it is later used as the surface on which the sun and moon move, which might suggest some such shape. In any case, the text goes on to say that this surface is the heavens (1:8), which the NRSV understands as "Sky". The waters below it are then collected into one place, allowing dry land to appear (1:9), so that plants can flourish on it. The sun and moon are set into the dome (1:14-18), and then animals begin to swarm in the sea, to fly in the air and to cover the face of the earth. Eventually, humans are created in God's image (1:26-27), and are told to "subdue" the earth and to "have dominion" over its creatures (1:28).

In all of this it is extremely difficult to identify three putative tiers. The surface of the dry land and the sea might be considered a possible tier, but it is not clear that the waters which are gathered "into one place" under the dome are the sea or if they extend further, below, around and perhaps even *above* the dry land in some way. In any case, there is no mention of a tier underneath, of an underworld. The dome itself might perhaps be considered a kind of tier, but its function is really that of an impermeable boundary to divide the waters, and to provide a kind of fixed surface for the sun and moon to travel upon. There is no sense of a further boundary beyond the upper waters, an outermost limit which might qualify as an upper tier, upon or beyond which God might dwell. And if it is objected that we are reading this rather literally, then it should be pointed out that this is exactly how the three-tiered cosmology of modern scholarship has arisen (Chapter 5). All of this means that when we look at the text closely, there is rather little to suggest the three-tiered picture. That is not, of course, to suggest that the three-tiered picture cannot be identified elsewhere in the Bible, rather that it is by no means obvious here in Genesis 1, where the cosmology is set out perhaps more carefully and methodically than anywhere else.

But even here it is relatively imprecise, and it might be better to see the Genesis 1 cosmology in a looser, even more metaphorical fashion, such as that of Jaki, who suggests that what we have so far called the "dome" is actually best thought of as the surface of a tent (Jaki 1987: 139). In other words, the world is conceived of as a well-known dwelling of ancient times, with the earth and the sky as its main structures, not tiers so much as boundaries which envelop and secure the dwelling space for creatures and humankind.

We will look at interpretations of P that highlight metaphor shortly, but for the time being let us continue to read the physical elements in it literally and see how they might be representative of "ancient science". The outstanding items are the waters above the dome, and the dome itself, both of which bear no relation to anything in our modern scientific view of the world. The waters above the dome presumably provide rain, and a later text describing the great flood tells us that, "on that day all the fountains of the great deep burst forth, and the windows of the heavens were opened" (Gen. 7:11). This picture suggests that the solid dome has "windows" to allow rain through. Note also the mention of "the fountains of the great deep", which is suggestive of the waters *under* the dome from Genesis 1:9, and which must extend underneath the earth, as well as forming the sea.

Clearly these ideas do not tie in with our understanding of the world at all, and it is interesting to note that even creationists do not read them literally. Whitcomb and Morris (1961: 238–9) are keen to assert that the narrative is a divinely inspired and inerrant record of the creation event, couched as a "simple, literal truth". Nevertheless, their treatment of the text is far from literal. For instance, they equate the dome with the "expanse" of air above the earth, i.e. the earth's lower atmosphere, which is of course anything but solid (*ibid.*: 229). Likewise, they believe that the waters above the dome were not fluid, but were originally a gigantic canopy of water vapour, which eventually precipitated and fell on the earth as torrential rain during Noah's flood, adding to the waters coming from the "fountains of the great deep". This canopy must have been hugely voluminous compared to our contemporary cloud cover, they claim, since our clouds are simply not capable of producing enough water to cover the earth to the depth required for a global deluge. And while the surface of the earth was being flooded, enormous geological changes were taking place so that dry land eventually began to appear again in due course. The ocean basins deepened, and the mountains became higher, so that the water which once formed the canopy became a large proportion of the new oceans that we know (*ibid.*: 77, 121, 240–58, 326).

In other words, according to Whitcomb and Morris the earth went through an enormous geological and meteorological transformation at the flood. But the biblical text says nothing of this. In fact, the only suggestion of a potentially new feature is the rainbow (Gen. 9:13). But the waters beneath the earth, and the solid dome in the sky, appear to be very much still in place after the flood, according to the text (8:2).

Whitcomb and Morris frequently admit that their ideas are speculative on scientific grounds, but they do not admit that they are also going beyond what the biblical text tells us. In any case, they are clearly offering an attempt to marry the Genesis cosmology and the flood story of Genesis 6–9 with their own brand of science, which borrows from the terminology of conventional modern geology and meteorology. But whether it does justice to the biblical texts is another matter. The Jewish rabbis of the early centuries CE bequeathed an enormous wealth of interpretations of the creation stories, and they generally appear to have been content to read Genesis 1 as indicating that the dome was a very solid barrier put in place to save the earth from being flooded by the heavenly waters (Ginzburg 2003: 12; *Genesis Rabbah* IV: 2). For instance, it was suggested that Noah's flood was caused by God removing two stars out of the constellation of the Pleiades, so that the flood waters rushed through the two holes created in the dome and engulfed the earth (Ginzburg 2003: 147).

It is easy to see how these two cosmological elements of the dome and heavenly waters might originally have arisen. If water is seen to appear from the skies (in the form of rain) and also to well up from beneath the earth (springs and rivers), then it would be natural to suppose that there are repositories of water in the sky, and beneath (or in) the earth. In that sense, the "ancient science" displayed here was arrived at by observation and hypothesis. It is not too much to say that this is much the same methodology used in modern science. It presents a working model of the world based on observation and explanation, albeit one which is now vastly outmoded. And in case we are tempted towards a feeling of superiority on this point, we should note that our current cosmology may in turn be vastly outmoded by the science of future generations. The history of science teaches us repeatedly that supreme confidence in our own scientific paradigms might well turn out to be misplaced.

In any case, we are clearly reading these elements in Genesis 1 rather literally as we try to construct a cosmology. But there are indications that they are not meant to be taken so literally. The separation of the waters in 1:6-7 may well be an echo of the ancient mythological motif of God's victory over the sea (Chapter 4) rather than a kind of scientific supposition, and this is perhaps what the similar passage in Proverbs 8:28-29 is hinting at (Day 2000: 100).

Moreover, there are plenty of passages elsewhere in the Bible which demonstrate that the ancient Hebrews understood rain very much as we do, coming from the clouds (e.g. Prov. 16:15; Isa. 5:6; Jer. 10:13). One intriguing passage is even suggestive of the perpetual water cycle – evaporation from the earth followed by the formation of clouds, followed by precipitation (Job 36:27-29). If it is true that the authors of the Bible had a more sophisticated view of the natural world than our putative cosmology drawn from Genesis 1 might suggest, then we are certainly making a category mistake in reading it so literally as to construct a hard and fast physical cosmology from it. In short, it probably does not represent "ancient science" in the sense that we habitually take the term "science" to mean, namely a materialistic explanation for the physical form of the world. There is more going on, as we shall see.

Time

Having looked at the physical cosmology described in Genesis 1, its description of space and matter, we must then return to the question we put off earlier concerning its description of *time*, and especially the six "days" during which everything was made. Although six-day creationists take this as a period of six literal 24-hour periods, and alter their scientific outlook of the world to suit, there have been various attempts by more moderate scholars to harmonize these six days with the vast age of the earth seen by modern science. These harmonizations were first made in the nineteenth century in response to the new science of geology (Wilkinson 2009a: 135–6), but they are still being suggested today (e.g. Lennox 2011). The most obvious (and least contrived) way of harmonizing is simply to say that "day" is not meant literally, but is a symbol for a new stage of creation. In which case we could interpret it to be as long as we wish, perhaps seeing each day roughly in terms of a geological stage in the earth's history. Indeed, this is a relatively popular option in conservative scholarship (Barr [1977] 1981: 40–42).

It is worth mentioning one especially ingenious attempt to make the six days of Genesis cohere with science, by Schroeder ([1990] 1992: 52–4), who invokes Einstein's theory of relativity to point out that time runs at different rates in different frames of reference. If God was in a different relativistic frame from the earth, moving much closer to the speed of light, then it is possible that six periods of 24 hours in God's frame of reference might correspond to billions of years upon earth. The timescale of Genesis 1 therefore records events in God's time, not ours. There are problems, though. Schroeder does not explain why God should be in one frame of reference over another, except to say that the six days were measured in a frame of reference which "contained the total universe" (*ibid.*: 53). But it is not clear in physical terms what it means to say that a single relativistic frame of reference contains the whole universe, nor is it clear in theological terms what it means for God to be "in" this frame of reference, travelling close to the speed of light. Sadly, Schroeder does not pose these questions, still less answer them, and we are left with the kinds of problems that beset many scientific interpretations of biblical narratives; namely that scientific

ideas are applied loosely to "explain" the narrative, but the further questions which arise are not worked through, leaving the proposal theologically incoherent.

Moreover, for all Schroeder's ingenuity in preserving the literal six days
of Genesis 1 intact, all that he has done is effectively to redefine them in
terms of billions of our earth years. Like other attempts to cohere the six
days with science, he has overlooked the overwhelming symbolic importance of the six days. The six days make the point that God's working week
is exactly the same as the human working week. Redefining the days in
terms of geological periods, or as the accident of relativistic physics, completely misses the point made by the text that the days are to be read as literal human days as experienced on earth, since it repeatedly mentions the
phrase "And there was evening and there was morning, the nth day" (Gen.
1:5, 8, 13, 19, 23, 31). The story is clearly arranged to fit into one working
week, with the seventh day (i.e. the Sabbath) as the crowning point of the
week, respected by God and humans alike.

The inescapability of this point is one reason why most critical biblical
scholars do not even attempt to harmonize the narrative with modern science. There is evidence of ancient scientific thinking there, but as we have
seen it is of such a kind that we cannot even be confident that it was meant
to supply a literal physical cosmology. And the fact that the timescale of
six days and one rest day evokes the human working week, and so patently
reinforces the portrait of God the master builder already implicit in the
narrative, suggests that in any case we should be looking at more symbolic
readings of the scheme of space, matter and time.

Mythology

Further confirmation that we are right to be cautious before reading a
physical cosmology out of Genesis 1 can be found in other ANE cosmologies such as Sumerian, Babylonian and Egyptian, where the same cosmological elements appear. Indeed, the idea that the world originated
from water, which was then separated to form the heavens above and the
earth beneath is very common, as is the idea that the heavens are marked
by the presence of a tangible firmament or dome (Gunkel 1997: 108–9;
Westermann 1984: 33–4, 115–17; Wenham 1987: 8). However, we should
note that scholars must reconstruct these cosmologies from religious and
mythological texts which are often much more allusive than Genesis 1, and
in the aim of simplicity scholars have not been shy of assigning them to the
ubiquitous three-tiered cosmology (e.g. Dobson 2005). The question arises
whether this is a case of the tail wagging the dog.

The connection between Genesis 1 and creation myths of other cultures
might lead us to ask whether the cosmological elements in Genesis might

not be better labelled as "mythology" instead of "ancient science". Indeed, perhaps they form part of P's polemic against Babylonian mythology and cosmology, not necessarily a literal view of the world which was taken for granted. Perhaps, and there was a time when scholarship used to operate with a definition of "myth" that it was "a story about the gods". Genesis 1, being resolutely monotheistic and therefore "a story about God", was considered to be above the level of myth. No longer though, and the level to which P works and reworks elements from other creation mythologies is widely acknowledged in critical scholarship, such as the motif of the conflict between the creator god and the sea (Chapter 4).

Furthermore, it is realized that "mythology" and "myth" are notoriously fluid terms, and very difficult to define precisely (Rogerson 1974; Oden 1992b; Segal 2011). Some definitions of "myth" overlap, for instance, with our use of the term "science", as an explanation for the world. Likewise, modern science, in its widespread use of imaginative models to represent reality, makes use of creative analogizing in a way not unrelated to myth (Averbeck 2004: 330–34). The difference between modern science and myth lies in the fact that science relies on the empirical method, so its creative models and narratives are in principle *revisable*, when they can be tested. It is worth remembering that some important scientific ideas *cannot* be tested though, at least at present. A highly topical case in point is that of the multiverse (see § "Space, time, and matter" in Chapter 2, above), indicating that the distinctions between modern science, ancient science, and mythology are not always as sharp as we might like to think, and that they all function(ed) to some extent as best-guess explanations of reality.

The upshot is that, although we have attempted to build a cosmology from the physical elements described in Genesis 1, we have had difficulty in determining whether they were understood as a comprehensive, literal description of the world. Part of the difficulty has been the uncertainty surrounding our understanding of "myth" and of "ancient science", of what was based on faith and what was open to question, testing, and revision in ancient Hebrew culture.

The cosmic temple

The connection between Genesis 1 and mythology can be pressed further. Recent historical-critical treatments of Genesis 1 have alleged that the text is less about ancient scientific views of the material world than about God's consecration of it as the cosmic temple, resembling ANE mythological accounts such as *Enuma elish* or the Baal Cycle, which also describe the building of a cosmic temple for the enthronement of the conqueror god. The difference between Genesis 1 and the other myths is that in Genesis the conflict part of the myth is downplayed or absent altogether, perhaps as a deliberate commentary on those other myths.

Walton (2009) argues that Genesis 1 sets out a *functional* view of the beginnings of the world, not a *material* view. In other words, God is not described as making material out of nothing, so much as ordering and inaugurating what is already there. It is therefore quite possible to interpret the six days of Genesis 1 as six literal 24-hour days: God takes a conventional human working week to establish the functionality of the (already existent) world so that it can operate as the cosmic temple. Walton (*ibid.*: 84) points out that in the ANE the temple was often viewed as a microcosm of the world, designed with imagery reflecting the functions of the world to provide a resting place for God's presence on earth. Hence the importance of the seventh day in Genesis 1 as the day of divine rest after God's work has been completed (*ibid.*: 92).

Walton is not alone. Barker (2010) makes similar points. Genesis 1 is not ancient science so much as a holy vision of the world inspired by the reality of the Jerusalem temple. Like Walton, Barker sees the design of the Jerusalem temple (1 Kgs 6-7) and Moses' tabernacle in the desert (Exod. 25–27) as reflecting the pattern of creation. In the same way, the worship which went on in them was designed to express the relationships between God and all created things, and especially the well-being of both creation and human society (Barker 2010: 22). There are clear implications here for our own regard for creation, and for our need to recover the biblical vision of awe and responsibility towards God's created world.

Likewise, W. P. Brown (2010) sets forward a case for seeing Genesis 1 as paralleling the architectural structure of the Jerusalem temple. The six days fall into a schematic arrangement which mirrors the temple's sacred space. Although depiction of the physical likeness of God was forbidden in the temple, yet humans are declared to be made in the image of God on the sixth day. The seventh day inhabits the most holy day of all, reflecting the holy of holies at the heart of the temple (*ibid.*: 40–42).

These three studies all reject the widespread reading of Genesis 1 as an account of material origins, and offer in its place symbolic accounts where the text describes the formation of order and relationship in society and the world. These accounts are grounded in the historical-critical approach, seeking to put forward something of what might have been in the original author's mind, but they also have a message for our times, chiming with our growing awareness of environmental issues, by emphasizing the societal and ecological concerns of the text.

Layers of reality

The cosmic temple approaches demonstrate that there are more layers of potential meaning in the text than of material origins, in spite of most modern attitudes (see § "Genesis 1 and modern science" above). Modern science has inspired a restricted hermeneutic – that it is all about how physical reality came into being – but it is important to be expansive in reading Genesis 1. The fact that the text may be read in terms of ancient science as well as ancient mythological and religious motifs means that it is much more complex than might at first sight appear. And pigeon-holing it as a "metaphor" of creation (or, worse, as "poetry") simply introduces confusion, because it is not said clearly what the text should be metaphorical of. What is more, this complexity is whitewashed over, and the reader only encounters the tip of the iceberg in terms of the wealth of the text. The same is true if the text is simply labelled as a "cosmology", even an ancient cosmology. A more careful consideration of Genesis 1 should acknowledge its status as a richly fertile exploration of the idea of beginnings, and of the complex network of relationships between God, creation and humankind.

Much of what we have said concerns the *genre* of the text, and how this relates to ancient and modern views of science. We have pointed out how multi-layered must any answer to the question of genre be. In that light, genre is probably not a helpful term to use, since it suggests that the text might be conveniently categorized, if only we could hit upon the correct category. Our approach has been to suggest that this would be a misunderstanding of the text: Genesis 1 resists categorization. But if a description is insisted upon, then it is a theological portrait of God as Creator before it is anything else.

Summarizing the many motifs we have touched upon, a fully comprehensive approach to Genesis 1 would need to acknowledge that the text potentially impacts on many levels of reality and meaning, and that there is no single incontrovertible "answer" for how to read it. The following list is by no means exhaustive:

- The nature of God as the transcendent Creator who orders and makes the world as "very good"; it is judged, and found to satisfy all requirements admirably.
- This suggests that *value* is an important aspect of the narrative. Far from being a dispassionate ("scientific") account of physical origins, the sense is of God's work as an act of aesthetic pleasure, and the product as a thing of almost moral perfection and fundamental beauty, to be cherished.
- Nevertheless, cosmological and material beginnings of the world are set out, especially in terms of "ancient science", which represent working attempts to rationalize the world.

- Incorporation of mythological elements of other ANE cultures, and reaction to others.
- The setting-up of boundaries to space and time.
- The hallowing of space as God's cosmic temple.
- The hallowing of time through the establishment of the Sabbath.
- The ordering of the network of functions and relationships which make up the cosmos and its creatures.
- The special status of humankind made in God's image.
- Their special responsibility for creation.

Clearly, few of these motifs have much bearing on modern science and its reading of Genesis 1; the text is truly expansive. And these motifs are only a first brief attempt at appreciating the depths of this first chapter of the Bible, and of the ways in which it is still able to inspire reflection on God and creation.

THE SECOND GENESIS CREATION ACCOUNT: GENESIS 2:4b–3:24 (J)

The "Yahwist"

The "Yahwist" account of creation was thought by Wellhausen to be significantly the earlier of the two (perhaps tenth century BCE). We refer to this account for convenience as J, and as earlier, we do not intend by this a commitment to any specific historical formulation of the Documentary Hypothesis. Quite distinctively, J uses a different name for God (*YHWH Elohim*) from P (*Elohim*), and does not attempt to describe the creation of the heavens and the earth, but simply life on earth. The style is also quite different. There is none of the stately repetition of P, but instead an epic prose style which is echoed in many other long sections of narrative through the Pentateuch, also attributed to the Yahwist. The sense that creation proceeds through an ordered and intricately planned sequence of events is less evident in J. Instead, there is an element of improvisation in God's creative action in J, as two of the significant stages (the creation of animals and then the woman) come about to correct the fact that "it is not good that the man should be alone" (Gen. 2:18). It is only with the creation of the woman that this deficiency is resolved and creation is perfected. Instead of God pronouncing that creation is "very good" at its completion (as in P; Gen. 1:31), this functional role is given to the man, who takes on God's evaluating role (Fretheim 2005: 40–41), and assesses the woman as his perfect complement: "This at last is bone of my bones and flesh of my flesh" (Gen. 2:23).

In fact, the way that this motif of the "goodness" of creation is played out differently in P and J illustrates the point we made at the beginning of this chapter, that P and J offer distinct, but in some ways complementary, accounts of creation. There is a complex relationship between them, and while it is too much to say that they are independent of each other, it is too little to see them as a piece.

Notably, J is said to develop a particularly anthropomorphic portrait of God. If P likens God to roles such as that of the skilled builder (albeit one of cosmological dimensions), then J describes God performing more everyday human tasks, such as planting a garden (Gen. 2:8), and walking in it, "at the time of the evening breeze" (3:8). And if P is potentially cosmological in its scope, then J is more anthropological in its focus, concentrating especially on the man, his geographical context and relationships with other creatures, and with the woman, created last. This makes for quite an important distinction from P since in its description of the creation of living things J follows a quite different sequence of events: the man is made before any other living things on earth, then the plants, animals, and finally the woman.

The way in which God and humankind play such central roles in both P and J suggests that both texts were both written primarily for theological reasons, although they also contain traces of scientific thinking of the time. Both set out the special relationships of humans with respect to both God and the rest of creation, but while P also gives a theological reflection on the utter transcendence of this one God (strict monotheism), and an explanation for other cultic/cultural issues such as Sabbath observance, J contains an aetiology of sin, death and hardship. Indeed, it is important to recognize in this that the J narrative does not end after Genesis 3 either, but more clearly than P dovetails into the longer story of primeval beginnings which follows (Gen. 4–11), and which sets out to describe the primeval context for humankind, existing not only in relationship with God, but in relationship (and conflict) with itself and the world. If humankind has failed in one, it has failed in the other too (Westermann 1974: 17–19).

J may be very different from P in style and content, but literary structures have been discerned in it, just as they have in Genesis 1. Westermann (1974: 190), for instance, visualizes the narrative as an arch, seeing it begin with God's first command to the man, not to eat of the tree of the knowledge of good and evil (Gen. 2:16-17). It then ascends to a climax with the man and woman disobeying the command, and descends to the consequences: discovery, trial and punishment. The final component, where God expels them from the garden, mirrors the beginning, forming a palistrophic structure (Wenham 1987: 49–51).

If P is a modern ideological battleground between creationists and more liberal interpreters, then J is even more so. Centuries of Christian interpretation have read J in terms of the "Fall", a fundamental demotion in the human condition thanks to the disobedience of the first man and woman.

The Fall is often said to have been the source of death in the world, as well as other "natural evils" such as corruption, decay, suffering, predation, disease, natural catastrophes and every kind of "fallenness" in which the present state of the human and non-human natural worlds depart from the original "good" creation (Bimson 2009: 120–22; Murray [2008] 2011: 74–80). Indeed, the canonical placing of J directly after P, where creation was repeatedly said to be "good", must have been significant in inspiring this reading of J as the reversal of the "goodness" of creation, and the onset of "fallenness". But whether J (or the rest of the Bible) actually says this is another matter, and it will be seen that many of the arguments surrounding the text, and its relationship with modern science, arise from Paul's and Augustine's readings of it (Chapter 7).

J and science

We noted broad parallels between P and modern scientific accounts of beginnings, but J flies completely in the face of modern science, especially biological science. This is apparent straightaway when we see that it describes creation beginning with a single developed (and adult!) male first, then plants, then animals, and finally the woman (also an adult).In addition, there are the not inconsiderable challenges of explaining how the woman could be generated from one of the man's ribs (Gen. 2:21-22), how a tree could produce fruit which, when tasted, results in an eternal curse for humankind (2:17), and how a snake could talk (3:1)!

Attempts are sometimes made to salvage some scientific respectability from the narrative. One good example is the creation of the man from "the dust of the ground" (Gen. 2:7), which plays on the similarity between the Hebrew words for "man" ('adam) and "ground" ('adamah). The image being suggested is probably that of God forming the man's body as a potter moulds clay (Hamilton 1990: 156), and then breathing life into it through his nostrils. The "dust" has been related to the modern scientific idea that biologically important molecules such as proteins and amino acids may have been synthesized naturally on the surface of clay particles in the early history of the earth, thus forming the raw materials for life (W. P. Brown 2010: 95). This is an interesting parallel to draw, although hardly one that the author of J would have grasped. The general scientific impossibility of so many other aspects of J explains why only the most committed fundamentalists even attempt to read it as possessing scientific credence (e.g. Whitcomb & Morris 1961: 464–6 on the snake that deceived the man and the woman, and Pimenta 1984: 112 on the surgical operation which God performed on Adam to make Eve).

In spite of these difficulties, there has been a widespread desire to retain one particular aspect of J as historically authentic, namely the existence of a historical first human couple. The theological and scientific issues which surround this are so convoluted that we shall devote a whole chapter to them (Chapter 7).

Genre, history and mythology

As with Genesis 1, much of the discussion around how to interpret J centres on how we define its genre. And as with Genesis 1, J contains evidence of ancient scientific and mythological thinking. Perhaps the most obvious idea attributable to "ancient science" – which appears in both P and J – is that life is created out of the earth (Gen. 1:11-12, 24; 2:9, 19). This is nowhere more apparent than in the J account of the creation of the man, fashioned from the dust of the earth (clay?). This is also one of the more prominent parallels with other ANE mythologies, especially some Egyptian and Babylonian myths of beginnings, where the first humans are made from clay (Hamilton 1990: 156–8). And there are other ANE mythological motifs found in J too, such as the existence of a lush paradise where the gods lived, or the motif of food which confers immortality, and a snake which deprives humans from eating it (cf. Gen. 3:22; see Wenham 1987: 52–3). However, although J has features in common with a number of ANE myths, it is similar to P in that there is no evidence of direct borrowing, but rather of subtle influence. And as with P, some scholars regard J as "anti-myth", a deliberate theological attempt to challenge some of the accepted mythologies of surrounding cultures (Bimson 2009: 108).

Discussion of the mythological parallels in Genesis 2–3 masks the fact that there is a sense in which it attempts to offer a kind of historical narrative. In the context of the Pentateuch (and even of the whole Bible), it is clearly placed to chart the beginnings, to set the scene in universal and primeval terms for what is to come more particularly in the story of Israel. And in the book of Genesis, much of which is taken up with the patriarch Abraham and his descendants, Adam is linked genealogically all the way through Noah to Abraham (Gen. 5; 11). For that reason, although few scholars are willing to refer to J as "historical" – as though it told a series of factual events in history which had been observed, reported and passed on – yet it might be referred to generically as "proto-historical" (Wenham 1987: 91), or part of "the primeval story". Westermann (1984: 196–7) points out how Genesis 2–3 provides an "overture" to the whole of the Yahwist's work in the Pentateuch, since the themes of rebellion and punishment, the promise of land, the importance of community and family which recur throughout, first appear in Genesis 2–3. Therefore, Genesis 2–3 is not easily detachable from the Yahwist's later writings, much of which might be labelled less controversially as historiographical in style if not content.

Scholars also refer to the narrative using generic terms such as "paradigmatic" and "aetiological" (Wenham 1987: 91; Bimson 2009: 109). A paradigmatic story is more like a fable or parable, than it is a historiographical narrative. On the other hand, an aetiology presents in narrative terms a putative event in the past which has an impact on today. Although it is straightforward to distinguish between a paradigmatic and an aetiological text in principle, it is not so straightforward to determine whether Genesis 2–3 is one or the other, or perhaps both simultaneously (Bimson 2009: 109).

It is clear that many modern approaches to Genesis 2–3 do not take these subtleties into account, but assume that, as with Genesis 1, it is either historiographical, or else metaphorical of beginnings. There are modern theological presuppositions behind these approaches. But like Genesis 1, the text is more complex and multi-layered, defying easy categorization and description. Moreover, it sets up threads which are woven tightly into the material which follows, even into the more plausibly historiographical material in Genesis 12–50. This is why it is unwise to see Genesis 2–3 too much as a self-contained literary unit with a genre all of its own, which is, after all, exactly what Western Christianity has done with it since Augustine, seeing it as the "Fall". The wider narrative context suggests that it should be seen as part of a longer story telling of the many ways in which humankind oversteps the boundaries imposed upon it by God, and of how God responds both with judgement and blessing (Chapter 7). Like Genesis 1, then, Genesis 2–3 is also a portrait of God.

J and God

If P evokes a picture of God as the skilled builder or architect who follows an intricate blueprint stage-by-stage, J gives us a completely different picture, although it is characteristically "anthropomorphic". Creation takes place over stages again, but they do not appear to be as carefully planned out and thought through. Instead, in at least two of the significant stages (the creation of animals and then of the woman), God appears to create in order to make good an earlier deficiency. God realizes that the man needs a companion and so creates animals (Gen. 2:18-19). When it becomes clear that these are not up to the task, God creates the woman (2:20-22), and so completes the story of creation. In each case, what is created comes about through adapting and improvising upon what has already been achieved.

Both P and J describe God's commission to the first humans, but they are very different. P's God tells them to "be fruitful and multiply", to "fill the earth and subdue it" (Gen. 1:28), and that they may eat of any plant or tree on the earth (1:29). J's God on the other hand does not encourage the man to travel the earth and "fill" it, but instead places him in the limits of the garden in order to tend it. This is perhaps out of care for the man rather than to confine him, since the rest of the earth was relatively barren. Indeed, J's God shows a considerably degree of concern for the man's welfare, and not just for food, since God goes to some trouble to create a suitable companion for him.

J's God only makes one command to the man – he may eat the fruit of every tree in the garden, except the tree of the knowledge of good and evil, "for in the day that you eat of it you shall die" (Gen. 2:16-17). Of course, the nature of this tree is shrouded in mystery, and it does not appear to be paralleled in other mythologies either, nor even elsewhere in the Bible outside of Genesis 2-3. Also present is the "tree of life" (2:9), which appears to confer immortality upon those who eat its fruit (3:22-24). Although this tree does not appear in the main action of the narrative, it does appear elsewhere in the Bible (e.g. Prov. 3:18; Rev. 22:2), and parallels exist with Babylonian myths. There is a great deal of uncertainty about these two trees (Westermann 1984: 212–14; Wenham 1987: 62–4; Hamilton 1990: 162–6), and about "the knowledge of good and evil" and why it might bring death, but the suggestion appears to be that the trees are counterparts to each other: the fruit of one brings life, and the other death. And despite the many questions surrounding them, it is the questions which they pose around the character of God in the narrative which are most enticing.

For instance, Barr (1984: 33–4) explains how inaccurate are the predictions of God in J. God warns the man that if he eats the fruit of the tree of the knowledge of good and evil he will die. But the man and the woman actually suffer a considerably more lenient punishment for their disobedience: expulsion from the garden and an increase in hardship and pain. God's prediction is incorrect, but the snake's is spot on (Gen. 3:4-5). As Barr puts it, "If one is to evaluate utterances by the scale of their correspondence with actual events, God's utterance does not come very high in degree, and that of the serpent comes as high as it is possible to come" (Barr 1984: 34).

This ambivalence surrounding God's nature can be seen as a component of J's "anthropomorphism". It also features elsewhere in the great narrative sequences of the Pentateuch, where God appears to be changeable in attitude, uncertain, and imprecise rather like any human being, only on a much more serious scale. On other occasions where judgement is nigh, God can express regret about previous decisions (Gen. 6:6), or uncertainty (Gen. 18:22-33), or a change of mind (Exod. 32:11-14). This changeability is not haphazard or fickle, but always a reasoned response to a human situation, and is very often more moderate or more merciful than what is expected. The point being made in J is that God is not static and monolithic, but dynamic and personal, someone with whom one might converse, or at least could pray to and hope for a favourable answer.

This is, of course, a considerably more sophisticated and subtle picture of God than that of P. And it introduces the moral chain of cause and effect which is such an important part of the human condition. J may not place boundaries on contemporary humans in the way that P's aetiology of the Sabbath does, but it indicates the ambiguity involved in moral judgements and their outcome, the human tendency towards disobedience, and God's nature in response.

P ends with God's verdict that all of creation was "very good" (Gen. 1:31); J's account ends with the opposite: the blessing is withdrawn from human-kind and they are expelled from God's presence in the garden. God's ver-dict describes human life as we know it, with hardship, suffering and death (3:15-19). Morally, it introduces questions and problems which require fur-ther exploration, and this is just what the rest of Genesis 1–11 seeks to do as the lives of all families of the earth come into view, before Genesis 12 focuses in again on one chosen family, that of Abraham (Hamilton 1990: 52). And the notion of obedience to God based on a supportive relation-ship between God and humans, followed by punishment for disobedience, is basic to the covenant theology developed elsewhere in the Pentateuch and the Bible. If P is relatively self-contained, J is anything but.

CONCLUSIONS

There is a complex relationship between the Genesis 1 account of creation (P) and the Genesis 2–3 account (J) which science does little to clarify. Both offer considerable challenges to any approach that attempts to har-monize them, either with each other or with modern scientific accounts of beginnings. Once we begin to recognize their own distinctive charac-ters, in part owing to their different historical and theological contexts, we begin to see their very considerable depths. It is often noticed that both of the Genesis creation accounts are rarely echoed explicitly in the Bible, but the fact that these passages stand at the head of the Pentateuch, and thereby of the Bible, shows their significance. The J account, for instance, might be echoed explicitly in the Bible only rather seldom after Genesis 3 (C. J. Collins 2011: 66–92), but it clearly sets the scene for many of the same concerns and motifs of sin, obedience and judgement which are repeated again and again throughout the Bible. This is why "no adequate theology can avoid coming to grips with this passage" (Rogerson 1976: 30).

These texts may be controversial in our modern times, but they are of enormous significance to the Bible, since they set out basic features of its *worldview* (Carlson & Longman 2010: 134–41).We have discussed the genre of the texts at some length here, and have not come to any firm conclusion, partly because of the difficulty of articulating this very point, that the texts are fundamentally expansive since they concern a whole worldview. If we fail to appreciate this point, and unthinkingly impose our own worldview on the texts, we will quickly misunderstand them, along with their claims about key worldview issues such as cosmology, (ancient) science, and the human condition and its relationship with the Creator and other creatures. Without awareness of this point, we will learn relatively little from the texts.

This has been a very selective and brief overview of an enormous area of research. The motivation has been to shed light on those aspects of the Genesis creation narratives that have a bearing on how science is used in interpretations of the Bible. This is by no means the end of the creation motif in the Bible, though, and in the next chapter we will attempt to cover the relevant additional material. We will be able to do so more briefly than here, since this additional material is rarely considered by scientists. That is not to say that it is not important though. As we have seen, interpretation of the Genesis accounts is considerably more open-ended than simple comparisons with modern science might suggest, and this picture only becomes more complex as we look at other aspects of the creation motif.

Chapter 4

CREATION ACCORDING TO THE BIBLE II:
THE CREATION MOTIF

CREATION AND NARRATIVE

Although the Genesis creation texts are usually regarded as the primary sources of biblical creation thought, there is far more creation material spread throughout the Bible. When taken together with the Genesis accounts, it makes for a very diverse account of creation, which we will refer to as the biblical "creation motif" (see § "Creation in the Bible" in Chapter 1, above). Furthermore, while some of the additional creation material coheres with P or J (usually P), there are many other elements. This means that there is less a "theology of creation" in the Bible so much as "theologies of creation". As Brueggemann (1997: 163–4) has explained, these theologies are united by the fact that they are *testimony* of "Yahweh who creates". God does so by word (e.g. Gen. 1, but also including the prophetic word), by wisdom (e.g. Jer. 10:12) and by spirit (Gen. 1:2). We might be tempted to unite this into a single doctrine of creation, but this would abuse the integrity of the biblical witness in its diversity. The view taken in this book is that the creation motif is focussed on the *nature* of God, which is never easily pinned-down nor systematized in the Bible; consequently, biblical creation theology is always diverse and multi-dimensional.

In his study of the Old Testament creation motif, Fretheim (2005) makes the important points that (1) creation thought is central to everything said about God, and that (2) Old Testament creation thought is relational; that is, it sees the formation of relationships as basic to God's nature, and to God's formation of creation. Everything exists in a state of interrelatedness, reflecting its maker (*ibid.*: 16). This is a valuable idea, and Fretheim does much to explicate it. We will do so in our own way in this and subsequent chapters, eventually through focus on God as Trinity.

The relevant creation texts are very extensive in scope, and we will largely aim to flag up their diversity in this chapter, extracting the most useful components of the creation motif for comparison with scientific views of creation. The first type of text to be considered here are the great narratives of the Old Testament, of which Genesis 1–11 forms the introductory and primeval story of beginnings. Taken together, from Genesis 1 to 2 Kings 25 and beyond, this varied anthology of largely historiographical prose tells a gigantic story from the beginnings of humankind to the beginnings of Israel, and then beyond to the effective end of Israel and Judah at the Exile, and the tentative re-birth at the rebuilding of Jerusalem (Ezra–Nehemiah).

From the point of view of the creation motif, key moments in this grand narrative sweep take place in the story of the Flood, in the Exodus, and in the giving of the law at Sinai.

In the Flood (Gen. 6–9), God destroys much of the P and J creation, and establishes a new creation, marked by a covenant with Noah and every living creature (9:1-17). This covenant sets limits on humans and animals, but also on God, who resolves never to undo creation in such a way again. It is not too much to say that this furthers the relationship of *inter-dependence* between Creator and creature which had already begun in 1:26-30: God freely commits to be constrained to some degree by the actions of human and animal, while bestowing some of the responsibilities of creation upon them (Fretheim 2005: 270–72).

In a similar way, the creation of Israel as a nation at the Exodus is marked by the establishment of the covenant at Sinai, which binds both God and people to a further state of inter-dependence. Again, we are guided by Fretheim (*ibid.*: 110–31), who points out that God's *creative* activity provides the basis for understanding much of what happens here, even though the story of the Exodus is customarily categorized as "redemption" rather than "creation". A key verse for Fretheim is Exodus 1:7, which indicates that, as the story begins, the Israelites in Egypt are obeying P's creative injunction to be fruitful and multiply (Gen. 1:28). Pharaoh's attempts to limit them, which move towards genocide (Exod. 1:8-16), are therefore a threat to creation. In response, God provides a series of signs, pre-eminently the plagues of Exodus 7–10, and the crossing of the sea (Exod. 14–15). These signs match the cosmic threat of creation's enemy (Pharaoh) by being similarly creational in scope; the sea crossing in particular provides spectacularly for Pharaoh's ultimate vanquishing. Creation thus restores itself, and the Israelites enjoy abundant provision of food and water in the wilderness (Exod. 15–17), through a series of miracles which are in fact a return to the divinely ordered scheme of providence.

The narrative moves on to describe the building of the tabernacle for worship (Exod. 25–31; 35–40). Parallels have long been noted between this account and P's creation narrative, making a similar point to that which we noted in Chapter 3 about creation as the cosmic temple. Moreover, the tabernacle narrative sits alongside the complex story of the giving of the law at Sinai, carried on through the books of Leviticus, Numbers and

Deuteronomy. Relatively few modern readers study these texts in detail, owing to their perceived obscurity and complexity, but they contain a wealth of insight into the Israelite worldview, and a great deal that informs a view of creation. As we shall note later (§ "The ancient Israelite 'mindset'?" in Chapter 5, below), the law sets up an ordered system for the entirety of life, memorably through distinctions such as those between the "clean" and the "unclean", and between that which is "holy" and that which is an "abomination". The human social and ritual worlds are entirely included in this system, but so are the agricultural and natural worlds; they exist symbiotically, and rely on each other for their preservation and flourishing.

It is difficult to overstate the importance of law (Torah) to the Jewish religious worldview, and here we see it seamlessly integrated into the great formational narrative of creation and redemption which runs from Genesis to 2 Kings and beyond. Many of the distinctions and boundaries enshrined in Torah stem from a worldview very distant from our own, but there is much that can be learned from this worldview as we go through this book, especially its holistic understanding of law, creation, religion and science, and its resistance towards glib categorization.

As we turn now to consider the creation motif in the Bible's poetic literature, we conclude this section with a quotation from Psalm 19, which relates a law of nature (the rising of the sun) to Torah so closely that it is clear they are to be seen as complementary ways of relating to the Creator, and of viewing the Creator's nature. If God and the human and natural worlds are inter-dependent upon each other, then so are abstract concepts such as law and creation:

> [The sun's] rising is from the end of the heavens,
>   and its circuit to the end of them;
>   and nothing is hid from its heat.
> The law of the LORD is perfect,
>   reviving the soul;
> the decrees of the LORD are sure,
>   making wise the simple.
>
>   (Ps. 19:6-7)

CREATION AND POETRY

Some of the most glorious psalms express praise of God's handiwork in every aspect of nature (e.g. Ps. 33), perhaps even showing resonances with the Genesis accounts of creation. Psalm 8 is a good example, bearing close similarities with P's assessment of the place of humankind in creation, where they are said to have "dominion" over it (compare Ps. 8:3-8 with Gen. 1:26-30). Since many of the Psalms exhort *humans* to praise God because of God's works (e.g. Ps. 9) or because of God's divine nature (e.g. Ps. 117), so there are also passages which describe *all of creation* praising God for the very same reasons (e.g. Pss. 65; 98). It is equally in the nature of humans and all of creation to give due recognition to the Creator. This illustrates the contingency that we discussed in Chapter 2 as basic to the Christian doctrine of creation. The whole of creation is dependent upon God as Creator for its existence in the beginning and throughout its history (i.e. its existence is not *necessary* but thoroughly reliant upon God), and praise is recognition of this simple fact. To fail to recognize one's contingency upon God is to fail to give praise to God for all there is, and vice versa.

Others psalms though, praise God's work in history (e.g. Ps. 105), expressing a similar sentiment of the recognition of contingency. If the whole of creation is contingent because it is dependent upon God for its initial and continued existence, then Israel is contingent as a nation because it is dependent upon God for its initial formation as a nation, its salvation at the Exodus, and its continued deliverance from enemies. A particularly interesting example is that of Psalm 136, which expresses praise to God for both creation *and* redemption. This psalm illustrates some close links with the P creation account (compare Ps. 136:8-9 with Gen. 1:16-18), but immediately goes on (vv. 10-16) to connect the creation motif with another important theological pattern, namely the idea of God's redemption in history, in the form of the Exodus.

> O give thanks to the Lord of lords,
>   for his steadfast love endures forever...
> who made the great lights,
>   for his steadfast love endures forever;
> the sun to rule over the day,
>   for his steadfast love endures forever;
> the moon and stars to rule over the night,
>   for his steadfast love endures forever;
> who struck Egypt through their firstborn,
>   for his steadfast love endures forever;
> and brought Israel out from among them,
>   for his steadfast love endures forever;
> with a strong hand and an outstretched arm,
>   for his steadfast love endures forever;
> who divided the Red Sea in two,
>   for his steadfast love endures forever;
> and made Israel pass through the midst of it,
>   for his steadfast love endures forever;
> but overthrew Pharaoh and his army in the Red Sea,
>   for his steadfast love endures forever;
>
>   (Ps. 136:3, 7-15)

This connection between creation and redemption is used to particularly good effect in "'Second Isaiah" (Isa. 40–55), the portion of the prophet which is thought to have been written in the Babylonian Exile (sixth century BCE), as the Israelites longed for a return to their homeland and a restoration of their former monarchy and temple worship. Second Isaiah is often said to be the most trenchantly monotheistic part of the Old Testament, perhaps like the Priestly creation account having been formed in reaction to the polytheistic Babylonian cult. As part of the prophet's proof that there is only one god, and that this god is Yahweh, his status as the sole creator is strongly emphasized (e.g. Isa. 40). At the same time, a return to the homeland from exile in Babylon is predicted, which will be a new and glorious exodus across the desert (Isa. 40:3-5; 41:17-20; 42:16; 43:14-21; 48:20-21; 49:8-12; 52:11-12; 55:12), and a "new thing" (Isa. 42:9; 43:19; 48:6-7). It is clear that the prophet has in mind a "new creation", which links together deliverance from Exile with the original foundational event of the Exodus. (A related "new creation", which involves a restoration of Jerusalem and the homeland, is described by the other major exilic prophet, Ezek. 40-48.) The theme of new creation, and especially its connection with modern science, will be discussed more fully in Chapter 9, and at this point we simply flag it up as a further component of the biblical creation motif.

Some of the relevant texts in Second Isaiah describe Yahweh as both redeemer and creator, in terms familiar from P (e.g. Isa. 44:24). But other passages appear to tap into a different pattern of creation, making use of *mythological* terms that do not surface explicitly in Genesis 1. The reference to "Rahab" here is especially significant:

> Awake, awake, put on strength,
> O arm of the LORD!
> Awake, as in days of old,
> the generations of long ago!
> Was it not you who cut Rahab in pieces,
> who pierced the dragon?
> Was it not you who dried up the sea,
> the waters of the great deep;
> who made the depths of the sea a way
> for the redeemed to cross over?
> So the ransomed of the LORD shall return,
> and come to Zion with singing;
> everlasting joy shall be upon their heads;
> they shall obtain joy and gladness,
> and sorrow and sighing shall flee away.
> (Isa. 51:9-11)

Here we see the prophet bringing all of the themes we have discussed so far into a single movement. The first creation and the redemption of Israel in the first Exodus become historical staging posts in the new exodus and the formation of the new and everlasting creation oriented around the return to Zion. But in order to recognize that the first creation is in view here in the reference to Rahab, we need to examine the mythology of creation.

CREATION AND MYTHOLOGY

Several mythologies of the ANE tell of a cosmic battle between a principal god and the forces of chaos. Before the discovery of the Canaanite Baal Cycle at Ugarit in Syria, the main source for this tradition was the Babylonian creation epic, *Enuma elish*, where the god Marduk fights with the goddess of the sea, Tiamat, defeats her and cuts her body in two, thus making the heavens and the earth. Egypt too, had a similar creation myth, involving the creator god Re doing battle with the serpent Apophis. Although there are some telling similarities between *Enuma elish* and Genesis 1, such as the creation of the dome above the earth to separate the waters (Gen. 1:6), there is no explicit parallel in Genesis 1 to the intriguing idea of a cosmic battle between the creator god and a dragon which personifies chaos, although Gunkel claimed to find one in the similarity between the Hebrew word for "deep" (*tehom*; Gen. 1:2), and the name Tiamat. There is, on the other hand, a prominent serpent or snake who personifies evil in the story of Adam and Eve (Gen. 3). A careful reader, immersed in the mythological culture of the ANE, would presumably have identified this serpent with the ancient cosmic enemy of Yahweh (Averbeck 2004).

These parallels between the Genesis creation accounts and other mythologies are rather sketchy though. More substantial connections with ancient mythological thought can be found elsewhere in the Bible, especially when we consider the mythological Baal Cycle discovered at Ugarit. This describes a battle very much like that between Marduk and Tiamat in the *Enuma elish*: Baal is the equivalent of Marduk, and Yam the equivalent of Tiamat (who also seems to be identical with the dragon Leviathan or Rahab described in the Old Testament). John Day, who has done much to publicize the recognition of this mythological theme (Day 1985; 2000: 98–127), refers to it as "God's conflict with the dragon and the sea". In the Bible, the theme may appear as a conflict that occurs at the time of original creation, but it may also be linked with reference to God's salvation, or God's enthronement over the world (e.g. Pss. 29; 65; 74:12-17; 77:17-21 [ET 16-20]; 89:6-18 [ET 7-19]; 93; 104:5-9). Related mythological parallels are seen in what is known as the "Divine Warrior" theophany (Cross 1973: 91–111): like Marduk and Baal, Yahweh is often portrayed as a storm god, manifest in storm, wind and rain, even in contexts where creation is not clearly in view (e.g. Exod. 15:1-18).

The mythological conflict theme is used to especially good effect in the book of Job, which, perhaps because of its subject matter (theodicy, explaining God's ways in the face of the inexplicable), has a particular interest in God's role in creation. There are a number of references to the conflict theme where the original act of creation is clearly in view (Job 9:8, 13; 26:12-13; 38:8-11), and the Divine Warrior theophany features prominently too (Job 38:1). But in the detailed and fantastic descriptions of the two beasts Behemoth and Leviathan (Job 40–41) we see an imaginative development of the theme, which makes no clear link with the primeval battle as the act of creation. These two beasts have often been interpreted as the hippopotamus and crocodile, respectively, but Day (2000: 102–3) points out that they are probably intended as mythical monsters. Leviathan in particular appears to be a dragon, with deadly and fearsome power, and both creatures are said to be impossible to master by anyone except God, who regards them as defeated and tame. The message conveyed by the text is that, just as the mythical monsters are far beyond human control or even understanding, so God's ways are much more so. W. P. Brown (2010: 141) points out that Psalm 104 forms an interesting counterpiece to Job 38–41, since like the Job text it describes the teeming diversity of creation, and includes Leviathan "playing" in the sea (Ps. 104:26). The contrast with the original mythological symbol of deadly combat between God and the sea could hardly be greater, and in both accounts Leviathan is no longer an enemy pitted against God but is one of God's creatures, with a natural place in the world ordered by God. That the symbol of the mythological dragon goddess can be domesticated and naturalized illustrates the degree to which the ANE mythological background to creation remained resistant in Israelite culture despite bitter invective against other ANE cultures.

This is further illustrated by the fact that the motif of combat with the dragon becomes something of a stock metaphor, which can be used in comments on current politics (e.g. Ps. 87:4; Isa. 30:7), or it may be projected forward in time, as a statement of eschatological punishment for those who are opposed to God (e.g. Amos 9:3; Isa. 27:1). The motif even informs the picture of the four monsters which come out of the sea and oppose God in Daniel's vision (Dan. 7). This, in time, was appropriated in Christian circles to become the image used for the Devil (Rev. 12; 13; 20), who also appears here in close association with the sea.

The image of God's conflict with the dragon and the sea is therefore subtle but highly significant because of its flexibility, and it gives us a way of seeing how the creation motif coheres with other theological themes. The Red Sea crossing, with its obvious motif of God's mastery of the sea by separating the waters (Exod. 14), is especially pertinent, and we may return to Isaiah 51:9-11, which connects the original act of creation through mythological combat with Rahab with successive exoduses, and a new and eternal creation when the exiles return to Zion.

It is also possible to "demythologize" the motif, to extract a sort of scientific meaning out of the story of God's conflict with the dragon/sea. In which case, we would construe it not as a creation story telling of a making from nothing, but as a story telling of *order from disorder*, and we might therefore connect it with other creative motifs in the Bible that speak of God establishing order in a formerly amorphous mass (McGrath [2002] 2006a: 146). There is, for instance, the image of God bringing about creation through working clay like a potter (Isa. 29:16; 45:9; 64:8; Sir. 33:13; Rom. 9:20-21). But perhaps the most notable example of creation as order from disorder comes in P. In Genesis 1:2, God begins the creation of the heavens and earth with the "formless void" and darkness over the face of the deep, all of which are symbols of disorder. Just as order is imposed by the creation of light, which is separated from the darkness, so order is imposed upon the earth by the separation of waters and the formation of dry land. And we will see that this motif, of creation as order from disorder, turns out to have an appealing analogy in the many emergent properties of nature described by modern science (Chapter 9).

CREATION AND WISDOM

There is a further very significant component to the creation motif, and this appears in the biblical Wisdom literature (especially Proverbs, Job, Ecclesiastes, Sirach, Wisdom of Solomon). The importance of this literature to the Bible's creation motif should not be underestimated, because not only is it as venerable as other creation traditions (Oden 1992a: 1166–7), it provides the foundation for much of the New Testament's creation theology, and is particularly amenable to comparisons with modern scientific views of the laws of nature, as we shall see.

We have already mentioned how the book of Job makes use of the mythological motif of God's battle with the sea. And in common with the other biblical books in the Wisdom category, Job 38–41 makes a great deal of God's role as Creator of the natural world. Interestingly, W. P. Brown (2010: 133) compares Job's gleaming description of natural life with Darwin's epochal voyage on *The Beagle*, which was so formational in the modern realization that life exists in a "multiversity of biodiversity". Job was already pointing this out millennia before Darwin.

If God is Creator of all there is, then God is also the originator of all wisdom. Therefore, by placing humankind in the context of the enormity and the awe of God's act of creation, we are better placed to appreciate our (in) significance, our own lack of human wisdom, and our dependence on God's wisdom and laws. This is a recurring theme in Job, as well as in Ecclesiastes, which is also notable because it emphasizes an orderliness in creation to be compared with other creation accounts, such as P of Genesis 1, or of Proverbs 8:22-31. But where these latter accounts emphasize order through the stages in which God carefully makes the world, Ecclesiastes describes creation in terms of the endlessly repetitive cycle of seasons and time:

> A generation goes, and a generation comes,
>   but the earth remains forever.
> The sun rises and the sun goes down,
>   and hurries to the place where it rises.
> The wind blows to the south,
>   and goes around to the north;
> round and round goes the wind,
>   and on its circuits the wind returns.
> All streams run to the sea,
>   but the sea is not full;
> to the place where the streams flow,
>   there they continue to flow.
>   (Eccl. 1:4-7)

Such a view of nature reinforces the writer's pessimism that "all is vanity and a chasing after wind" (Eccl. 1:14). As well as good, there is suffering in life, and it must inevitably come to an end for each of us (Eccl. 12:1-7), while the world of creation continues relentlessly and remorselessly. Despite the fact that these sentiments were first recorded well over two thousand years ago, there is much that resonates here with the modern scientific view of the world (W. P. Brown 2010: 186), and especially with Darwin's idea of natural selection through survival of the fittest. Nature develops through cycles of endless struggle and competition, oblivious to the fate of the individual or even of whole species. If the seeming futility of this view of life inspires the New Atheists to argue in our day against religion, then it is worth noting that the author of Ecclesiastes acknowledged the same sense of futility thousands of years before, but concluded that it made religion and the confession of God, who is above everything, all the more important (Eccl. 12:13).

Ecclesiastes notes that, in spite of this futility to life, it is evident that there must be meaning in it, a wisdom which ultimately comes from above. But, as in the book of Job, it is a wisdom which is elusive to mere human minds (Eccl. 8:16-17). And in Job, even though humans may search for it as though they were digging the deepest mine in search of precious metals, yet still they will not find this wisdom (Job 28). As von Rad (1972: 148) says of it: "This 'wisdom', this 'understanding' must, therefore, signify something like the 'meaning' implanted by God in creation, the divine mystery of creation."

In some parts of the Wisdom literature, Wisdom becomes heightened beyond a "meaning" implanted by God, or even the agency through which God created the world (Prov. 3:19), to the status of a personified female being. The possible divine status of Wisdom and her relation to creation reaches a particularly high point in the famous hymn of Wisdom in Proverbs 8, which has Wisdom making the significant and central statement: *"Yahweh created me at the beginning of his journey, the foremost of his works from that time"* (v. 22). The passage goes on to describe how Wisdom accompanied God through all of the making of creation; and in verse 30 she is described as like a "master builder" or "architect" (or perhaps even a "young child", the meaning is uncertain). In any case, she is God's "delight" (v. 30).

But how exactly does she relate to God? There is uncertainty over how to translate the verb in the crucial verse of Proverbs 8:22 – was she "created" (as in the rendition given above), or would "begot", or even "acquired" be more appropriate (Oden 1992a: 1167)? This uncertainty, and the potentially divine status of Wisdom which flows from it, clearly bears on the question of Israelite understandings of monotheism (and it became a particularly vexed issue in the much later Arian debate of the fourth century CE, concerning the divinity of Christ). Is Wisdom being spoken of metaphorically as an aspect of God's very personality or being, perhaps a feminine side? Or is Wisdom something like a goddess consort of the male creator god (as is found in other ANE religions)? Or is Wisdom a separate but created entity, like an angel, who accompanies God (Dell 2000: 20)? These are very difficult questions to answer with confidence, but scholars have tended to highlight the fluid and metaphorical nature of Wisdom's description in 8:22-31, generally seeing Wisdom as a literary device describing an aspect of God's personality as both born from God, with God, and in God (R. L. Murphy 1992: 927).

The Wisdom of Solomon 7–9 takes this motif of Wisdom personified even further, with an extended passage on the centrality of Wisdom in creation: "She reaches mightily from one end of the earth to the other, and she orders all things well" (Wisdom 8:1). This association of Wisdom with the *ordering* of the world might put us in mind of the chaos myth of creation (§ "Creation and mythology", above). It is certainly a possible allusion, albeit a distant one, for it has been noted that apart from Job (and also perhaps Prov. 8:29), the chaos myth is "remarkably absent" in the Wisdom literature (Day 2000: 100). In any case, what is remarkable about the Wisdom of Solomon compared with Proverbs 8 is that we find an even closer association between Wisdom and the personality/being of God:

> For she is a breath of the power of God,
>   and a pure emanation of the glory of the Almighty;
> therefore nothing defiled gains entrance into her.

> For she is a reflection of eternal light,
>   a spotless mirror of the working of God,
>   and an image of his goodness.
>
>   (Wisdom 7:25-26)

If after having read Proverbs 8 we were unsure as to whether Wisdom has a divine status or not, then the Wisdom of Solomon seems to clarify the situation. Wisdom is not identical with God, and she is certainly not an attribute of the created world either, such as its "goodness". Rather, she is an outflowing of God's personality, a gift of God (8:21) who inhabits and orders the world. And she is more than the divine meaning implanted into the world, giving it purpose and harmony, since she is also its "fashioner" (7:21-22), taking an active role in its making.

A similarly exalted description of Wisdom personified comes in Sirach 24, where Wisdom is said to be transcendent over creation in the way that only God is. Indeed, we might be forgiven for thinking the passage was God's own self-description, if the passage did not say clearly that Wisdom was created by God, and is at God's beck and call:

> I came forth from the mouth of the Most High,
>   and covered the earth like a mist.
> I dwelt in the highest heavens,
>   and my throne was in a pillar of cloud.
> Alone I compassed the vault of heaven
>   and traversed the depths of the abyss.
> Over waves of the sea, over all the earth,
>   and over every people and nation I have held sway.
> Among all these I sought a resting place;
>   in whose territory should I abide?
> Then the Creator of all things gave me a command,
>   and my Creator chose the place for my tent.
> He said, "Make your dwelling in Jacob,
>   and in Israel receive your inheritance."
> Before the ages, in the beginning, he created me,
>   and for all the ages I shall not cease to be.
>
>   (Sir. 24:3-9)

One feature of these portraits of Wisdom which is particularly appealing in our modern scientific age is her relationship to the laws of nature. She is described as forever ubiquitous in the natural world, something like its fashioner as well as its blueprint, purpose, meaning and order, and yet also dwelling especially in God's enlightened people, in Israel. This bears a great deal of similarity with some modern estimations of the laws of physics, where they are elevated to semi-divine status (see § "The laws of nature" in

Chapter 2, above). But there is more to Wisdom than the laws of nature. Not only is she an outpouring of God's character active in fashioning creation, but when we consider the rest of the Wisdom literature we see that moral, ethical and social wisdom come into consideration too: she is more than science. It is, however, her embodiment of natural law that points towards a way to appropriate these texts theologically in our scientific age. There is a clear bridge that can be built between Hebrew conceptions of the divine underpinning of the world and modern ideas of the laws of nature. And this becomes particular clear when we turn to interpretation of the New Testament, with the advent of Christ and the doctrines of the incarnation and Trinity.

CREATION AND CHRIST

In the New Testament we find that, apart from a few references to the Genesis creation stories in order to develop a moral point (e.g. Mk 10:2-12; 1 Cor. 11:7-12), and a notable reworking of the chaos myth through the figure of the "Dragon" (Rev. 12; 13; 20), talk of creation is focused largely on and through the person of Christ. There is a heavily eschatological flavour to this theme, but we also find that many of the sentiments which were expressed in the Wisdom literature are now captured and amplified in talk of Christ. The best-known example comes in the famous Prologue to John's Gospel (Jn 1:1-18), with its hymn to "the Word" (*logos* in Greek), which, it becomes clear, is the pre-existent Christ, the "Son" (Jn 1:14, 18).

There has been much scholarly speculation about the religious and intellectual background to John's choice of the term *logos* (Tobin 1992). *Logos* was, for instance, used extensively in Greek philosophical circles, and the Stoic concept of the *logos* as the rational principle of order built into the universe is suggestive of John's use of the term. And the fact that the Stoic concept of *logos* bears a resemblance to some of the more exalted assessments of the laws of physics in our own time is perhaps one reason why interest has developed in the science–theology field of seeing Christ as embodying the laws of physics (§ "The *logos* and the laws of physics" in Chapter 10, below).

But for all the attraction of seeing the Stoic concept of *logos* behind John's *logos*, the Jewish Wisdom tradition presents a more likely basis. Close parallels are seen between what John says of the *logos* and what the books of Proverbs, Wisdom and Sirach say of personified Wisdom. And we find a similar ambiguity in discerning the status of the Word with respect to God, because John tells us that the *logos* was both with God at the beginning, and is also very actually God (Jn 1:1). And as Wisdom personified was said to be vital in making the world, so John tells us that it was through the *logos* that all things were made: "All things came into being through him, and without him not one thing came into being" (Jn 1:3a). Like Wisdom, the *logos* is compared with light (Jn 1:4-5, cf. Wisdom 6:12; 7:26), and is said to be the source of life (Jn 1:3-4, cf. Prov. 8:35; Wisdom 8:13). And like Wisdom, the *logos* was in the world (Jn 1:10, cf. Sirach 1:15) but the world by and large did not know him (Jn 1:10, cf. Baruch 3:31).

John's Prologue can also be seen to be a Christological interpretation of the Genesis 1 creation account (Barton 2009: 194–5). Both passages begin with the unmistakeable and resounding phrase, "In the beginning ..." And John's identification of the pre-existent Son with the *logos* recalls the way in which God *speaks* in Genesis 1 and the world comes into being (Gen. 1:3, 6, 9, 14, 20, 24, 26). Here, the spoken word is all-effective. God does not need to actively fashion the world in Genesis 1, but simply *commands* it to come into being. In fact, even saying that God *commands* is perhaps too strong, because the relevant phrases in Genesis 1 are often rendered in terms of the divine fiat, or "letting-be" (e.g. "Let there be light"). If so, the spoken word of creation is more an act of divine encouragement than command, and gives us the paradoxical picture of the transcendent Creator who is simultaneously in close relationship with Creation, prompting it to spring into life. And once God's spoken word of encouragement in Genesis 1 becomes personified in the divine *logos* of John 1, who works alongside God in creation and yet becomes a part of it as "flesh" (Jn 1:14), the sense of partnership comes even more to the fore. This means that, although the motif of creation through the *word* of God is known elsewhere (e.g. Pss. 33:6, 9; 119:89; 148:5; Heb. 11:3), it reaches new heights in John 1. Moreover, while John's use of the term *logos* makes clear the parallels with Genesis 1, it also connects the motif of creation with the prophetic *will* of God, as also expressed through speech, "the word of the Lord" of the Hebrew prophets (Macquarrie 1990: 43–4, 107–10; Peacocke 1996b: 327).

And this is perhaps how we are in part to understand the most celebrated phrase in John's Prologue, "and the Word became flesh and dwelt among us" (Jn 1:14). It is in Jesus of Nazareth that God's creative purpose and divine will, which are the same purpose and will expressed by the law and the prophets – together with the duo of "grace and truth" (Jn 1:14, 16) – are embodied in the form of a human being (Ward 2010: 78–9). God is revealed in such an unprecedented way in this human being that he may even be said to be the "only begotten God" (*monogenes theos*): "*No one has ever seen God; the only begotten God, who is at the Father's heart: he has made him known*" (Jn 1:18).

The intimacy pictured here – coupled with revelatory purpose – is reminiscent of the relationship between God and Wisdom in Proverbs 8. And although we have focussed here on John's Prologue, the connection between Jesus and the Jewish Wisdom tradition is by no means unique to John's Gospel: we find traces of it also in the Synoptic Gospels (e.g. Mt. 11:19, 25-30) and in Colossians 1:15-20 (Deane-Drummond 2009: 100–107).

In terms of the historical development of Christianity, this identification between the man Jesus of Nazareth and the divine pre-existent Son/Wisdom/*logos* must have come about in the first generations of Christianity as the disciples and early followers sought to make sense of the legacy of Jesus, especially his death and resurrection. It is difficult to know how this identification occurred, whether through some sort of evolutionary chain of theological reasoning over a number of years (e.g. Dunn [1980] 1989: 251–8), or perhaps through a much more sudden ("explosive") set of circumstances early on (e.g. Hurtado 2003: 78), perhaps including revelatory experiences (e.g. Hurtado 2005: 29–30). But certainly, the New Testament letters of Paul (the earliest Christian writings we possess) indicate that the processes by which Jesus came to be recognized as divine were already well under way by the 50s CE. One of the most intriguing questions to arise from this observation is how the early Christians managed to accommodate the divine status of Christ within the monotheistic framework of early Judaism. For, faced with a ready polytheistic solution to the divinity of Jesus in the models of the Roman and Greek pantheon of deities, the early Christians chose rather to continue working within Judaism. It has been argued that they were able to do so perhaps through the interest in semi-divine figures shown by Jewish apocalyptic literature (e.g. the Son of Man in 1 Enoch 48), but the Jewish Wisdom tradition must have been at least as important, since it provided a scriptural and theological basis for seeing Jesus as the pre-existent Son of God alongside God at creation (Dunn [1980] 1989: 259). This made the natural link between Christ and creation.

And so it is that we find an amazing series of statements in the New Testament, such as in John's Prologue, which assert that long before the humble carpenter from Nazareth was ever born into this world, the *logos*/Son of God already existed and had even created the world at its beginning (Jn 1:1-4, 10; Col. 1:15-20; Heb. 1:2-3). John's Gospel is difficult to date, but most scholars place it towards the end of the first century, partly because it is said to show a more highly developed Christology than much of the rest of the New Testament. On the other hand, there are some very highly developed Christological statements in Paul. Within only about twenty years of Jesus' crucifixion, Paul could write: "*but for us there is one God, the Father, from whom are all things and we exist for him, and there is one Lord, Jesus Christ, through whom are all things, and we exist through him*" (1 Cor. 8:6). And so the connection was made very early on that the God who created the world also stooped to join humanity: in taking on responsibility for the redemption of the world as Christ, he is correspondingly to be worshipped by every creature "in heaven and on the earth and under the earth" (Phil. 2:10).

Paul developed other theological pictures to explain the mystery of Christ, and one which is particularly useful in connecting creation and redemption is that of Christ as the second Adam (Rom. 5:12-21; 1 Cor.

15:21-22, 45-49). Like the first Adam, Christ becomes linked with the Genesis creation story and the origins of humanity, but his role in redemption brings a *new* creation into existence (2 Cor. 5:17; Gal. 6:15). Which means that Christ, by virtue of his redemptive act of death and resurrection, becomes both the fulfilment of the initial creation which began in Adam, and something new again, ushering in a new age. Thus we see, through this simple allusive motif of the new Adam, that the theological themes of creation, redemption and eschatology are bound together. In the final scene of the Bible this idea is portrayed with rich symbolism as the fulfilment of all things when the new Jerusalem comes down from the new heaven to form the centrepiece of the new earth (Rev. 21–22).

We will explore the eschatological dimension more fully in Chapter 9, so we will simply highlight here the key role played by Jesus' resurrection in substantiating claims about Christ's role in creation, a point which Pannenberg (1968: 390–97) has developed. In Pauline theology, Jesus' resurrection is important not simply because it is the miracle which vindicated Jesus' death on the cross, but because of its wider significance in the Jewish context of the time. The apocalyptic sects of early Judaism (such as the Pharisees) believed that the dead would be resurrected at the Last Day for judgement, and so Paul, who had spent his early life as a Pharisee, interpreted the resurrection of Jesus in something of these terms, as the "first fruits" of the general resurrection which would soon come. Jesus' resurrection therefore became the sign that the end of the ages is now upon the world (1 Cor. 15:20, 23), and that Christ is the universal King (1 Cor. 15:24-25; Phil. 2:11). Pannenberg's point is that the resurrection, seen as an *eschatological* event, is the key to interpreting all theological statements made about Jesus. So the resurrection of Jesus is the reason why the *human* Jesus of Nazareth is credited with *divine* pre-existence as the Son of God, who took part in creating the world in the beginning. His resurrection is the fulfilment of all creation, and therefore it is right to see God's eternal purposes (including those at the beginning of creation) crystallizing in him and finding their meaning through him:

> The incarnation of God in Jesus of Nazareth forms the point of reference in relation to which the world's course has its unity and on the basis of which every event and every figure in creation is what it is. Because Jesus' unity with God is first decided by his resurrection, only through Jesus' resurrection is the creation of the world fulfilled.   (Pannenberg 1968: 396)

If this might tempt us to take a very human-centred view of creation and redemption, then we should remember that the New Testament material is clear that creation is focussed on Christ as the incarnate Son, not on humankind as a biological species (Fergusson 1998: 18). In any case, there is a highly important passage in Paul which broadens the picture considerably – Romans 8 – which has been used extensively in recent years to develop ecological theologies (e.g. Southgate 2008; Edwards 2009). This passage develops the theme of Christ's resurrection as the beginning of the future eschatological era of life where God's Spirit is bestowed on believers and lived in the present: "If the Spirit of him who raised Jesus from the dead dwells in you, he who raised Christ from the dead will give life to your mortal bodies also through his Spirit that dwells in you" (Rom. 8:11).

Paul goes on to describe the relevance of this kind of new life for now, speaking of the present in terms of a period of suffering, an eschatological phase predicted by Jewish apocalyptic to presage the general resurrection of the dead on the Last Day:

> I consider that the sufferings of this present time are not worth comparing with the glory about to be revealed to us. For the creation waits with eager longing for the revealing of the children of God; for the creation was subjected to futility, not of its own will but by the will of the one who subjected it, in hope that the creation itself will be set free from its bondage to decay and will obtain the freedom of the glory of the children of God. We know that the whole creation has been groaning in labour pains until now; and not only the creation, but we ourselves, who have the first fruits of the Spirit, groan inwardly while we wait for adoption, the redemption of our bodies.
>
> (Rom. 8:18-23)

Although it is clear that this eschatological process is designed primarily with the benefit of humans in mind (the "children of God"), it is the whole of creation which is caught up in it, with the word "creation" (*ktisis* in Greek) emphasized no less than five times. If Paul is referring here to the "Fall" of Adam and Eve (Gen. 3) when he speaks of creation being subject to "futility" and in "bondage to decay", then he sees the outcome which God has in hand as similarly cosmic in scope. The redemption of "the children of God", signalled by the resurrection of Christ and the "first fruits of the Spirit", is not just for the children of Adam and Eve but for the whole of creation. For the present though, the creation is "groaning in labour pains"; that is, it is going through a necessary time of suffering before the new creation is birthed. In other words, the whole of creation has suffered the common fate of humankind, but it will also benefit from its common redemption in the future. In this way, Romans 8 develops a cosmic perspective on the theme of Christ's resurrection which is anything but anthropocentric.

Romans 8 also makes it abundantly clear that all of this takes place by the power of the Holy Spirit. It is the Spirit who fills believers with the life of the new creation (e.g. v. 9), who is also the life of the risen Christ (v. 11).

It was the same Spirit who was present at the original creation, hovering or sweeping over the face of the deep (Gen. 1:2). Since the Hebrew and Greek words for "Spirit" can also mean "breath" and "wind", we might say that this was the same Spirit who became God's breath of life in the first man (Gen. 2:7) and then left the generation which perished in the Flood (Gen. 7:22). Quite simply, the Spirit/breath is the source of biological life (Ps. 104:29-30), but also of new eschatological life: this same Spirit gave life to the new church at Pentecost (Acts 2; cf. Jn 20:22).

Mention of the Holy Spirit calls to mind the third person of the Trinity, and so if it seems that we have strayed some way from the work of Christ, it should be noted that the Pauline letters (a) see Christ's work in creation as an idea which must be developed eschatologically, and (b) associate the eschatological work of Christ and the eschatological work of the Spirit very closely. We therefore find that we are unable to account sufficiently for the work of Christ in creation without beginning to relate it to that of the Holy Spirit. It is somewhat inevitable that talk of God as Trinity arises from this point.

Of course, it goes without saying that much of what we have said here about Christ and creation has benefitted from the concentrated theological reflection and controversy which took place after the first century CE. It took the early church several hundred years to develop a mature Christology which was able to interpret consistently such theologically advanced ideas as those contained in texts such as Colossians 1, where Christ could be said simultaneously to have created the world and to have reconciled it to God by dying as a common criminal on the cross (Col. 1:20). It was discovered that these paradoxical ideas were best interpreted not by explaining them so much as re-articulating them in sharper paradoxical terms, of Christ's simultaneous humanity and divinity. Thus the Council of Chalcedon (451 CE) was able to speak on the one hand of Christ's divine nature, whereby he was "born from the Father before the ages", and on the other of his human nature, whereby he was "born in the last days from the Virgin Mary". These two natures exist "unconfusedly, unalterably, undividedly, inseparably" in one Christ (Norris 1980: 159). Such language is worlds away from that of first century Christianity, but it is difficult not to read the New Testament texts in its light, that is, anachronistically: reading back into the texts concepts and realities which were only fully recognized later. This is nowhere more true than in what we will discuss in the next section, the idea of God as Trinity.

CREATION AND THE BEGINNINGS OF THE IDEA OF GOD AS TRINITY

If the Council of Chalcedon sharpened the paradox which is implicit in New Testament Christology by speaking of Christ's two natures, then we can see from our remove of nearly two thousand years that there is sound theological reasoning behind all of this. According to the New Testament, the Son of God who died on the cross as a human being (Mt. 27:40-43; Mk 15:39; Rom. 5:10) was the same Son of God who had played a part in making the world in the beginning (Col. 1:13-20). Putting it more bluntly, if the Son of God is sufficiently God as to be able to save the world, then he is sufficiently God to have created it. The two are therefore placed together – creation and redemption – as equal and complementary acts of divine love. And here we have the beginnings of the idea of God as Trinity, perhaps the most paradoxical aspect of the Christian faith, but borne out of the observation that the God who saves humankind did so by appearing on earth as a human being, and must therefore be the same God who had made the world in the beginning, and is the same God who is present working in the world as Spirit even now.

This approach may make good theological sense to us, but it is never stated as baldly as this in the New Testament. The most obvious New Testament text which appears to point to the Trinitarian reality of God is Jesus' command to his disciples to baptize "in the name of the Father and of the Son and of the Holy Spirit" (Mt. 28:19), which echoes the baptism of Jesus, a Trinitarian moment in all but name (e.g. Mt. 3:16-17). There are others though, such as the so-called Farewell Discourse of John's Gospel, where Jesus tells his disciples that his Father will send the Holy Spirit to them to remind them of Jesus and testify on his behalf (Jn 14:26; 15:26). Paul's letters contain one passage which appears to be explicitly Trinitarian (2 Cor. 13:13), and he also makes very close associations between Father, Son and Holy Spirit elsewhere, not least in the verses leading up to the crucial passage from Romans 8 which we cited earlier (Rom. 8:15-17). And there are further aspects of Paul's theology which may be seen as thoroughly – if not explicitly – Trinitarian (Dunn 2011: 180), not least his teaching on the Church (the representation of the new creation on earth): it is the "Church of God" (e.g. 1 Cor. 10:32) and the "body of Christ" (e.g. 1 Cor. 12:27), and brings about fellowship/participation in the Spirit (2 Cor. 13:13).

In short, there are hints of the beginnings of a Trinitarian theology in the New Testament, and it is largely expressed in *economic* terms, that is, associating Father, Son and Holy Spirit closely through their complementary roles in the "economy"/"plan" (Eph. 1:10) of creation and redemption. The doxological statement in Romans 11:36, for instance, can be interpreted as an economic view of God as Trinity, saying, "For from him [the Father] and through him [the Spirit] and to him [Christ] are all things."

On the other hand, articulation of God as Trinity in *immanent* terms, that is, by means of the inner relations and workings of the Godhead, was more or less impossible until the development of appropriate terminology was made in the later centuries. Tertullian (*c.*160 to *c.*220 CE) is especially important here, since he brought to prominence the terms "Trinity"

(*trinitas* in Latin) and "person" (*persona*), which form the basis of all immanent Trinitarian discussion in Western theology.

It is even possible to infer the idea of God the Holy Trinity in Old Testament texts, although historical critics could well complain that this is
tantamount to gross anachronism. Still, this has not stopped theologians
since at least the time of Irenaeus in the second century CE from attempting to demonstrate that Christian faith in Father, Son and Holy Spirit can
be supported by texts such as the Genesis creation stories (e.g. Irenaeus'
likening of the Son and Holy Spirit to the "hands" of God fashioning Adam
from the clay; *Against Heresies* IV: pref. 3). And modern scholars have done
something of the same, albeit more cautiously. We have already noted (§
"Creation and narrative", above) Brueggemann's warning (1997: 63) that
the Old Testament creation motif cannot be formulated into a doctrine of
creation as such, since it is too "inchoate", but it contains all of the materials necessary for a Trinitarian understanding of creation, since Yahweh is
said to create by word (Gen. 1:3), by wisdom (Jer. 10:12) and by spirit (Gen.
1:2). And Mackey (2006: 39–40, 47–8) has pointed out that Word, Wisdom
and Spirit are used as three interchangeable agencies throughout the biblical creation motif in both Old and New Testaments, an observation which
inevitably leads us to speculate about their theological status along Trinitarian lines.

So, although we might be reluctant from a historical point of view to
develop the Old Testament (or even New Testament) creation texts along
Trinitarian lines, yet there are elements in the texts which lend themselves
to such an approach. Moreover, a Trinitarian approach offers a number of
advantages from our perspective several millennia – and many theological
revolutions – after the texts were first set down.

The first point to make is that, while we wish to avoid historical anachronism, there is a venerable tradition of theological interpretation of the
Bible, going right back to the early church, which stands by the belief that
both Old and New Testaments testify to a progressive revelation of fundamentally the same God. And we can see this standpoint in the New Testament itself, which takes a number of Old Testament texts and interprets
them as speaking of Christ. This is representative of the method of biblical interpretation known as *typological*, which sees the content of the
Old Testament as prefiguring or anticipating what is to come in the New.
And hence we have Augustine's famous maxim: "In the Old Testament the
New is concealed, in the New the Old is revealed" (Augustine, *Questionum
in Heptateuchum* 2: 73; translation from Kelly [1960] 1977: 69). In case
we are tempted to prioritize the New Testament over the Old because of
such statements, we should remember that the New cannot in any way
be understood without the Old. It is therefore appropriate to emphasize
the interconnectedness of both testaments if a theological approach like
this is to be taken, that Old and New Testaments are seen to inform and

guide readings of each other, because they are part of the same canon, the Christian Scriptures. Indeed, we have already begun to do just this, by incorporating the New Testament creation material seamlessly alongside the Old in this chapter. In its defence, if modern historical scholarship is insistent that we should attend to the *historical* context in which a text originated (with all that implies for later concepts such as God as Trinity), then a Christian reading could well respond that we must also attend to the *canonical* context. After all, the text is a component of the foundational basis of Christianity, which maintains faith in God as Trinity at its heart. As a result, reading the biblical creation texts theologically requires that tacit hermeneutical decisions be taken with respect to belief in God as Trinity, whatever sense is made of those texts from a historical perspective.

The second point to make concerns the hermeneutical usefulness of a Trinitarian reading. In this book, which seeks to explore the biblical creation motif partly from the perspective of modern science, there is an attractive simplicity in associating the *logos* with the organizing principle behind creation (including the laws of nature), while the Holy Spirit can be developed as the immanent God present in the perpetual workings of creation, with all that this suggests concerning modern evolutionary science.

This relates to a third point concerning the merits of a Trinitarian reading. As we shall discuss in the next two chapters, it is difficult in our modern scientific age to resist the spirit of deism, which sees God as detached from the workings of the world. There are many ways in which our religious thinking is tinged by it, either consciously or unconsciously. A thoroughly Trinitarian view, on the other hand, insists that God has been actively involved in both redeeming and in creating the world throughout history. Such a Trinitarian perspective is, of course, thoroughly in tune with the *theistic* atmosphere of the Bible, so although it is a later and more developed view of God than that of the Bible it arguably offers us the best way to appropriate its atmosphere in our more deistic age.

Webster (2003) has made an important point about this in his theological exploration of the idea of Holy Scripture. He argues that all too often the Bible is read either from the perspective of an overt naturalism or its opposite, an overt supernaturalism. The naturalist insists that the text should be read primarily in terms of its human origins as a historical document, and so effectively subordinates to secondary interpretative levels the possibility that the text might have a role in God's self-communication. And the supernaturalist attempts the reverse, by emphasizing the role of divine revelation in the production of the text over historical factors. Both, claims Webster, are fatally flawed, not only in their understanding of Scripture but in their understanding of how God relates to the world. In particular, they reveal a dualism which separates God from the world in a way which is hardly theistic. We are back at something rather like deism. Webster says:

The plunge into dualism is inseparable from the retrenchment of the doctrine of the Trinity in theological talk of God's relation to the world. When God's action towards the world is conceived in a non-trinitarian fashion, and, in particular, when Christian talk of the presence of the risen Christ and the activity of the Holy Spirit does not inform conceptions of divine action in the world, then that action comes to be understood as external, interruptive, and bearing no real relations to creaturely realities. God, in effect, becomes causal will, intervening in creaturely reality from outside but unconnected to the creation.

(*Ibid.*: 21)

The solution must be to uphold both the transcendence and the immanence of God simultaneously, something which the doctrine of the Trinity affirms straightforwardly. And as far as the Bible is concerned, Webster is right that we must perform a similarly dialectical affirmation where we uphold the "creatureliness" of the biblical text simultaneously with its sanctified status as a medium of God's self-revelation.

Taking Webster's comments to heart we can say that, although the discussion in this section on the connection between the biblical creation motif and the idea of God as Trinity has been rather tentative, it has begun to set up the hermeneutical approach that will be important later on, as we look at scientific interpretations of the Bible's creation material.

CONCLUSIONS

The biblical creation motif does not consist of single concise and well-defined concept or principle; it is not "*a* theology" as such. The creation stories of Genesis 1–2 are often taken as the definitive biblical statement, but we have seen that they not only make distinct and different theological emphases from each other, but that there are many other relevant texts in the Bible, from Genesis to Revelation. These point to further strands in the creation motif. Therefore, a single doctrine of creation cannot be derived from this material; it is simply too varied in genre, aim and content. Nevertheless, all of this material is united by the fact that it proclaims the supremacy of the God of Israel as the sole Creator.

So although our natural tendency might be to read the biblical creation material as theological articulations about the *world* and how it came into being, yet it can equally be read as theological articulations about the *nature of God*. The last few sections of this chapter have made that abundantly clear, as we have briefly reviewed ways of understanding the Wisdom and New Testament creation material. We have seen that it begins

to suggest a theological depth to God's being which Christians still struggle
to conceptualize after several thousand years.

Before we turn to scientific and philosophical treatments in the next
chapter, it is important to raise one point, rarely made in the science–theology field but essential for understanding the biblical portrayal of God
as Creator, and that is about the place of worship, awe, and wonder as the
proper human response. In the biblical texts, consideration of creation
inspires praise. Indeed, the theological fact of creation is sometimes given
in the Bible as a sufficient reason for worship alone, even before God's work
in redemption is taken into account:

> You are worthy, our Lord and God,
>   to receive glory and honour and power,
> for you created all things,
>   and by your will they existed and were created.
>   (Rev. 4:11)

Some of the most notable expressions of praise on account of creation are
found in the Psalms. Psalm 8, for instance, paints a picture of the utter
dependence of humankind on God and their resulting duty of praise, while
Psalm 104 does something of the same for all created life, Psalm 98 for the
landscapes of the earth and Psalm 19 for the voiceless heavens. We therefore see in the biblical view that, in participating in the universal movement of praise towards the Creator, the various components of creation
stand as witnesses to each other to spur each other on. This offers a valuable corrective against our inevitable human-centred prioritizing, as for
instance, God's speech to Job in chapters 38–41 illustrates. This is a point
in favour of recent ecological theologies which seek to present a more universal perspective (e.g. Horrell 2010: 60–61).

As with the Old Testament creation material, that in the New Testament
does so in the context of praise. But what is notable about the New Testament material is that it concerns Christ, and makes startling claims about
his divinity, his pre-existence, his role in creation, and the obligation to worship him in a way that is reserved for Yahweh alone in the Old Testament
(e.g. Phil. 2:5-11). This reveals something of profound but subtle importance about the Christian view of creation and the necessity of worship.
As Wilkinson (2009b: 20) puts it: "The universe cannot be fully understood
as creation without Christ". From the perspective of a natural theology
(that is, one based on reason and experience of the "natural" world), such a
statement cannot be substantiated empirically in any straightforward way;
it is a postulate. The Revd William Paley (1743–1805) articulated one of
the most famous examples of a natural theology by comparing the Creator to a watchmaker of superlative skill. Such arguments from design have
always been vulnerable to the charge that they construct the god of the

philosopher – the god of human logic and analogy – and not the Christian God of Golgotha, who must be apprehended by *revelation*, rather than by *observation* of nature. On the other hand, modern evolutionary theologies often combine the two angles by suggesting that the suffering Christ "redeems" the evolutionary suffering of creation (Chapter 8). For now, we note that Christ's centrality to creation is another way of articulating the mystery of incarnation: it is a revealed mystery, but it is the keystone to the architecture of Christianity (McGrath [2002] 2006b: 246), allowing for the recognition that in Christ, he in whom "the Word became flesh" (Jn 1:14), Creator has become creation and creation has become Creator. This is a point that the New Atheism, in its attempt to cut the ties between Creator and creation by negating natural theologies, has largely failed to recognize. To a Christian, any hypothesis is incomplete that puts forward arguments for or against the existence of God based on science or creation, and that does not also take into account the fact that through Christ's life, death and resurrection God has entered into an intimate relationship with the universe and so also redeems it.

This means that God as Creator cannot straightforwardly be treated either as a scientific hypothesis to be reasoned about or an entirely objective other. And it means that the Christian cannot properly respond with cool logic alone to a consideration of creation, but with praise. In bestowing the divine riches of Son and Spirit upon creation, creation is bound to respond with its utmost riches of gratitude in return to God: "Creation and eschatology return glory to God – the very glory they are given through the *Trinitarian movement* of God toward and in them" (Hardy 1996: 169). Purely scientific perspectives of creation founded in *naturalism* are unable to take this point on board since they have no means to do so. They can describe the material nature of the created world and can even suggest many reasons why creation is to be respected and wondered at, but they cannot describe it in terms of a relationship with the Creator. So they cannot of themselves enter into the movement of glorifying between Creator and creation. As it turns out, this is a significant drawback when interpreting the biblical creation texts.

Chapter 5

THE FRAMEWORK OF BIBLICAL CREATION

Through the next two chapters we will explore how the Bible's creation texts may be integrated into modern discussions in the science–theology field, first by discussing ways of understanding the *scientific* framework of the biblical texts, and then the *theological* framework.

Although we might find it straightforward to distinguish scientific from theological talk in our culture, it is not so straightforward when we come to the Bible, since much of the scientific framework of ancient Hebrew thinking was couched in theological terms, and vice versa. Take the categories *natural* and *supernatural*, our standard vocabulary for speaking of the material world against the idea of a spiritual world; of the ordinary scheme of things ("natural") as against miracles ("supernatural"). There is a degree of ambiguity in these terms, just as there is ambiguity in the term "nature" (McGrath [2002] 2006a: 81–133). Does "nature" refer to the world of wild-life – the flora and fauna of the earth which exist apart from humankind – or is it a technical term for all that comes under the remit of science? Or is it a theological term meaning all of creation which stands apart from God?

Here we will take a *natural* event to be an event which is describable by science through the usual scientific method of experimentation and test-ing of hypotheses. In which case, we might be tempted to say that a *super-natural* event has no clear natural (scientific) explanation on any level; it is caused by powers above (*super*) this world; we would be likely to identify a spectacular miracle narrative as evidence of the supernatural.

Some of the biblical creation material might be described as "natural" straightforwardly, especially that which calls upon everyday events such as "the rising of the sun" (e.g. Mal. 1:11). Now it is worth noting that, even in an example like this, which calls upon the everyday regularity of the phe-nomenon in question, we moderns who come after Copernicus understand the scientific background to the rising of the sun very differently from those who first composed and read these texts. And that is even before we take account of the fact that this natural example is actually a *theological* metaphor for the universality of devotion to God: "For from the rising of the sun to its setting my name is great among the nations, and in every place incense is offered to my name, and a pure offering; for my name is great among the nations, says the LORD of hosts" (Mal. 1:11). Even in a seemingly straightforward example like this of "natural" language in the Bible, several interpretative levels are at play simultaneously which take us beyond scientific terms, and this is the case even after defining carefully what we mean by the term "natural".

Perhaps the best illustration of the ambiguity and overlap between natural and supernatural categories in the Bible comes in the word "spirit", which in both Hebrew (*ruah*) and Greek (*pneuma*) can equally be translated "wind". Although we might think of "spirit" as fundamentally supernatural, and "wind" as natural, the fact that the same word could refer to a reality in both categories in Greek and Hebrew suggests that the people of the Bible might not have thought of reality in the same ways as us (Sanders 1993: 142). Both "spirit" and "wind" were invisible but palpable forces in their own ways, and there was not necessarily a hard-and-fast distinction between them.

In short, there is often no easy division between the natural and the supernatural in the texts of the Bible. Such a division stems from much later philosophical developments and is more at home in our modern scientific worldview. Let us take an example. Can we say that Yahweh's creative work in making "springs gush forth in the valleys" (Ps. 104:10) is of a different kind from that which miraculously stopped the River Jordan flowing so that Joshua and the people could cross (Josh. 3:16)? While the first example is an everyday phenomenon, and sounds inherently naturalistic to our modern ears, yet there is no indication in the text that it is different in any *theological* respect from the second example, the miracle of the crossing of the Jordan. In any case, this miracle can easily be explained scientifically by occasional earthquakes which are known to cause landslips on the river banks of the Jordan and block its flow (Bentor 1989: 327–8). But whether we interpret either of these texts in terms of modern science or not, the point of both is that the phenomena they describe occur because God is "the Lord of all the earth" (Josh. 3:13). To distinguish God's *natural* activity from God's *supernatural* activity is thus to imply two mutually exclusive views of divine activity, which goes beyond what the biblical authors claim, at least in these two texts (Westermann 1984: 175).

And yet, the ancient Israelites must have been capable of regarding many features of their physical environment, such as the flow of streams and rivers, as regular (and therefore "natural") occurrences, rather as we would in our modern scientific worldview. They may even have recognized these as examples of laws of nature (Rogerson 1977: 73). It does not require a detailed knowledge of modern geology or physical geography, for instance, to understand that water usually flows downhill, and will cut a channel into sand or earth, forming a stream or river over time. Indeed, many aspects of agricultural practice, such as irrigation, rely on an understanding of basic science. In other words, naturalistic explanations for many regular phenomena in the world must always have been at hand well before the advent of modern science.

In fact, there is evidence in the Bible that regular phenomena were recognized as such, although it was not necessarily associated with our idea of "law" (as in "law of nature"). But consider this passage, which predicts, and then describes, the fate of those caught up in the rebellion of Korah:

> Moses said, "... If these people die a natural death, or if a natural fate comes on them, then the LORD has not sent me. But if the LORD *creates a new creation*, and the ground opens its mouth and swallows them up, with all that belongs to them, and they go down alive into Sheol, then you shall know that these men have despised the LORD." As soon as he finished speaking all these words, the ground under them was split apart. The earth opened its mouth and swallowed them up, along with their households – everyone who belonged to Korah and all their goods. (Num. 16:28-32)

This is a fascinating text. Note the distinction between a "natural death/fate", and a "new creation". Our modern scientific worldview means that one of the first questions we frame in approaching a story like this is "what really happened", i.e. what caused the earth to split apart? The obvious explanation which springs to mind is an earthquake. On the other hand, it is possible that the event was caused by the fragility of the hard desert topsoil, which in some places can split open dramatically and unexpectedly after rain (E. W. Davies 1995: 176–7). The text gives us few physical clues for deciding between the two interpretations, but we should beware of putting too much store on "what really happened". For one thing, the earthquake has a mythological significance, often appearing as a component in the Divine Warrior theophany (e.g. Judg. 5:4-5; Ps. 29; Hab. 3:6). There is therefore a mythological or symbolic dimension to this event in the desert which indicates a deeper significance beyond "what really happened".

Significantly, the event is described as an unparalleled creative act, a "new creation". Whether earthquakes (which were not unknown in the area) were *always* regarded as miraculous and symbolic is beyond the scope of the present discussion, but this particular event is clearly regarded as miraculous. Conversely, awareness is shown elsewhere that remarkable events might not be divinely caused, but might come about in the ordinary scheme of things "by chance" (1 Sam. 6:9). Also, we see the idea of a "natural death", or a "natural" fate in the text above, expressed literally in the Hebrew as "like the death of all people", or "the fate of all people". This idea, that death is universal and cannot be escaped except by divine providence, is perhaps the closest the Bible comes to a statement of a "natural law". Other traces of it appear, described as "the way of all the earth" (Josh. 23:14; 1 Kgs 2:2; including its converse – the conception of life: Gen. 19:31), or "the end of all people" (Eccl. 7:2). And in the Greek literature of the Bible, we find the noun *physis* (and derivatives) used to refer to something more akin to our idea of "nature", especially the notion that humans and creatures are created alike with certain "natural" predispositions, qualities and abilities (e.g. Wisdom 7:20; 4 Macc. 5:8-9; 5:25; Rom. 1:26-27; 11:21, 24; 1 Cor. 11:14; 2 Pet. 2:12). The oft-repeated phrase in some Priestly passages and in Ezekiel, which describes creatures "of every kind", makes a parallel recognition to our idea of "nature" as wildlife, of a diverse and rich world set apart from humankind (e.g. Gen. 1:12, 24, 25; 6:19; 7:14; Ezek. 17:23; 39:4, 17).

However, we must reconcile this evidence of an ancient view of "nature" with the observation that, when the biblical writers came to describe naturalistic phenomena such as the flow of streams and rivers, it was often a *theological* (supernatural?) explanation which was given, where God was seen to be the fundamental cause. In other words, the supernatural could be seen to be natural, and the natural seen to be supernatural. Such a viewpoint lies behind Ecclesiastes 3, for instance, which discusses the ordered and predictable (law-like?) regularity of all things, both in the human and non-human worlds ("For everything there is a season ..."), but underpins it all by God's unfathomable purposes. The people of the biblical world were capable of thinking in scientific ways not so far removed from ours in some respects, but also capable of expressing this using a thorough-going theistic theology when it came to literary expression.

THE ANCIENT ISRAELITE "MINDSET"?

Biblical scholarship has tended to drive an intellectual wedge between the ancient world and ours. Until relatively recently, it was commonplace for biblical scholars to assert that the ancient Hebrew mentality was more "primitive" than ours, occupying a worldview steeped in myth and superstition, more open to the miraculous, and substantially less rational.

The sharp distinction between the thought processes of ancient peoples and us owes much to the writings of Lucien Lévy-Bruhl (1857–1939), and especially to his widely influential book, *Primitive Mentality* (1923). However, this categorization of the ancient mindset is now criticized as a tacit judgement of inferiority and "gullibility" of ancient cultures (e.g. Douglas [1966] 2002: 93–5). But during the nineteenth and much of the twentieth centuries it was readily assumed that pre-modern thought was more or less "pre-scientific", and lacked critical rigour and potency compared to modern thought. The onset of postmodern awareness in recent decades has led to a decrease in confidence in our powers of objectivity though, and a re-assessment of ancient intellectual achievements.

It has also become apparent that we should not be too ready to emphasize our credentials as enlightened and critical moderns, free of gullibility. Science may have brought many technological advances and changes in understanding our world, and there has been a marked decline in traditional religious practices in western Europe over the past century, but there is no sign that basic spiritual belief is on the wane throughout the wider world. In fact, our world is not devoid of its own kind of mythology which reinforces cultural values, national stereotypes and so on, quite apart from religious beliefs (Wyatt 2005: 172). For instance, even in this age of science, belief in the miraculous is still widespread, as is shown by the popular cult of Padre Pio, for instance, and there is extensive devotion to horoscopes and alternative (usually individualistic) affirmations of spirituality (Corner 2005: 179–95). One might even add belief in UFOs and conspiracy theories as other aspects of "faith" at play in our modern world which demonstrate that we are not all as thoroughly sceptical of unproven ideas as scholars might think.

As Corner points out (*ibid.*: 179), critical scholarship has too often tended to assume that everyone else in the modern world shares its general scepticism towards the miraculous. And Willis makes a similar comment after noting that a survey conducted in 1994 indicated that eighty-seven per cent of the American population affirms faith in the resurrection of Jesus:

> A careful observer might conclude that, while scholars today are debating the meaning of a postmodern existence, the people in the pews have not yet entered what scholars refer to as the modern era, a time when all traditional beliefs must be criticized and possibly rejected. Lay Christians easily believe what academic types were taught that modern people could not believe.
> (Willis 2006: 187–8)

If modern people are capable of investing faith in the miraculous, then the ancients were equally as capable of full-blooded scepticism. First, consider Josephus, who, in telling the story of the Red Sea crossing by Moses and the children of Israel (Exod. 14), tries to defend it by recounting a similar sea crossing by Alexander and his army from more recent times (*Antiquities* II: 16.5). Importantly, Josephus concludes with the formula "However, on these matters, everyone is welcome to his own opinion", conceding that many will remain sceptical of the Exodus story, even with the later story of Alexander to support it. Second, consider a much more recent example, from a religious author who complains of the extent of scepticism towards the spiritual in British society: "There are many people who consider only what they can see and do not believe there are good and bad angels nor that the souls of man lives on after the death of the body nor that there are any other spiritual and invisible things." Without knowing, one could be forgiven for thinking that this opinion had been voiced by a modern-day church spokesperson, but in fact the author was Peter of Cornwall, an Augustinian prior writing in England around 1200 CE, complaining of the scepticism of his peers well inside the supposedly pre-critical "Dark Ages" (Bartlett 2008: 110).

In any case, there is evidence that the ancient Hebrews were not incapable of making observations about the natural world and of cataloguing them and seeking to explain them in ways we might recognize as "scientific". There was the recognition, for instance, that Solomon's legendary wisdom included a sound knowledge of the natural world (1 Kgs 5:13 [4:33 in the Vulgate and in many English translations]). And some of the poetic literature of the Bible contains list-like passages of natural phenomena, or of creatures of the earth, with astute observations of their behaviours and natural habitats (e.g. Job 38–41; Ps. 104; see W. P. Brown 2010: 17–18). In that sense, there is a ready awareness of the natural world in no way limited in scope compared with ours, even if it was vastly deficient in terms of a much deeper scientific understanding. It is also clear that the authors of the Bible possessed a good working knowledge of many aspects of agriculture, mining and astronomy (e.g. Job 9; 28). They must have had an elementary mathematics too; it was presumably not as sophisticated as that of neighbouring cultures such as those of Babylon or Egypt, but the Bible tells us of various accomplished engineering and building projects which must have required mathematical skill, and it even shows awareness of the special geometrical properties of the number we call *pi* (1 Kgs 7:23; 2 Chron. 4:2; see Høyrup 1992).

Important criticisms of the idea of a "primitive mentality" have been made by John Rogerson (1974: 182–3, 187; 1977; 1983). With regard to the basic scientific idea of causality, for instance – the relationship between cause and effect in describing an event in the world – Rogerson argues for caution against digging too great a gulf between our thought world and that of the ancient Hebrews. It has often been said that while we possess a sophisticated scientific and historical framework which means that we do not have to call upon God as an explanation (a cause) for events in the world, yet the ancient Israelites attributed everything to God. However, while it is quite possible that the Israelites saw the regularity of the natural world more in terms of God's promises and faithfulness (Gen. 8:22) than we do in our more mechanistic worldview (Rogerson 1976: 5), one should not go too far with this line of arguing, since it acts to negate the many technological advances which were made between Neolithic times and the Iron Age (when the Old Testament largely came into being). These advances show that the ancient Israelites were perfectly capable of developing basic technological and agricultural skills.

On the other hand, with regards the age-old problems of how to explain evil, of free-will and determinism, Rogerson believes that the Old Testament is certainly distinctive, attempting to approach these problems theologically within the broad picture of monotheism. Indeed, these are still problems in our day, and largely theological problems at that; our approach to them is certainly indebted to the Bible. Abiding problems of evil and morality demonstrate all too well that intellectual progress is anything but linear (Ward 2008: 217–18). We may have developed a refined moral agenda in the West which emphasizes universal human rights and equality, and we may enjoy the benefits of enormous medical and technological progress, but these are by no means universal, even in our world. Furthermore, modern civilization has also relapsed into the most extreme forms of barbarism at times, dwarfing in scale and inhumanity anything of which the ancient world was capable. Science has brought the end of the material world within human reach as well as its technological salvation.

There is a further important difference between modern and ancient thought (Rogerson 1983: 56–7). We have already flagged-up interpretations of Genesis 1 which see it as a description of *ordering* over *making* (§ "The first Genesis creation account: Genesis 1:1–2:4a (P)" in Chapter 3, above). While our view of cosmic order is heavily influenced by the natural sciences, Israelite thinking sees creation in terms of distinctions between order and disorder which we barely recognize, especially between "clean" and "unclean" states of existence, prescribing social and ritual interactions, which foods can and cannot be eaten, and so on. It is not that the Israelites lived in a mystical world where myth was inseparable from reality (as scholars have sometimes thought in the past, e.g. in the supposition of the "mythopoeic" worldview; cf. Frankfort *et al.* [1946] 1949), but in a world which was differently conceived from ours in terms of order and propriety.

In fact, the differences between the ancient Hebrew worldview and ours are probably best expressed in religious terms rather than as a modern scientific mindset versus a so-called "primitive" mindset. One of the most relevant factors to account for is belief in God, since it is optional in our society, even if the broad majority of modern people opt for it in some way. In ancient Hebrew culture on the other hand, it would have been taken largely for granted. Why this difference? To my mind, it must get to the heart of the issue, but to discern it we need to be reminded of some of the historical issues about the changing patterns of religious thought. For one, we should not underestimate the influence which the Newtonian view of the universe has had on our religious thinking. Even though Newtonian physics has been largely superseded by developments in twentieth-century physics – developments which have brought about a new open-ness and uncertainty in our view of the physical world – the deistic view of God which arose from Newton is highly influential in forming modern religious beliefs, which makes Theism a correspondingly harder position to hold than in biblical times. This is an important point, since this book interprets the common ground between the Bible and modern science theologically. That is, it puts forward an understanding of the *divine nature* and of *divine works* in relation to the natural world as they are testified to by the Bible, in its characteristically theistic outlook. From that point of view, any tendencies towards Deism in our interpretations of the Bible should be carefully highlighted and evaluated.

Having begun to think through some of the preliminary issues which arise when we compare our scientific way of thinking with what we find in the Bible, we turn now to the key scientific concepts of time, number and space.

TIME

"In the beginning"?

One of the most decisive statements made about time in the Bible is its first: "In the beginning ..." (Gen. 1:1). We find many biblical echoes and allusions to the idea that God made the world "In the beginning" (e.g. Prov. 8:22-23; Isa. 40:21; 41:4; Jn 1:1; Col. 1:18; 1 Jn 1:1; Sir. 39:20). Genesis 1:1 is interpreted in terms of the beginnings of the *physical* world: before the creation there was nothing, and then after there was everything. This is the idea which has come to be referred to as creation "from nothing". But there is a clear paradox in speaking of creation in such before/after terms: how can we speak of time before the creation, if there is literally nothing to refer it to? Pondering this conundrum gave Augustine the opportunity to make the famous conclusion that God must be outside of time, and that God created time as part of the created world (*Confessions* XI: 1, 13-14; *City of God* XI: 6). Indeed, it is possible to read the creation of time out of Genesis 1 itself, since it declares that God made light and darkness, day and night, evening and morning, so that there could be "the first day" (1:4-5). And in the same way that God creates time by the *separation* of light and darkness, God makes space in vv. 6-10 by separating heaven and earth, sea and land (Westermann 1974: 43).

But Genesis 1:1 has not always been read as describing the absolute beginning of all things including time. For instance, the Jewish rabbis whose thoughts are recorded in the *Genesis Rabbah* (a midrashic document from the third to the sixth centuries CE) maintained that many things existed before the "In the beginning" statement of Genesis 1:1, and time itself had existed long before the evening and morning of the first day in Genesis 1:5 (*Genesis Rabbah* III: 7). The rabbis contended that God had experimented with making many worlds before ours, but had destroyed them all out of dissatisfaction, until hitting upon the solution that a satisfactory world could be made if it was provided with a means of salvation. Hence our world came to be created, which is where "In the beginning" of Genesis 1:1 begins. Or a related rabbinic interpretation: God created Wisdom and Torah two thousand years before the creation of the heavens and earth, together with other features important to Judaism such as Paradise, Hell, the Messiah's Name, and Repentance (*Genesis Rabbah* I: 4; Ginzburg 2003: 1; Graves & Patai [1963] 2005: 45). Indeed, such was the importance of Wisdom to rabbinic thought (against the relative unimportance of absolute beginnings) that Genesis 1:1 was sometimes rendered not "In the beginning ..." but "In Wisdom God created the heavens and the earth" (Kugel 1997: 53–6).

Clearly, there were alternative ways of looking at the "In the beginning" statement of Genesis 1:1 *without* needing to see it as the beginning of time and of all created things. And if this was how the rabbis of the early centuries CE interpreted it, then we must wonder what the author of P intended. He may well have considered the formation of light and darkness to mark the beginning of time (the "First Day"), but it is quite possible that he also considered the "formless void" of Genesis 1:2 to have pre-existed all of this (Chapter 6). But for us, more than two thousand years later, it is difficult to escape the many centuries of Christian thought which have read Genesis 1:1 as a statement of absolute beginnings of the physical world. And the immense appeal of the Big Bang model in recent decades has provided further impetus for reading Genesis 1:1 in this way, capturing the popular imagination so successfully that the Big Bang is irreconcilably connected with phrases like "In the beginning" and "Let there be light".

Subsequent development of the Big Bang model has brought further complications though. As we have already mentioned (§ "The Big Bang model" in Chapter 2, above), attempts to understand the earliest quantum phase of the Big Bang have raised questions about whether it is correct to speak of a beginning to time as such. In connection, recent work has speculated on what came "before" the Big Bang, or what caused it, seeing it entirely in physical and mathematical (i.e. contingent) terms. Perhaps the Big Bang was the consequence of an even more primeval phase described by physics, such as an earlier universe (Stoeger 2010: 178–80). The widespread contemporary interest in the hypothetical possibility that our universe is simply one of many – part of a much larger "multiverse" (§ "Space, time, and matter" in Chapter 2) – makes a related point, that our universe is believed by many cosmologists to be set in a wider created matrix described in terms of mathematics, if not the laws of physics we know. If so, the rabbis were not so misguided in their insistence that Wisdom and Torah (i.e. Law, cf. the laws of physics) preceded "In the beginning".

The upshot of this discussion is that, although there may be questions of interpretation regarding P's "In the beginning" seen in its historical perspective, the science has not illuminated the picture of absolute beginnings either, because it is a *theological* idea. However, we can see that time is not infinite in the Bible: it is defined at one end with a beginning. We cannot tell whether this beginning was considered as an absolute, but it is a beginning nonetheless. The implication is that time – at least as we experience it – is a created entity. The fact that it also appears to have an end in view (the new creation), indicates that time is a thoroughly contingent reality; that is, it depends utterly upon God. A similarly contingent view of historical time appears repeatedly in the prophets. And there is an analogy in physics: the second law of thermodynamics points out that entropy (disorder) must always increase, meaning that time can be defined in terms of the direction of increasing entropy in the universe ("the arrow of time"). Time is therefore irreversible, and is entirely contingent upon what came before.

There is one final point to make about "In the beginning" time and the seven days that follow it. They do not represent neutral, objective time: the seventh day shows that they stand apart, since it is "blessed" and "hallowed" by God (Gen. 2:3), and its weekly celebration as the Sabbath is to stand at the heart of Israel's future distinctiveness (Exod. 20:8-11; Deut. 5:12-15). Such is the significance of this day that Moltmann can say: "The sabbath opens creation for its true future. On the sabbath the redemption of the world is celebrated in anticipation. The sabbath is itself the presence of eternity in time, and a foretaste of the world to come" (Moltmann 1985: 276). The seventh day is thus pivotal to the act of creation: it signals the possibility for time to be holy, and for all creatures to enjoy it alongside God, and it signals the consummation of time to come. Finally, it is the outstanding sign that God has entered into time (Fretheim 2005: 63), a point that we shall explore shortly (§ "God's time", below).

The end of time?

As Peters (1989: 86–7) has pointed out, to exist is to have a future. We might be historical beings rooted in what has happened in the past, but there is a forward-looking perspective which must not be lost, since God can be said to create from the future, continually marking out a future for the cosmos to inhabit. Indeed, this is arguably the most important perspective for Christian theology, with its central focus on the eschatological significance of the resurrection of Jesus.

Some of the most dramatic eschatological texts in the Bible indicate a catastrophic end to the world which matches its beginning (e.g. 2 Pet.

3:10-13). Only, as with the ambiguity over the question of beginnings, it is perhaps not a final end so much as a completion or fulfilment: the beginning of the new creation (Isa. 65:17; 66:22). For many texts see eventual triumph and salvation lying beyond the coming catastrophe (e.g. Amos 9), perhaps even invoking the creation of a new world (e.g. Rev. 21–22). Therefore, when we consider the many eschatological passages in the Bible we see that there is a sense in which time repeats itself on a grand scale.

On the other hand, Cullmann's influential work *Christ and Time* made the claim that early Christianity established a *linear* view of time over and against the more cyclical Greek view, where time is a never-ending circle which must be escaped from in order to achieve redemption (Cullmann 1951: 52). According to Cullmann, the early Christian view saw a beginning to time at the initial creation, and an end at the final redemption. In between, God's works of revelation and salvation were made decisively in history through Christ, so that all events past, present and future "are connected along the course of an ascending time line" which leads to the final redemption (*ibid.*: 32). This effectively connects to another straight line, since eternity is endlessly extended time (*ibid.*: 63).

The linear view of time is widely contrasted with Eastern thought, which is seen as fundamentally cyclical (Albright 2009: 991; Wilkinson 2010: 120). But this is only true up to a point. For sure, biblical texts do not speak of endless cosmological cycles of death and rebirth, as in the idea of reincarnation. On the other hand, they do not put forward an entirely linear view of time either, and Cullmann's view has been criticized as having been influenced less by the New Testament texts than by "Newtonian absolute time laced with a stiff dose of belief in progress" (Jackelén 2006: 966).

It is possible to argue that there is indeed a kind of cyclical view of time in the Bible (Chapter 9), especially if, as we shall suggest, Cullman underestimated the importance of eschatology in the biblical view of eternity. Taking the longest possible view, a single grand cycle can be discerned: the end of our period of the first creation becomes the beginning of the new creation. And so we find that redemption is achieved through an effective recycling of time. And if time is recyclable on a grand scale, there is a sense in which it is recyclable on a smaller scale too. The Flood (Gen. 6–9) represents one possible eschatological cycle where the old world ends and a new begins, as is clear from the fact that God effectively re-creates time after the Flood (Gen. 8:21-22). Smaller cycles of time are discernible too, especially in the lives of individual believers and Christian communities, which are not only the new creation (2 Cor. 5:17; Gal. 6:15) but are also lived in the "in between times". Thanks to the saving work of Christ and the gift of the Spirit, believers already experience the life of the world to come, but they also live for the present in this world; time for them is "already" but "not yet" (Jackelén 2005: 74). Less a single linear view then, time begins to look complex, dynamic and multi-dimensional (Wilkinson 2010: 129).

This is true when we look at Old Testament views of time too, and scholars have seen a distinction between *prophetic* eschatology – which looks for deliverance in real historical time concerning real social, political and historical situations – and *apocalyptic* eschatology, which looks for deliverance beyond history and beyond this world, perhaps seeing it in terms of a dramatic end to this cosmos followed by new creation (Hanson 1975: 11–12). In some cases these two kinds of eschatology overlap and we find some very difficult interpretative questions arising, especially around some of the more bizarre apocalyptic prophecies. In short, are they simply metaphors for political salvation in historical time, or do they literally expect a full-blown, once-for-all cosmological redemption?

We shall look at this problem of interpretation in some detail in Chapter 9, but will note here that, if there is a sort of beginning to biblical time, there is also a sort of end too, which in some ways may also be a new beginning. In short, biblical time is not strictly linear. And if the Newtonian worldview conceived of time as linear and eternal (§"Space, time, and matter" in Chapter 2, above), then the scientific revolution of the last hundred years has provided a totally new perspective which in some ways meshes with the complexity we see in biblical texts.

Historical time

And what of time between the beginning and the end (i.e. historical time)? To what extent might this be linear?

We should bear in mind that both biblical Hebrew and biblical Greek express time differently from each other and from modern English. For instance, biblical Hebrew does not contain a general term for abstract time, and neither does it contain past, present or future tenses as we know them. Instead, it maintains two aspects to its system of verbs, roughly corresponding to whether an action is completed or not. For this reason, the two Hebrew aspects are often compared with the Indo-European tenses of "perfect" and "imperfect", respectively, although these are only rough approximations which still do not do justice to the Hebrew. Is this evidence that the people of the Old Testament thought about time differently from us? One scholar suggests it might be:

> Many scholars argue that the Hebrew verb system does not have "tenses" ... The storytellers and poets of ancient Israel must have, nonetheless, been familiar with some notion of time, even if it was not mathematical and linear; they wrote passages filled with references to past, present, and future events.
>
> (Nash 2000: 1310)

Here we see the linear view of time appearing again, albeit in the negative, that the Hebrew verb forms constitute evidence that the Old Testament view of time was "not mathematical and linear".

I am inclined to agree that the Old Testament view of time was "not mathematical and linear", but not on this evidence alone. Certainly, it is true to say that Hebrew thought, as we find it expressed in the Bible, did not explore abstract time in the way that classical Greek philosophy was equipped to do, still less we in our modern times have done, with our more developed understanding of historical method and of scientific views of time. Furthermore, the people of the Bible possessed little or nothing in the way of artificial timepieces, and as far as we can tell they did not need to keep diaries in order to fulfil busy social and business engagements; their pace of life was clearly very different from ours, which would no doubt have coloured their subjective experience of it differently from ours. But all the same, as physical human beings, governed by the same physical cycle of days, weeks, months, seasons and years, we must all experience something of the same *flow* of time. Certainly, the narratives of the Hebrew Bible – using just two aspects for its verb forms and no tenses as such – show as sophisticated a development of human story-telling as anything in our modern age. And the biblical assessment of the human lifespan certainly chimes with our own view of steadily "flowing" time, captured bleakly in the famous verse from Psalm 90:

> The days of our life are seventy years,
>   or perhaps eighty, if we are strong;
> even then their span is only toil and trouble;
>   they are soon gone, and we fly away.
>   (Ps. 90:10)

Hence, while we should be cautious about claims that the Israelites knew linear time (as though they had something of our precise, mathematical conception of it), it seems reasonable to suppose that they nevertheless experienced "flowing" time rather like we do (§"Space, time, and matter" in Chapter 2).

The Bible does though, show awareness that there is a theological significance to historical time which we do not share. If the Bible can harken back to "In the beginning" as a fixed point in time, then it can also harken back to key moments in history as fixed points, such as the Exodus (e.g. 1 Kgs 6:1; 2 Chron. 6:5; Heb. 8:9). This is not a linear view of time, nor cyclical, nor repetitive like the seasons and regularities of the natural world. In fact, this view sees time as anything but an impersonal and objective parameter. Rather, it is the arena in which God's personal will and purposes are revealed. Festivals and holy days (including the Sabbath) represent related fixed points through which theological time can be regularly realized in daily life while still retaining something of the "one-off" character of the original event (e.g. Exod. 12). And finally, the widespread prophetic motif of the "day of the Lord" (e.g. Amos 5:18, 20; Ezek. 30:3) is a similar kind of theological fixed point in the future, where historical time becomes eschatological. In the New Testament, this future fixed point is sometimes spoken of using the Greek term *kairos* (e.g. Mt. 8:29; Mk 1:15; Rom. 13:11). Usually translated into English as the neutral word "time", *kairos* actually has no exact equivalent in English but often tends to mean something more like the "opportune time", or the "expected season". *Kairos* therefore exemplifies this idea of the fixed point in the future which is of the utmost theological importance, and in the New Testament it is preeminently the Day of Judgement (Mk 13:33; 1 Pet. 4:17).

God's time

There is a further component of theological time in the Bible, God's own time:

> For a thousand years in your sight
>   are like yesterday when it is past,
>   or like a watch in the night.
> (Ps. 90:4)

> But do not ignore this one fact, beloved, that with the Lord one day is like a thousand years, and a thousand years are like one day.
> (2 Pet. 3:8)

These passages claim to express God's experience of time through a paradox which is surprisingly state-of-the-art, since it bears comparison with the scientific "block" view of time, often raised in the science–religion dialogue, where all times are experienced simultaneously as part of the four-dimensional "spacetime continuum" of relativistic physics (Chapter 2). The two biblical passages cited above may not say this in so many words, but they imply that our sense of flowing, inescapable time is not truly objective since it is not shared by God. Might we then say that God experiences time as a "block"?

Ward (2008: 120–23, 132–3) advocates this, constructing a view not unlike Augustine's, where God is "outside" of time in uncreated "eternity", which Augustine thought of as the absence of time, a state where there is neither past nor future but only a continuous present (*Confessions* XI: 1, 11, 31). Effectively, in Ward's solution God looks in on time from the outside, creating it all as a block and experiencing it as such.

Ward's explanation is appealing in that it makes use of modern physics to explain some of the paradoxes of God and time. They are not paradoxes from the perspective of physics but from ours as humans, since we are bound within a subjective and local "flowing" view of time. There is, however, the difficulty with Ward's suggestion that we are no wiser as to how God might interact with time if God is not in it; the causal link between God and the world is still totally unknown, and we are left with something rather like the God of Deism, "outside" of time. It is also not clear whether such a view reflects what the biblical texts are saying, which instead appear to suggest that God is *inside* time, experiencing it in ways totally outside our ken. God engages fully with it and in it, but is by no means constrained by it (Fretheim 2005: 25). It might be better therefore, to use a relational metaphor rather than a spatial one, to say that God exists *in relationship with* time rather than outside it. God relates to time in analogous ways to those in which God relates to other created entities including space, being both transcendent and immanent with respect to it. And one possible way of relating this to scientific ideas is to think in terms of developments in physics such as string theories, which attempt to model the universe by introducing as many as twenty-six dimensions. If so, God might be said to exist metaphorically in further dimensions of time in addition to our one, and so relates as higher dimensions to a lower dimension (Wilkinson 2010: 126).

There is more, though. We find, for instance, occasional hints in the Bible that time is seen as being in God's possession:

> Yours is the day, yours also the night;
>   you established the luminaries and the sun.
> (Ps. 74:16)

Time is also something to be commanded by God:

> Have you commanded the morning since your days began,
>   and caused the dawn to know its place?
> (Job 38:12)

And time can be said to be continuing because God has made a covenant relationship with creation through Noah (Gen. 8:22). The response of time to all of this is to praise God:

> ...you make the gateways of the morning and the evening shout
> for joy.
> (Ps. 65:8)

And here we see that time's relationship with God is to be characterized by worship, as with the material universe.

One last aspect of God's view of time needs to be thought through, namely the concept of eternity. Augustine thought of eternity as the total absence of time, but it is not clear that this idea can be found in the Bible, since the Hebrew and Greek terms which tend to be translated into English as "eternal" and "eternity" are specifically time-related terms referring to far-flung continuance into the future (or past). Such a view is conveyed by this description of God's longevity, for instance:

> Long ago you laid the foundation of the earth,
>   and the heavens are the work of your hands.
> They will perish, but you endure;
>   they will all wear out like a garment.
> You change them like clothing, and they pass away;
>   but you are the same, and your years have no end.
>   (Ps. 102:26-28 [ET 25-27])

Instead of speaking of eternity as a state of timelessness, of a state of perpetual stasis or torpor then, biblical texts tend to see "eternity" as never-ending time, as Cullmann pointed out. Only, there is also a decisive eschatological twist which Cullmann did not emphasize sufficiently. We can see this by considering the concept of "eternal life", so important in the New Testament (e.g. Mt. 19:16; Jn 6:54; Rom. 6:22; 1 Jn 2:25). As Pannenberg has pointed out, this does not imply that eternity is simply the continuation of time *ad infinitum*: "If [life everlasting] means a life that is going on without end, but otherwise similar to our present form of life, there is no idea of eternity at all, only of time without end" (Pannenberg 2005: 102). In fact, eternity in New Testament terms implies a decisive act of transformation. In the New Testament, the Greek terms for "eternal" and "eternity" derive from the word *aion* (e.g. Sir. 18:10; 2 Pet. 3:18), which can also mean "age" or "period". This is consistent with the heavily eschatological tone of the New Testament, where eternity is by and large seen as the imposition of the coming new age to redeem the "present evil age" (Gal. 1:4). The idea that Christ will come again at this point is an important part of the scheme, so that it will constitute "the end" (1 Cor. 15:24). Likewise, it is possible to see in the New Testament that all times have their fruition – their beginning and their end – in Jesus (Mt. 1:1-17; Lk. 3:23-38; Col. 1:18; Rev. 21:6; 22:13). In that sense, "eternal life" in New Testament terms is an eschatological concept; it is "life from the next age", i.e. life which has God's new creative transformation as its source. That "eternal life" might include immortality ("imperishability") is a reasonable inference to make (1 Cor. 15:50-54), but it is to be seen as a consequence of the universal eschatological transformation, not a thing to be desired in itself alone.

In this way, we can see that New Testament talk of eternity is not of a state of timelessness, nor even perhaps of never-ending time as such, but is rather seen as the goal of time, realized through the person of Jesus first rising again in historical time as the "first fruits" of the age to come (1 Cor. 15:20) and secondly returning in the unspecified future. It might be unspecified, but it is expected soon (1 Cor. 7:29), and in part it is already realized for Christian believers, upon whom "the ends of the ages" have come (1 Cor. 10:11). In that sense, believers are already living eternal life, the life of eternity now.

The upshot of this is that it is difficult to describe the views of eternity which we find in the Bible in terms of a single abstract conceptualization of time; at least in the New Testament it must be done eschatologically through the person of Christ, seen as the result of God's action of salvation from the future which nevertheless completes the past and present too (Russell 2002a: 275, 301–2; Pannenberg 2005; Jackelén 2006). Such a conception of time is far from linear, and to call it cyclical hardly does it justice either. If we are to suggest a way of understanding how God relates to this view of time, it is clear that there is only one way to summarize it: God relates to created time from eternity by reaching back and redeeming time, so as to bring it into eternity. And as for what constitutes eternity itself: there seems little point speculating when it is still "to be revealed" (Rom. 8:18; 1 Pet. 1:5; 5:1).

In any case, Jackelén (2005: 82, 116–17) has put her finger on the truth of the matter by explaining that the Bible views neither time nor eternity as abstract entities, but in terms of what fills them, i.e. their content. They are signs of dynamic relating: God is in eternity, but God is in time too if God is present to both. In the same way, the Christian believer lives in the eschatological tension between the "already" and the "not yet". Time and eternity can be seen as different facets of God's dynamic interaction with the created world. An ontological view of time is replaced by a relational view. God's transcendence relates to eternity, while God's immanence relates to time.

Dates and numbers

A final component of this discussion concerns the way in which dates are recorded in the Bible. There is often a symbolic significance to time and numbers in the Bible which may surprise us who are accustomed to seeing numbers as representing objective, impartial quantities. Archbishop Ussher's famous dating of creation and the flood relied on the dates and genealogical data recorded in the Bible, such as the ages of the patriarchs (Gen. 5). For much of the seventeenth and eighteenth centuries Ussher's chronology was regarded as definitive, but the development of geology through the eighteenth and nineteenth centuries rapidly demonstrated its inadequacy as a reliable chronology of literal scientific beginnings. It slowly became clear that Ussher's date of 4004 BCE for the creation of the earth was out by not just a few thousand years, nor by a factor of ten, but by an unimaginable number of years (4.5 billion to be more precise). And this was not through any fault in Ussher's methodology: he was simply doing what a number of scholars had done before him since at least as early as Theophilus of Antioch (second century CE) in taking the numbers given in the Bible at face value (Cohn 1996: 94–6). Rather, the fall of the house of Ussher came about through an epistemological shift in how the Bible was read. The roughly concurrent developments of geology, evolutionary biology and biblical studies as critical disciplines called into question the old consensus that Genesis had been written by Moses with the aid of divine revelation.

As a result, the biblical numbers which formed the backbone of Ussher's approach have been exposed to a high degree of critical scrutiny. It is now clear that we no longer share much of the Bible's conception and meaning of numbers; sometimes it sees codes and symbols for deeper realities where we might see simply neutral quantities. Many of the dates given in the Bible have clearly been systematized at some stage in the formation of the text. For instance, there is the general trend that most of the generations before the flood are said to have lived between 900 and 1000 years, while after the flood, the ages given slowly diminish until after Moses, when they reach present-day levels (Miller & Hayes 1986: 58–9). Apart from the general unlikelihood that such extreme ages should be taken literally, given what we know of human biology, these ages are clearly designed to make the theological point that, since creation, humankind has steadily lost its vitality, withdrawing further and further from divine favour. Looking more closely, there are good indications that the ages of the patriarchs before the flood (Gen. 5) have some kind of symbolic significance, using multiples of 5 and 60, for instance, which also feature in Babylonian numerology (Bailey 1989: 124).

Another example of the way in which the biblical authors had a grasp of the significance of numbers unlike ours is given by the many appearances of the number forty and its multiples. To mention just three of many possible examples: in the flood, rain fell on the earth for "forty days and forty nights" (Gen. 7:12), and Moses was on Mount Sinai for "forty days and forty nights" (Exod. 24:18), as was Jesus in the wilderness (Mt. 4:2). Many scholars have come to the conclusion that in this kind of context forty is a biblical synonym for "many". But forty is also used schematically as a synonym for a generation, as in the instance when Moses and the Israelites are said to wander in the wilderness for forty years (Num. 32:13). Connected with this is the very significant date given in 1 Kings 6:1, which all biblical chronologies must take into account, for the interval from the Exodus to the building of Solomon's temple. It is given as 480 years, which, if taken literally, would put the Exodus in the fifteenth century BCE. But many scholars prefer the thirteenth century as the most likely timeframe for the Exodus (Provan et al. 2003: 131–2). And it is quite possible that the figure of 480 years is typological in origin anyway, since $480 = 40 \times 12$, and so it may represent twelve generations; perhaps twelve leaders of Israel from the time of Moses through to Solomon, representing the twelve tribes (Cogan 1992: 1005).

From these examples and many more, it can be seen that the dates which may be calculated from the numbers of the Bible should be treated with a degree of historical caution, and certainly never taken unquestioningly at face value. The biblical authors were not bound by our scientific worldview and our concern for technical and literal accuracy when citing numbers. But we should not set up too strong a distinction between them and us, for two reasons:

1. The Israelites were as capable as we are of performing accurate calculations using elementary mathematics; their architectural achievements alone prove that. The differences concern more their interest in the *significance* of numbers and dates, and the six days of Genesis 1 are a good example of this, making the symbolic connection between the working week of God and humans, with the exemplification of the Sabbath (Chapter 3).

2. It should not be concluded from this discussion that every number and date recorded in the Bible is of symbolic value only, since some narratives show signs of careful historical research not unlike that of modern-day historians. This is particularly clear in the ages and lengths of reigns given for the kings of Israel and Judah in the books of Kings and Chronicles. They are cited carefully, often with supporting evidence, so that we read something like this: "Manasseh was twelve years old when he began to reign; he reigned fifty-five years in Jerusalem ... Now the rest of the acts of Manasseh, all that he did, and the sin that he committed, are they not written in the Book of the Annals of the Kings of Judah?" (2 Kgs 21:1, 17). The text is apparently referencing genuine court archives in pre-exilic Jerusalem or Samaria, rather like footnotes in a modern-day historical work. What is more, we can verify some of these narratives independently, using archaeology and other ANE records (as did Ussher, in his own day). Perhaps the best known is the campaign of the Assyrian king Sennacherib against Judah in 701 BCE, described in 2 Kings 18–19, which may be compared with an independent Assyrian account (Miller & Hayes 1986: 353–65).

The conclusion is, of course, that examining the dates and numbers of the Bible is by no means a straightforward exercise. On the one hand, the Bible contains texts which illustrate a view of historical dates and time rather like ours, with a concern to preserve historical accuracy. But on the other, it contains texts which show an interest in the symbolic significance of numbers. Many texts fall somewhere in between, and so are notoriously difficult to interpret, and the date given in 1 Kings 6:1 mentioned above is a good example. In its awareness of science, its awareness of time, and its awareness of history, the Bible is anything but clear-cut, showing both similarities and glaring discrepancies with our modern worldview. The same is true of its awareness of space.

SPACE

The three-tiered cosmos

We turn now to the ancient Hebrew view of "space". As with the understanding of time expressed in the Bible, its conception of space and the cosmos is bound up with its view of God's relationship with the world as Creator. In our culture we are fully capable of picturing the full scope of our universe without needing to see God as present in it; but this is not true of the biblical view. And here we underscore one of the main points of this book, that the difference between our religious mindset and that of the ancient authors of the Bible boils down to different views of the relationship between God and the world; namely, that ours is inescapably tinged with deistic influences compared to theirs. We are more likely to think of the natural world as a closed self-sufficient system than they. However, even this point needs careful thought. It is not true to say that, if our age effectively places God outside of our modern cosmology, then the Bible incorporates God fully within it. As will become clear, one of the biblical devices for describing God's relationship with the physical world is the simple metaphor of distance. Sometimes God is described as being near, sometimes unreachably far off, representing immanence and transcendence, respectively.

The Bible's cosmological references are often interpreted to mean that the cosmos was believed to be limited in extent. This might not be so far from the truth – one possible solution to the Big Bang model suggests that the universe has boundaries (§ "The end of the universe" in Chapter 9, below). If we take references to the "ends of the earth" literally (e.g. Isa. 41:8-9), the suggestion might be that the earth is a flat disk (or a flat shape of some kind with "corners") and that one could reach its edges if one went far enough. For that matter the sky was said to be limited in extent too (e.g. Ps. 19:4-7). Scholars often interpret these statements literally as speaking of a flat earth at the heart of a cosmos which consists of three levels or tiers: the heavens above, the earth beneath, and the primeval waters and Sheol beneath that (e.g. P. S. Alexander 1992: 979). Such a view is suggested, for instance, in this passage found in the Ten Commandments: "You shall not make for yourself an idol, whether in the form of anything that is in heaven above, or that is on the earth beneath, or that is in the water under the earth" (Exod. 20:4; Deut. 5:8). Similar expressions can be found in the New Testament. The ascension of Jesus (Lk. 24; Acts 1), for instance, is suggestive of the idea that heaven is to be found literally in the sky (or at least, accessible via it), and the famous Philippian hymn contains a three-fold cosmological statement: "that at the name of Jesus every knee should bend, in heaven and on earth and under the earth" (Phil. 2:10).

The three-tiered model is able to make sense of statements such as these, but in general it is something of a scholarly approximation. There is a widespread modern urban myth that people in the Middle Ages believed the earth to be flat, a myth which is demonstrably false (Cormack 2009). It is possible that there is something of this urban myth in the scholar's three-tiered model. Tiers are usually flat, for one thing, but with the possible exception of the ambiguous image "the end(s) of the earth" (e.g. Ps. 135:7), the Bible makes no explicit comment on the earth's roundness or flatness. Moreover, the three-tiered model is unable to account for all of the complexities that arise in the biblical material. A good example comes with the term "heaven". The belief is expressed in various texts that it is a solid boundary (a literal "tier") in which sun, moon and stars are set, and above which are the heavenly waters (Gen. 1:7-8; 7:11; see § "Time" in Chapter 3, above). Other references to the heavens being "stretched out" or "beaten out" by Yahweh – rather like the work of a craftsman working on a sheet of metal – may also testify to the belief that the sky is a solid "dome" or expanse (e.g. Isa. 42:5; 44:24; see van Wolde 2009: 9). On the other hand, the Hebrew and Greek words for "heaven" can equally mean "sky", so that we might understand it as being roughly equivalent to our own understanding of "sky" as the whole expanse above the earth. And for sure, the "heavens/sky" are described as the place where the birds fly (Prov. 30:19); it is the created space above the earth which contains the clouds (Dan. 7:13), and the sun, moon and stars (e.g. Deut. 4:19). This is hardly a "tier". Furthermore, there are some descriptions of "sky/heaven" in the Bible which go beyond that of a physical reality and begin to describe something of a *theological* or symbolic reality, rather like our modern term "heaven". This idea is seldom found in the Old Testament beyond occasional texts which cite heaven as the place where God's throne is to be found (1 Kgs 22:19; Ps. 11:4; Isa. 66:1). But when we come to the later Jewish apocalyptic literature and to the New Testament we see something more like our own view of heaven taking shape (e.g. 1 Enoch 14; Mt. 18:10; Rev. 4), where "sky/heaven" is a theological location of special holiness. It is the natural abode of God, the blessed Paradise where the faithful departed are to be found, far transcending the physical "sky" above our heads.

If there is a degree of subtlety concerning the understanding of "heaven" which goes beyond what the three-tiered model is able to express, then there is further subtlety concerning how many tiers there should be.

Returning to Genesis 1 again (which is, after all, the most complete cosmological description in the Bible), it is not clear that tiers or levels are being described at all so much as a different kind of picture altogether (§ "Cosmology" in Chapter 3). The salient cosmological feature of the description (which is strongly emphasized by the flood narrative in Gen. 6–9) is that the earth is surrounded by water both above and below, with a "dome" to hold back the upper waters. This is not a three-tiered model so much as a description of a "bubble" surrounded by water (or a protective "tent"), and it highlights an important feature of the Hebrew worldview which is lacking in the three-tiered model, namely the cosmological importance of water, which appears so prominently in the biblical creation motif through Yahweh's mythological conflict with the dragon and the sea (§ "Creation and mythology" in Chapter 4, above). The inhabitable universe is like a submersible, preserved and protected by Yahweh deep within the disordering waters, so that his created order can flourish. Other texts include the sea as a fourth tier in addition to heaven, earth and Sheol (e.g. Job 11:8-9; Ps. 139:8-9; see Oden 1992a: 1169). And in the book of Revelation we find a doxology not unlike that cited above from Philippians 2:10 which, instead of pointing to three tiers, points to four including the sea: "Then I heard every creature in heaven and on earth and under the earth and in the sea, and all that is in them, singing" (Rev. 5:13). Here we see the cosmos described not in terms of tiers so much as realms of habitation. Moreover, if we return to the writings of the rabbis of the early centuries CE, some of the earliest recorded interpretations of Genesis 1, we find evidence of cosmological speculation which involves not three tiers, nor four, but *many* tiers – seven heavens and seven earths to begin with, as well as water (Ginzberg 2003: 5–6).

The point of this discussion is not to complicate the picture unduly but to point out the shortcomings of the three-tiered model as a *literal* description of the ancient Hebrew cosmology: the texts describe a view (or perhaps views) which is/are more subtle and more complex than such a simplistic model can account for. But there is a further potential difficulty for the three-tiered model, since most of the cosmological statements which are interpreted as evidence in its favour are in fact metaphorical allusions to God's relationship with the world. Should they really be understood as statements of a literal cosmology, or would they be better read as metaphors of divine presence?

The location of God

To investigate this question, let us look more closely at the cosmological language which describes God's location. There are numerous examples of texts which locate God in heaven, and some which even suggest that God can look down from there at people on the earth (e.g. Pss. 14:2; 33:13-14). This would suggest an understanding of "sky/heaven" where God is literally above our heads. Indeed, popular Christian language often locates God in "heaven" (e.g. "Our Father in heaven", Mt. 6:9), but few, if any, modern people would think of "heaven" as a locale in the material universe, even if that might have been the case in ancient times. Effectively though, both ancient and modern cosmological views of heaven make the same point, that God's place of abode is completely out of reach to human beings under normal circumstances. Bultmann (1960: 15, 20) argued that the three-tiered universe of Hebrew cosmology was evidence that the primitive "mythological thinking" of the Bible should be demythologized for our modern scientific age. However, not only is the idea of a primitive mentality barely sustainable, but it is unlikely that the ancients interpreted their myths as literally as modern scholars do. As Caird puts it:

> Biblical man may indeed have pictured the world to himself with heaven above it and Sheol below; but as A. M. Farrer has pointed out, he was not silly enough to imagine that aviation could reach the one or excavation the other. Anybody who has ever accepted the three-storey picture as a description of the world he lived in has done so because it was also a permanent and universal symbol without which certain aspects of religious truth could neither be apprehended nor expressed.
>
> (Caird 1980: 120–21)

If Caird is right, then the three-tiered cosmology of modern scholarship is not a cosmology so much as a symbolic way of expressing "religious truth", or in other words, the relationship between God and the world, symbolized by distance and geography. Mascall (1956: 26) made a similar point many years before, speaking of the "real and pernicious period of literalism" which arose through the scientific revolution of the seventeenth century. It had the result that the Bible's language of spatial separation of God from the earth, always understood *qualitatively* as the distinction between creatures and their Creator, was now read literally and therefore became highly problematic:

> the displacement of the earth from the centre of the universe by Copernicus and Galileo, and still more the unification of the sublunar and supralunar world by Newton's discovery of universal gravitation, abolished all qualitative differences between different regions of space.   (*Ibid.*: 27)

It was now no longer possible to understand biblical references to the qualitative difference between God and the world without taking them literally.

And hence we find scholars reading such references in terms of a hypothetical three-tiered cosmology, as if such references were actually scientific statements about the nature of physical space.

It is safer to conclude that many of the cosmological statements in the
Bible are symbolic, rather than scientific, statements: if God is in heaven,
then God is utterly out of reach and transcendently different from the
world. This point can be pressed further by taking an example such as
Psalm 57, which contains a number of different spatial statements about
the location of God. On the one hand, God seems to be in heaven, because
the psalm contains a prediction that God will "send from heaven and save"
(v. 4 [ET 3]). But other images of space and location about heaven and
God's virtues are used which make it clear that the language was always
intended as metaphorical:

> Be exalted, O God, above the heavens.
>   Let your glory be over all the earth.
> For your steadfast love is as high as the heavens;
>   your faithfulness extends to the clouds.
>   (Ps. 57:6, 11 [ET 5, 10])

The prepositions used in this passage are particularly revealing. God is to
be exalted *above* the heavens (the sky), and God's glory to be *over* all the
earth, since God's love and faithfulness extend *as high as* the heavens, and
as far as the clouds. Taken literally, God appears first to be located above
the sky, but then on the earth and no further than the clouds. But clearly,
this is not meant literally; the psalm is a series of poetic allusions to God's
absolute transcendence and universal faithfulness, using spatial metaphors
for emphasis.

Something similar may be said of the counterpart to the heavens,
namely that which is beneath the earth, the underworld (often called Sheol
in the Old Testament). This need not be seen as a literal description of a
physical tier below the surface of the earth but could just as easily function in an entirely metaphorical way, as the symbolic status of the dead.
They are completely out of the reach of the living, and also unable to reach
God themselves. The underworld therefore becomes a metaphor of separation from the living (e.g. Job 7:9) and perhaps even from God (e.g. Ps. 88:5
[ET 4]; Isa. 38:10-18).

An even clearer example of heaven being used as a spatial metaphor of
transcendence comes in Solomon's prayer of dedication of the Jerusalem
Temple (1 Kgs 8). Solomon implores Yahweh to hear his prayer "in heaven
your dwelling place" (v. 30), while at the same time expressing the awareness that God will no more dwell in the Temple which Solomon has just
built than literally in heaven: "But will God indeed dwell on the earth? Even
heaven and the highest heaven cannot contain you, much less this house

that I have built!" (1 Kgs 8:27). This is one of the clearest indications in the Old Testament that a primary function of the references to God being in the heavens is to point metaphorically to God's utter transcendence over the world.

Theophany

The view that we have put forward so far is that many of the biblical descriptions of physical space are metaphors for the Creator/creation relationship. This is supported by the fact that God's presence is associated with various distinct physical locations in the Old Testament, not just the sky/heaven. The theophany of Yahweh occurs pre-eminently on mountains (e.g. Mount Sinai, Exod. 19), and mountains are connected strongly with manifestations of the divine presence in its transcendent mode, such as Mount Zion (Micah 4), Mount Zaphon (Isa. 14:13-14) and various notable mountains in the story of Jesus (Mt. 5:1; 15:29-31; 28:16-20; Mk 9:1-9). But other features of the natural landscape are also important as locations for theophany, such as trees (e.g. Gen. 18:1; Exod. 3:1-6), streams (e.g. Gen. 32:22-32), and rivers (e.g. Pss. 36:8-10; 46; Ezek. 1:1; Mk 1:9-11). Within the three-tiered model we might read these locations as "bridges" between the three physical tiers. On the other hand, if we take a more figurative approach, these various natural locations of theophany can be read as suggesting that the distinctions between cosmological domains are actually much more fluid and itinerant than the terminology of "tier" might suggest; they shift along with talk of God's presence, which can be both mobile and adaptive. In short, they are metaphors again of God's nature and relationship with the created world. In a similar way, Levenson argues that Old Testament references to an "earthly Jerusalem" and a "heavenly Jerusalem" point to a world picture made up of two tiers which are open to each other, and interpenetrate on Mount Zion (Levenson 1985: 141–2). The sense is not that the boundaries are sharp, but that there are locations in our world which reveal God's presence and holiness more clearly than others. They are physical locations which also encapsulate or symbolize divine transcendence, rather like the metaphor of "heaven".

In addition to geographical *locations* like mountains and springs, God is also said to be manifest in natural *phenomena*; primarily the thunderstorm (e.g. Exod. 15:1-18; Judg. 5:4-5; Job 37:2-38:1), fire (e.g. Gen. 15:12-21; Exod. 3:1-6) and earthquake (e.g. 2 Sam. 22:8), but even in human structures (the Jerusalem Temple and religious liturgies, e.g. 1 Kgs 8). The point is that if we moderns hardly believe that God has a literal resting place in our universe, then neither did the biblical writers; rather God's presence is associated with different kinds of places and different kinds of phenomena in different kinds of ways, pointing to a breadth of understanding of God's revelation and work in the world. It is entirely possible that different images and motifs had their roots in different mythological aspects of Israel's past, but the fact that they have been combined almost seamlessly in many texts, and canonized all together in the Bible, suggests that no one image should be taken as exhaustive or historically authoritative. The different images build up the entire picture, which is multi-faceted and cannot easily be collapsed into a single conceptual pattern.

A final significant point about the language of theophany is that, as Fretheim (2005: 260–61) recognizes, it is intimately related to the language of creation's praise of God (see also my conclusion to Chapter 4). God is revealed in mountain, earthquake and storm in much the same way that mountain, earthquake and storm praise God, through their exercise of natural but intensely revelatory functions. Far from being merely colourful metaphors to express *human* praise of God, such texts illustrate that every non-human corner of creation has a holiness of its own which reveals the nearness of God's presence. If theophany expresses something of God's transcendence, then nature's praise expresses something of God's immanence.

Immanence

There are many other ways in which God is said to be intimately close to the world, communicating an *immanent* view of divine presence. We will mention some of these in the next chapter, when we discuss the possibility of locating the *creatio continua* category in biblical texts, but other metaphorical descriptions of God's closeness (Ps. 145:18) can be found, such as in certain Psalms, where God is described as our shepherd (Ps. 23), our shelter (Ps. 91), and our keeper and shade (Ps. 121). A similar degree of intimacy is found in expressions of God's renewal of covenant, and of love for the people (e.g. Exod. 29:45-46; Isa. 42:6; 43:1-2; Jer. 31:33-34; 32:37-40; Ezek. 37:26-28; Hos. 11).

It must be admitted though, that the immanence of God is not spoken of in the Old Testament so explicitly as is the transcendence of God. However, there is an important and more subtle trend at work because, roughly from the eighth century BCE with the beginning of written prophecy, there seems to have been a tendency for God's revelation to be sought in wisdom, prophetic word, voice, and oracle, that is, in forms of human utterance. These motifs speak powerfully of divine immanence, as illustrated with the story of Elijah on Mount Sinai/Horeb (1 Kgs 19:11-12), which some scholars (e.g. Cross, Levenson) propose as a significant narrative development describing the evolution of Israel's attitude towards prophecy. In the narrative, Elijah waits for God's revelation on the mountain, but God is not revealed in the great wind, nor the earthquake, nor the fire, which strike the mountain (i.e.

in traditional signs of theophany), but in the "sound of sheer silence" which follows (Cross 1973: 193–4). The voice of Elijah's inner conscience has replaced the tremendous and awe-inspiring spectacle of God which Moses and the earlier Israelites had been privileged to witness on the mountain (Levenson 1985: 89–90). In other words, the divine theophany has become internalized, and expressed through the prophetic voice. This perhaps goes some way towards explaining the developing focus in Old Testament times on the written prophets from the eighth century onwards, together with reflection on the law (e.g. Pss. 1; 119) and the Wisdom literature. Divine immanence becomes expressed in terms of the inner faith of the reflective community and individual.

Even more intimate expressions of divine immanence can be found in the New Testament, and in Paul's theology of the Holy Spirit the discussion of divine immanence reaches new theological heights. If the resurrection of Jesus can be said to have come about by the power of God at work (through the Spirit), then that same Spirit is directly at work in the lives of ordinary believers (Rom. 8:11), but as a work of "new creation" (2 Cor. 5:17), not of the old.

Perhaps the best example comes in Paul's discussion of spiritual gifts and the "body of Christ" in 1 Corinthians 12. Here, we find that, because of the immanent (and eschatological) work of God in believers, they are given the "manifestation of the Spirit" (1 Cor. 12:7). By displaying spiritual gifts such as the utterance of wisdom and knowledge, gifts of healing and prophecy, believers have themselves become the locations of divine theophany. It is hard to imagine a more comprehensive symbol of divine immanence than this, and any description of God's relationship with the created world must give it due consideration alongside the well-known symbols of God's transcendence (e.g. Gen. 1).

CONCLUSIONS

By this stage, we have clearly moved some way from discussing biblical conceptions of time and space. This is because so many of the Bible's statements which appear to describe the cosmos and its structure are actually symbolic references to the relationship between Creator and creation. As it is today, space was one of the main metaphorical devices used for describing the nature of God and God's relationship with the world. This means that the popular scholarly reconstruction of the three-tiered cosmology should only be used as a rough approximation at best, and should probably not be regarded as a hard and fast description of what ancient Hebrews believed about their physical world. It is possible that it captures something of the truth, but the texts on which it is based are better understood as metaphorical devices to describe the divine quality of transcendence with respect to three entirely distinct realms of being: (1) God, (2) the living and (3) the dead. A system of metaphysical boundaries is being described, and we might be reminded of the not-unrelated system of boundaries found in the legal and ritual material of the Old Testament which describes what is clean and unclean. Neither system bears relation to our modern scientific views of space or cosmos, but rather sees the cosmos in social, ritual, and theological terms.

In the same way, we have found it difficult to isolate a view of time in the Bible which is not in some way influenced by theological considerations. We have discussed biblical ideas of cosmic beginnings and of endings, as well as of historical time in-between, and we have found that they are all heavily symbolic in various ways of God's work in the world. Ordinary Israelites must have been capable of thinking about time and space in everyday pragmatic ways, without needing to incorporate God into their thoughts, but it seems that, when the bigger picture was in view, then God was never far from the scene. In the same way, we discussed ancient Israelite science, and asserted that a view of causality related to our own must have existed, otherwise early technology would have been impossible, but in the texts of the Bible it is often couched in heavily theological terms.

Our modern scientific worldview has clearly drawn us into a much more deistic frame of mind than the early Israelites, or least those who were active in the composition of biblical texts. If we find it straightforward to see the big picture of our world, of time and space, of boundaries and structures, without God active in it, then the early Israelites seem to have found it correspondingly harder to conceive of such a big picture. Their default big picture incorporated God's activity as a matter of course. Ours rarely does.

In the next chapter we will take the discussion further by looking at how God's relationship with the world may be understood in both biblical and more contemporary theological terms.

Chapter 6

CREATOR–CREATION:
HOW CAN A RELATIONSHIP BE DESCRIBED?

CREATION FROM NOTHING (*CREATIO EX NIHILO*)

The scientific revolutions of the last 150 years have had far-reaching implications for how we view God's relationship with the world. The emphasis upon evolutionary models in both physics and biology has led to a re-appreciation of the biblical perspective which puts God's intimate presence with the world alongside God's above-and-beyond transcendence.

In this chapter we will look at the *theological* framework of the biblical creation material in the light of modern science. We will do this by assessing two categories which have been widely used to distinguish different types of God's creative work – *creatio ex nihilo* ("creation from nothing") and *creatio continua* ("continuous creation"). These categories are often used in the science–theology field, but they are of uncertain status in biblical ideas of creation, as we shall see. Nevertheless, I will point out that they introduce important considerations for the models of God's relationship with the world which we see in the Bible. In other words, although the categories were constructed hundreds of years later than the biblical creation texts first came into written form, yet they introduce a useful way of reading the biblical texts theologically and in conjunction with scientific interpretations.

We have already introduced *creatio ex nihilo* (Chapter 1) – it is the idea that when God made the world at the beginning of time, God made it literally "from nothing" – a belief which has the important consequences that God is neither dependent on the world nor necessarily a part of it. The world, on the other hand, is necessarily dependent on God for its existence. This is one of the basic statements of "theism" – the orthodox belief in God as an objective being distinct from the world – as opposed to "pantheism" (the belief that the world is essentially identical with God), or "pan-en-theism" (the belief that the world is "in" or is a part of God). In contrast, theism maintains that God is both personal and active in the divine work of creation: God both created the world at the beginning of time *ex nihilo*, and continues to support and uphold (or sustain) it, and is active in it. Since the world was dependent upon God for its existence in the first place ("In the beginning"), it continues to be dependent upon God for its continued existence; it is contingent in the widest possible sense. In fact, if God is said *not* to sustain the world in every moment of its existence, then this suggests that the world exists by means of its own power and is in a sense equal to God. The theological position of *creatio ex nihilo* is therefore not only relevant for how things began, but for how they continue to be. In short, *creatio ex nihilo* is not an explanation of "In the beginning" so much as a statement that there is an ongoing *relationship* between the created world and its Creator. As Stoeger (2010: 181) puts it in his discussion of God and the Big Bang: "creation is not a temporal event, but a relationship – a relationship of ultimate dependence". The relationship is one of transcendence on God's part, and contingence on the world's. Other ways of putting this are to say that God is the one who exists necessarily, while the world exists in dependence upon God; that God is omnipotent and supports the world, being the means by which it continues to exist. We find this idea that God supports the natural order of the world expressed in biblical passages which praise God for the rhythm of the day and the seasons, and for the provision of harvest (e.g. Pss. 74:16-17; 145:15-16; Jer. 5:24). Likewise, the Gospels tell us that God's support is so sufficiently all-embracing as to care for every sparrow and lily of the field (Mt. 6:25-29; Lk. 12:6, 24-28). And the idea that without God's explicit support the world would be destroyed is found memorably in the covenant which God makes after the flood with Noah, with every living creature and with the earth, symbolized by the rainbow (Gen. 9:12-17).

It is important to understand clearly the idea of God's transcendence which flows from the *ex nihilo* view, and that when we speak of transcendence we do not necessarily mean that God is over and above the created world, as though so far beyond it as to be out of touch with it. In other words, we are not making a point about any spatial or temporal frame of reference in which God is either to be found or not to be found. By speaking of transcendence we refer rather to the idea that God is not constrained by time and space in the way that we are. Again, this does not mean that God is outside of time and space in the sense of not being present. Rather, God is omnipresent, so that every event or object in time and space exists through God's originating power (Ward 1996b: 290). It is God, and God alone, who prevents it from falling back into nothingness. In this way, we find that theism, and the assertion that God made the world *ex nihilo*, specifies a whole series of conclusions about God's supportive and sustaining relationship with the world. If modern science has caused us to believe that talk of creation is all about temporal beginnings, then the *creatio ex nihilo* category may help us to regain something of the idea which the Bible asserts, that it is equally about a relationship with the Creator.

Theism is not the only framework for understanding God's relationship to the world, though. The rise of modern science, and its success in explaining the world without calling upon a Creator, has meant that the God–world relationship has come under close philosophical, theological and scientific scrutiny. One alternative framework is that of deism. In common with theism, deism asserts the transcendence of God, and God's initial work in creation. But after that they depart, since deism believes that God plays no part in the fabric of the world thereafter. Indeed, deism emphasizes God's transcendence to such a degree that it posits a very real separation between God and the world after the initial beginning, insisting that God has not interacted with the world once it had come into being. Belief in miracles and revelation is therefore negated in the worldview of deism, since God allows the universe to proceed on the path initially set for it without divine interference or guidance. Deism does not necessarily deny the idea of *creatio ex nihilo* though, since a deist can affirm God's general providential support of the world without believing that God interacts closely with its activity. It is, however, safe to say that deism disagrees with much of the perspective of theism, which not only maintains the *ex nihilo* view throughout the history of the world, but also believes God to be *immanently* present in it (that is, inherent in creation, in close proximity to it).

Within the deterministic Newtonian worldview of the early modern period, deism was seen to be an attractive faith option, since it allowed science to be science – scientific processes could be understood as natural and regular without any need for divine interference. Although deism has declined in the meantime as a conscious faith option, yet it has left a more unconscious legacy which becomes apparent when we try to understand stories of miracle and revelation in our scientific context: it becomes extraordinarily difficult to avoid deistic talk of "intervention".

There are good reasons for seeking to maintain a theistic perspective over deism. First, science has moved on significantly since the early modern era of Newton. With the rise of Darwinism in the nineteenth century, and the New Physics in the twentieth (marked especially by the discoveries of relativity, quantum mechanics and chaos theory), the regular and almost mechanical worldview of Newton has largely been superseded by a much more open scientific view of the world which acknowledges novelty and freshness at its heart. Second, deism is a view which is largely alien to the biblical world. Although some passages suggest that "God is in the heavens" (Ps. 115), which might suggest that God is far out of reach, the God of the Bible also takes a close and active interest in history and in the natural world. Indeed, we find the astonishing idea that God has bowed down so close to creation as to actually become a part of it, in Christ, and continues to work immanently in it, as the Holy Spirit. If the biblical God is transcendent (suggesting an unimaginably sheer difference between God and the world), then this God is also immanent and present (or in other words inherent or intrinsic to the world, practically indwelling). Although the biblical texts do not strictly appear to know of *creatio ex nihilo*, yet they are consistent with it, as we shall see. And they certainly show plentiful signs of the theistic idea that God is both transcendent and immanent. Consequently, in the face of the difficulties for theism which are thrown up by modern science, and in spite of the concomitant attractions of deism, we will suggest that a theistic viewpoint matches the biblical worldview best.

Theism has one further point in its favour as a statement of faith, in that it holds a stronger position than deism in debate with New Atheism. Deism can be seen to be a form of dualism, moving God's sphere of influence from the material world to the spiritual. Affirmation of deism means that God's personal relationship with humans becomes restricted only to the spiritual dimension, so that belief in God, and worship, become human cerebral and spiritual activities. This dualistic affirmation means in turn that the affiliation between Creator and all of creation which we saw in the conclusion to Chapter 4, expressed so vividly in the call to the whole universe to participate in worship, is now denied. Non-human creation is emptied of divine meaning except that it points to "design" (which only humans can appreciate, and that only cerebrally), and there is no longer a sense in which it exists for its own sake to give glory to God or to receive God's glorying. So texts which suggest that the floods might "clap their hands", or the mountains "sing together with joy" in praise to God (Ps. 98:8), for instance, lose much of their richness. In a theistic position they are metaphorical expressions of universal worship of the Creator through fulfilment of the divinely created potential; they are the creature echoing the Creator's "very good" (Gen. 1:31). In a deistic position only humans can worship God, and so such texts become metaphors for human admiration of the world. And this means that religious arguments for the existence of God lose much of their force in deism, since they can no longer draw on the larger life of the universe standing in relationship with its Creator; the universe has instead become a passive and inert receptacle for the spiritual/intellectual life of humans. Deism, then, can do little more than point to God as an explanatory hypothesis for why the world has turned out as it has. But this is an inherently weak argument when placed against science, because science is able to explain much of the world without calling upon a designer.

Theism imbues the whole of creation with the presence of God's Spirit, giving non-human reality a spiritual significance of its own which it cannot have in deism. Ironically, the growing importance of the ecological perspective in recent decades has led to increased respect for the natural world. This is a scientific development, but nevertheless one which has a resonance with the theistic affirmation that all of creation possesses intrinsic merit in God's sight (Chapter 9).

For these reasons, we will be careful to maintain a theistic approach in this book. This is not to be pejorative of deism, which has, at times, been a fertile affirmation of faith in the modern period (Fergusson 2009: 77), but rather to steer a theological course as close as possible to that charted by the Bible.

CONTINUOUS CREATION (*CREATIO CONTINUA*)

If *creatio ex nihilo* is a foundational theistic statement of God's transcendence with respect to the world, then the term *creatio continua* can be used to express the equally theistic idea that God is immanent; that is, present in and with the world, participating in it in an actively creative sense. But these qualities of transcendence and immanence only describe the relationship from the world's perspective. Seen from God's perspective, we find that it is *contingency* which is emphasized: the *ex nihilo* view expresses the contingency of the world's very existence in the first place, while the *continua* view expresses the contingency of every new creation and event in the ongoing life of the world.

However, there has been some uncertainty around this point in the past, since the *ex nihilo* view already contains the idea that God is active in supporting and preserving the world throughout its existence, and this has been construed by notable theologians such as Aquinas as a form of continuous creation (Pannenberg 1994: 40). And in modern times, Schleiermacher preferred to downplay any distinction between God's initial act of creation and God's subsequent support of it by saying that it is all one divine act of "preservation" (*The Christian Faith*, §38; see Pannenberg 1994: 42). Others, on the other hand, have wished to distinguish sharply between God's original work of creation *ex nihilo* and God's subsequent work of conservation, maintaining that conservation is not the same as creation, and that it is only the original action which is truly creative (Copan & Craig 2004: 148–65).

If there has been ambiguity in this long-standing discussion over whether God's continuous support/conservation/preservation of the world constitutes "creation" (and "continuous creation" at that), then a new force has entered the fray, that of modern science. The contemporary dialogue between science and theology emphasizes the importance of evolutionary models to our understanding of creation, and therefore suggests that we should take seriously the term *creatio continua* as representing a distinct kind of creative activity from that of *ex nihilo*.

To clarify the distinction between the *ex nihilo* and *continua* categories, it is worth considering this comment of Pannenberg's (1994: 35): "To preserve something in existence presupposes that it exists". In other words, the continuing preservative role of *creatio ex nihilo* only applies to things that already exist. But what of entirely new forms that did not exist before? We might even ask about new lives that do not as yet exist. The implication is that "newness" requires the introduction of a new kind of category to supplement *ex nihilo*. *Creatio continua* is thus often used in the science–theology field to express the idea that God's creative activity is not restricted simply to the very beginning of the world, nor to its constant underpinning or preservation, but is ongoing, novel and fresh at all times.

Now *creatio continua* tends to presuppose *creatio ex nihilo* in the first place (i.e. God's prevention of the falling of time, space and matter back into nothingness), so we might regard it as dependent upon the *ex nihilo* view (*ibid.*: 122, n. 323). Nevertheless, *creatio continua* is still a useful category in its own right to represent the current scientific consensus that the world is in a state of continual becoming. In other words, God's creative plan for the world was not entirely completed (fulfilled?) in its initial Big Bang state, and neither is it fulfilled by God's support of what has existed since and exists now. Rather, *creatio continua* suggests that the creative work is constantly ongoing in order to reveal the world's full potential, which is perpetually novel and fresh. To use a scientific term, *creatio continua* sees God's creative activity as continually "emergent", and not simply the predictable outworking of well-defined laws and principles. *Creatio continua* has been associated in the science–theology field with writers such as Arthur Peacocke and Ian Barbour, influenced by the panentheistic God of process theology. (Note that process philosophy and process theology highlight relationships and processes between every entity in nature, down to the most minute level by which the world continually comes into being. God is seen as intimately caught up in this, to the extent that God may be said to change along with the world, and even to share in its suffering; Barbour 1997: 284–304.) But it is also possible to affirm *creatio continua* within a more conventional theistic approach, since God's immanence is seen in the creative work of the Holy Spirit (e.g. Ps. 104:30). As Polkinghorne has explained, "*Creatio continua* can be understood as the work of the Creator in the mode of divine immanence, just as *creatio ex nihilo*, the preservation of creation from ontological collapse, is the work of the Creator in the mode of divine transcendence" (Polkinghorne 1998: 81). So, although these two categories of *creatio ex nihilo* and *creatio continua* emphasize different views of God's relationship with the created world (and therefore different models of God too), ultimately both may be seen as basically compatible with the general the-istic view that God is both transcendent and immanent with respect to creation. While the *ex nihilo* view of creation is more foundational, yet it is useful to be able to affirm the *continua* view alongside it, since it read-ily incorporates elements of chance and emergence into our theological models of creation while preventing them from being seen from a deistic angle where all is effectively predetermined (Polkinghorne 1994: 79; van Huyssteen 1998: 105).

CAN SCIENCE SHED LIGHT ON *EX NIHILO* AND *CONTINUA*?

How might these two categories of creation be related to scientific under-standings of the beginnings and development of the world? Just as it is tempting to make a close identification between the Big Bang model and the opening verses of Genesis 1 (§ "Genesis 1 and modern science" in Chapter 3, above), so it is also tempting to connect the Big Bang model with the theological idea of *creatio ex nihilo*, since both suggest that the universe arose dramatically at a definite point in history. Copan and Craig, for instance, make this connection, on the grounds that the "abso-lute beginning of the universe" which the Big Bang model provides has "momentous theological ramifications". They go on to state that:

> Given the biblical and theological grounds for the doctrine of
> *creatio ex nihilo*, we should *expect* to observe something like a
> big bang universe rather than a steady state universe or an eter-
> nally oscillating universe. Given the evidence, the big bang does
> plausibly represent the creation event.
>
> (Copan & Craig 2004: 18)

However, there are several problems with making this identification (Russell 1996: 208–9). For one, in spite of what Copan and Craig claim, the Big Bang model is not an absolute beginning in the sense of *ex nihilo* since it does not posit a definite theological "nothing" before its initial state, which the *creatio ex nihilo* approach both positively asserts and requires. On the contrary, the Big Bang model requires "something" to be in place before our spacetime can be born, although there are various speculative possibilities as to what that "something" might be, such as the idea that perhaps our universe was created out of a previous universe, which was destroyed as ours was born. A further possibility is that our universe is one of many which co-exist as part of the grand ensemble known as the "multi-verse". At the bare minimum, some kind of conceptual quantum cosmolog-ical framework must be in existence to give rise to the Big Bang. Therefore, every scientific explanation must be contingent to some degree, and none can be altogether compatible with the theological assertion that there was literally nothing before there was anything, since the theological concept of "nothing" (the absence of creation) cannot be open to scientific enquiry by definition. In other words, Big Bang cosmology simply cannot reproduce the "nothing" which the *ex nihilo* approach asserts. At best, the Big Bang can be a vivid means of visualizing the beginnings of our universe, but it cannot help us to visualize our *ex nihilo* beginnings.

But there is a more significant difficulty behind attempts to link *creatio ex nihilo* with the Big Bang. They run the risk of saying that *creatio ex nihilo* is only relevant in the entire history of the universe at its conception. In other words, they restrict God's transcendent interaction with the world to its very beginning, thereby denying the world's need of God's transcendent support throughout time, and tending towards the viewpoint of Deism.

There is a similar temptation to identify the viewpoint of *creatio continua* with scientific models of cosmological evolution (which Big Bang cosmology provides) and biological evolution (such as neo-Darwinism). As we outlined in Chapter 2, both the Big Bang model and neo-Darwinism are of central importance in scientific explanations of the way the world is as it is today. Although there are elements of determinism in both models, the overall picture also highlights the operation of chance and emergent processes, which are responsible for the coming-into-being of fundamentally new entities at various stages in time, not just those predictable from the very beginning. These processes may be regarded as truly *creative*, since they suggest that the creation of the world is still unfinished and ongoing. Therefore, they are analogous to the theological idea of *creatio continua*. And the widespread recognition of this scientific viewpoint has been important in encouraging theologians to look afresh at the *creatio continua* category. Indeed, Polkinghorne (1994: 76) points out that, while belief in *creatio ex nihilo* will always be metaphysical, based on a perception that God is transcendent with respect to creation, belief in *creatio continua* is more directly motivated by our scientific perception that the world is evolving. This claim was famously made by Aubrey Moore well over a century ago, when he explained that Darwinism, despite prompting vociferous debate over the relationship between science and theology, had made the Deism of the previous age untenable:

> The one absolutely impossible conception of God, in the present day, is that which presents Him as an occasional Visitor ... Darwinism appeared, and, under the guise of a foe, did the work of a friend. It has conferred upon philosophy and religion an inestimable benefit, by shewing us that we must choose between two alternatives. Either God is everywhere present in nature, or He is nowhere.   (Moore [1889] 1891: 73)

And many contemporary theologians are fully in accord with this sentiment. Mackey (2006: 34), for instance has put it succinctly: "Evolution is just a name for continuous creation". And we should not ignore the very significant comments of the biologist-theologian Arthur Peacocke:

> Any notion of God as Creator must now take into account, that God is continuously creating, continuously giving existence to, what is new; that God is *semper Creator*; that the world is a *creatio continua*. The traditional notion of God *sustaining* the world in its general order and structure now has to be enriched by a dynamic and creative dimension – the model of God sustaining and giving continuous existence to a process which has an inbuilt creativity, built into it by God. God is creating at every moment of the world's existence in and through the perpetually endowed creativity of the very stuff of the world.
> (Peacocke 2001: 23)

Peacocke's encouragement is well put, but in spite of all this we should be cautious not to identify specific scientific ideas of cosmic or biological evolution too closely with the theological category of *creatio continua*. If we were to do this, we would run the risk of creating a similar problem to that which we saw above where we discussed attempts to link the Big Bang closely with *creatio ex nihilo*. We would be suggesting that God's continuous creative activity is manifest more in some ways (especially those described by evolutionary scientific models) than in others: God would appear to be more present immanently through the development of novel forms of life than in already existent forms. Furthermore, we would run the risk of amplifying an unhelpful distinction between *creatio continua* and *creatio ex nihilo*, of identifying the former primarily with *natural* mechanisms, and the latter with the *supernatural*. We must be careful therefore not to imply that when God creates continuously God's work comes within the remit of science and is natural, while when God creates from nothing it is theological and inherently supernatural. This distinction is largely unknown in the Bible (Chapter 5).

For these reasons, it is helpful to affirm both categories of *creatio ex nihilo* and *creatio continua* together as complements, and to affirm them primarily as *theological* categories without making them reliant on science. It may be that one category in particular (*continua*) shows tantalizing analogies with the discoveries of modern science, but this does not make it any less theological, or any more scientific, than the other (*ex nihilo*). Modern science has highlighted the importance of chance and novelty in our understanding of the evolution of the world, and *creatio continua* allows us to incorporate that idea quite generally into our theology, without pinning it down to specific scientific models. Indeed, it is important to incorporate such elements of unpredictability, against a tendency which assumes that God's creative activity is always law-like and orderly. Such a mindset gave us deism.

Both categories then, *ex nihilo* and *continua*, are fundamentally theological at the end of the day: they both describe God's creative work, one as immanent, and the other as transcendent. This can also be demonstrated from the reverse direction: if biological evolution may be seen as fitting particularly well within the remit of one category (*continua*), then it requires the other (*ex nihilo*) for the world in which biological evolution takes place to exist in the first place. The two categories complement each other, describing how God is both present in creation and transcendent with respect to it. And it hardly needs saying that this is the traditional solution known as theism.

WHAT DOES THE BIBLE KNOW OF ALL THIS?

Creatio ex nihilo

Having described in broad terms the state of discussion surrounding the categories of *creatio ex nihilo* and *creatio continua*, let us now look at the extent to which they are reflected in the biblical creation texts.

First, we must ask whether we are correct in applying these ideas to the Bible, since they stem from later historical debates and contexts. Westermann (1984: 108–9, 174), for one, urges caution in the application of the *creatio ex nihilo* category to the Genesis texts, for this very reason. Anachronism is, of course, one of the perennial pitfalls in interpretation of the Bible, or indeed of any ancient text: later interpretative categories should not be applied roughshod without sufficient consideration for the worldview and historical context of its authors. We raised this issue in a previous chapter, in the context of discussing the Trinitarian view of God (§ "Creation and the beginnings of the idea of God as Trinity" in Chapter 4, above). We can go on to say more generally that it is important to make sure that, as far as is possible, we should be reading theology *out* of the Bible, and not *into* it. But this does not mean that we are *prohibited* from using later interpretative categories, because this would be to exalt the text to such an un-approachable status from our point of view as to be practically unreadable. Indeed, it is an important point of theological interpretation that the biblical text cannot, by its very nature as Scripture, be preserved in historical aspic; instead, it must be interpreted afresh theologically in the light of new historical, scientific and cultural insights, while its historical origins are still respected and held foremost.

Historically, the idea that creation occurred *ex nihilo* did not begin to come to prominence *explicitly* until the second century CE, perhaps eight hundred or more years after the text of Genesis 1 was first set down. We find notions of creation which cohere with *creatio ex nihilo* particularly in the work of early church theologians Irenaeus, Tertullian and Theophilus of Antioch (Copan & Craig 2004: 124–45), who defended the Jewish basis to the Christian Creator God in the face of their sceptical Greek cultural context. Largely polytheistic, the Greek worldview tended to follow Plato in affirming that the universe was effectively eternal, having been made from pre-existent stuff, and that material reality was of a lesser significance than higher forms (and was perhaps even inherently evil, having been made by a lesser god, according to the gnosticizing thought of the early centuries CE). In the face of this, the early Christian theologians put forward the revolutionary idea that there was but one God, who had made the world as "good" *ex nihilo*. Now Theophilus, Irenaeus and Tertullian did not regard this as an innovation, so much as an explication of what the Old Testament said about the Creator God. But it is questionable whether the Old Testament really does assert anything quite like *creatio ex nihilo* – as we shall see shortly – and it is possible that these theologians insisted on the idea that creation came from nothing more because they wanted to make a clean break with Greek assumptions (which asserted that "nothing came from nothing") than from exegetical concerns alone (Young 1991). In any case, it allowed them to promote the notion, also running contrary to Greek thought, that the world was totally distinct from its Creator. We can see the apologetic logic behind this: only if it was grasped that the one God who had created the world through the Son was the same God who had redeemed it, now in the Son incarnate, could the universal significance of Christianity be appreciated (Louth 2009: 42).

Clearly, the historical context in which the *ex nihilo* idea grew up was some considerable distance from that of Genesis 1, although it is quite possible that Genesis 1 was also formed polemically against a polytheistic milieu, Babylonian rather than Hellenistic. But there is one important textual aspect of Genesis 1 which makes application of the *ex nihilo* idea difficult: it makes no clear statement that there was "nothing" before there was anything. As we saw in § "'In the beginning'?" in Chapter 5, the rabbis of the early centuries CE were convinced that a number of created things had existed before the "In the beginning" of Genesis 1:1, notably Wisdom and Torah. In other words, the Genesis creation story did not describe strict creation "from nothing" as far as they were concerned. Of course, this tells us nothing about what the author of P thought when putting the text together many hundreds of years earlier, but it does demonstrate that interpretation of Genesis 1 at the time of Irenaeus *et al.* was not uniformly *ex nihilo*.

There is a further consideration to take into account that bears on the question of whether Genesis 1 is compatible with *creatio ex nihilo*, namely that the crucial first two verses of Genesis 1 are notoriously difficult to translate, leading to four possible readings (Hamilton 1990: 103–8; Copan & Craig 2004: 36–49; Fretheim 2005: 35; Barker 2010: 131). Two in particular stand out, and tend to dominate published English translations. They may be represented like this:

1. In the beginning, God created the heavens and the earth. The earth was a formless void ...
2. In the beginning, when God began to create the heavens and the earth, the earth was a formless void ...

Option 1 suggests that the first act of creation was the making of the earth as a "formless void". Option 2, on the other hand, suggests that the earth already existed as a formless void when God began. In other words, God did not start "from nothing", which means that God's first creative act would actually be described in Genesis 1:3 ("Let there be light"). If we opt for 1, then, in the hope that it coheres best with the *ex nihilo* category, we find a further difficulty, because creation of a chaos is a contradiction in terms in the biblical view. We saw this in the mythological component to the creation motif which describes the story of God's conflict with the sea (§ "Creation and mythology" in Chapter 4, above). So the chaotic "formless void" of Genesis 1:2 (*tohu wabohu* in Hebrew) could never be the *result* of a creative act of God, since chaos is antithetical to God, but it would more usually be the *starting point* for creation (Fergusson 1998: 12–13). In which case, option 2 is looking more likely, and we may say that an important function of the first section of Genesis 1 (vv. 1-10) is to describe the *ordering* of the pre-existent chaotic waters, by God's imposition of boundaries upon them, rather than a *making* from nothing. In support, it is notable that the enigmatic Hebrew phrase *tohu wabohu* recurs in Jeremiah 4:23, when the prophet describes a reversal of creation (the emergence of chaos from order) as a cosmic symbol of God's judgement upon the people. Their wickedness – disorder with respect to God – is seen as a symbol of the primordial earth. If option 2 is the correct reading (and there is considerable uncertainty), Genesis 1 describes God as *ordering* pre-existent chaos as much as *making* new material reality, and we saw interpretations that cohere with this in § "The cosmic temple" in Chapter 3. However, there is still much ambiguity, which is why attempts to make Genesis 1 state the *creatio ex nihilo* view are often rather forced.

However, there are statements more amenable to the *creatio ex nihilo* view, such as this: "Before the mountains were brought forth, or ever you had formed the earth and the world, from everlasting to everlasting you are God" (Ps. 90:2); by no means explicitly *ex nihilo*, it is broadly compatible with it. The earliest biblical statement which can be taken as literally *ex nihilo* can be found in the relatively late text from the second or first centuries BCE, in 2 Maccabees 7:28: "God did not make [the heavens and the earth] out of things that existed" – although it has been claimed that some New Testament references affirm a *creatio ex nihilo* view too, notably Romans 4:17 and Hebrews 11:3 (Copan & Craig 2004: 79). But even in the 2 Maccabees text, this statement is not as unambiguously *ex nihilo* as it might appear, not least because Jewish thinking did not settle into an *ex nihilo* pattern until hundreds of years after Christians had begun to affirm it, perhaps not even until the fifteenth century (McGrath [2002] 2006a: 160–61). After all, we have seen that the rabbis of the first few centuries CE patently did not believe that the "In the beginning" of Genesis 1:1 was literally from nothing.

But in searching for affirmation of the *ex nihilo* view in the Bible, it might be that we are looking for the wrong kind of statement. There might be no unambiguous statements which say that before creation existed there was nothing but God, but there are many which are compatible with the idea which stands behind *creatio ex nihilo*, that God is utterly transcendent. After all, the biblical creation motif unfailingly sees God as the root and the basis for all that exists and continues to exist, which is what "from nothing" means. We also see – on almost every page of the Bible – the corollary of God's transcendence: the idea that creation, and especially God's people, are utterly dependent upon God. Doubts may be aired that the 2 Maccabees passage quoted above was intended as an explicit statement of the *ex nihilo* doctrine, but set in its narrative context – a mother's hope for the vindication and resurrection of her martyred son – it expresses a belief entirely consonant with *creatio ex nihilo*, that God alone is the source of life, and is alone to be entrusted with it (Louth 2009: 43).

In support of the *ex nihilo* view then, it is possible to say that, although it arises from later questions and later theological problems, it is entirely likely that the biblical writers would have affirmed it if need be, as Westermann concedes (1984: 108). If it had ever occurred to the biblical writers to ask if there was nothing before there was anything, they would presumably have pressed home their view that one should look solely and utterly to the Creator as the source of all that is. On balance, it may be said cautiously that *creatio ex nihilo* is incipient in the creation accounts, simply by virtue of the over-arching and transcendent presence of God described therein, and the trust and dependence upon God expressed throughout the Bible. And Copan and Craig present a strong case for seeing *creatio ex nihilo* as a thoroughly biblical doctrine, even if it is not stated as such explicitly. As they put it: "Even if the doctrine of creation out of nothing is not explicitly stated, it is an obvious inference from the fact that God created everything distinct from himself" (Copan & Craig 2004: 27). The biblical picture of God as transcendent, and as ultimately dependable as the source of all there is, offers probably the strongest evidence that the biblical creation motif may be cohered with the *creatio ex nihilo* view. And as long as we remember that the *creatio ex nihilo* doctrine is as much about

God's continued over-arching relationship with the world as it is about how things originally came into being, then there is no need to be unduly concerned about the exact translation of Genesis 1:1-2, whether it describes a creation from nothing or a creation from pre-existent chaos. The point is rather that God is transcendent over it, and remains so.

Creatio continua

If God is portrayed in the Bible as transcendent, we must turn to the other side of the coin and ask of the extent to which God is portrayed as *immanent*, making the world anew moment by moment. This is the position of *creatio continua*, inspired especially by modern cosmological and biological evolutionary ideas of creation. And although recent interest in the category of *creatio continua* has been inspired by scientific ideas, we have argued that it is best not to identify it too closely with any particular scientific model. In any case, if we are to look for evidence of *creatio continua* in the Bible, we will obviously not find discussions of evolutionary biology or cosmology. One intriguing exception is Genesis 1 itself, where the appearance of dry land and the various creatures follows roughly the order known from modern palaeontological research. We mentioned in § "Genesis 1 and modern science" in Chapter 3 that some authors have used this as evidence that the Priestly author was privy to divine revelation of modern evolutionary biology, but we concluded that this was a question more for biblical hermeneutics than biology or geology. Consequently, in order to test the *creatio continua* category we must look in another direction, for signs in the Bible that God is regarded as immanent and intimate in creative processes.

In support, it is certainly possible to identify biblical material which can be interpreted as suggesting divine immanence. God's lengthy description of the natural world in Job 38–41 suggests an intimate and active participation in it, as does Psalm 104, and for that reason both texts lend themselves especially well to ecological reflection (Horrell 2010: 49–61). Psalm 104 is especially notable as an extravagant hymn of praise on account of God's creative abilities, and speaks of the original creation of the stars, the deeps, and the heavens alongside God's work in the contemporary natural, animal and human worlds. In a sense, these texts mix and match God's transcendent and immanent qualities together, and there is little here to indicate that any of these creative acts – either in contemporary times or "In the beginning" – are regarded as fundamentally different from each other; they all appear to be contained within God's action of creating and making. Kraus has captured this well in his comment on Psalm 104: "But the entire creation is open to Yahweh: it is absolutely dependent on him, it dies without him. It lives on a creative act which is constantly effective in renewal"

(Kraus 1989: 304). The God of Job 38–41 and Psalm 104 may therefore be inferred as inherently creative, both at the beginning and continuously ever since. Furthermore, there are numerous passages which highlight God's intimacy with humankind in the creative process, since the act of human gestation and childbirth is connected with God's creative ("making"/"forming"/"begetting") activity (e.g. Gen. 2:7-8; Job 31:15; Ps. 139:13-16; Eccl. 11:5; Isa. 44:2, 24; 49:5; Jer. 1:5), and sometimes God's saving activity too (Isa. 66:9). All of this suggests that there is a role for the *creatio continua* category in emphasizing God's continuous everyday activity in the midst of creation.

There is some disagreement though, as to whether this everyday creative "making"/"forming"/"begetting" activity is truly creative in the same way that God's act of creation "In the beginning" is creative. At what point does an act of creation differ from an act of "making"/"forming"/"begetting"? Is there a real philosophical and theological distinction at stake, or is this a matter of semantics?

Westermann, for one, prefers to set creation apart as a primeval action distinct from all later work, so that we should not speak of divine creative activity at all after "In the beginning". Instead, we should speak of God's "blessing" (Westermann 1984: 175). This activity of "blessing" is greater, he says, than the mere talk of continual "preservation" which is implicit in the *ex nihilo* category, but is not as revolutionary as the idea that there is genuine *creatio continua*. One says too little, the other too much, in Westermann's view. But in contrast with Westermann, Fretheim (2005: 4–9) pushes for a *maximal* understanding of biblical creation material: much that Westermann would label as "blessing" Fretheim regards as evidence of continuous creation. Who is right?

Westermann's emphasis on "blessing" as an ongoing complement to the "In the beginning" creation theme is certainly insightful, and should not be abandoned. Here, blessing is described as the power of fertility, causing the creation to flourish (e.g. Gen. 1:22), and it appears at key points in the singling-out of humankind in creation (Gen. 1:28; 9:1). It even describes something of God's work in human history (e.g. Gen. 12:1-3). However, it is not clear that it can capture the full breadth of making and creating language in the Bible. To see this, it is necessary to look in more detail at the precise meaning of the Hebrew verb *bara'*, often translated "to create" in Genesis 1–2 and beyond: "In the beginning God when created [*bara'*] the heavens and the earth" (Gen. 1:1). It has long been noted that *bara'* is used extensively in passages where God's creative activity is in view (such as in Gen. 1 and in Second Isaiah, e.g. Isa. 40:26), and moreover it characteristically has God as its subject. In other words, it appears to describe a uniquely divine activity that involves bringing new things into being, sometimes at the beginning, but sometimes in history (e.g. Exod. 34:10; Jer. 31:22). And so the verb *bara'* is often rendered "to create" in English translation (e.g. Gen. 1:1, 27; 2:3, 4). But does it mean "create" in the sense of *ex nihilo* creation (i.e. to conjure up a material reality when previously there was none), or could it mean something more subtle? To discern the latitude of possible meaning, it is worth mentioning some recent studies. Walton (2009: 39–44) argues that *bara'* means "create" in a *functional* (rather than *material* sense): to assign a function to an already-existent entity, so that it comes to have a *modus operandi* in the scheme of things. Alternatively, van Wolde (2009) revives a suggestion that has been made occasionally since at least the nineteenth century (Westermann 1984: 34–5), that *bara'* in Genesis 1 should not be translated "to create" at all, but rather "to separate" In which case, it has a very concrete and material meaning, but refers to the spatial activity of *dividing* a pre-existent material entity. Likewise, we have already noted that the creative events of Genesis 1:1-10 may be seen not so much as a *making* activity so much as an *ordering* of the chaotic waters. On the other hand, Copan and Craig (2004: 49–59) maintain that, in the context of Genesis 1, *bara'* should be taken to mean true *ex nihilo* creation.

There is clearly considerable disagreement over how to understand this crucial verb, and it is made all the more uncertain by the fact that Genesis 1–2 also uses more commonplace words such as *'asah* ("he made") and *yatzar* ("he formed") in similar ways to *bara'* (e.g. in Gen. 1:7, 16, 26; 2:7). *'Asah* even appears in parallel with *bara'* in the crucial verse 2:4, the bridge between the P and J accounts of creation: "These are the generations of the heavens and the earth when they were created [using *bara'*]. In the day that the LORD God made [using *'asah*] the earth and the heavens ..." (Gen. 2:4). Consequently, *bara'* should not be loaded with too much significance over other words of "making"/"forming"/"begetting", since it is clear that these words too can have divine creation in view (Westermann 1984: 86–7, 98–100). But exactly what kind of divine creation is in view – whether it is "In the beginning", *ex nihilo*, *continua*, "separation", functional or some other kind – is a more complicated issue, and is probably best judged on a passage-by-passage basis. The same is true of the precise translation of these verbs, whether "making"/"forming"/"begetting" is really any different from "creating", given that the translation of *bara'* itself is debatable.

In terms of the *vocabulary* of creation then, we can see that it is difficult to set the narratives of Genesis 1–2 clearly apart from other texts that describe God's work of making/creating in the world. That Genesis 1–2 describes acts of making/creating "In the beginning" clearly places them first in the scheme of the biblical narrative, but whether these acts are inherently more "creative" than later acts of making/creating is a moot point. Which means that it is unclear if Westermann is right to downgrade later making/creating texts from the status of true "creation" and to subsume them under the banner of "blessing". Ultimately this seems to call for a value judgement concerning the type of nomenclature one prefers to use.

Certainly, if one wishes to include God's work in human history alongside all other divine activities in creation, such as the fertility and maintenance of the earth, or the making of human generations, then "blessing" seems to be as good a term to use as any other. But I remain to be convinced that "blessing" fully captures the essence of motifs such as the making and creating of life and of new forms of reality.

What is perhaps more relevant to the question of whether the *creatio continua* category should be applied to biblical material is the type of *relationship* being portrayed between God and the things being created. And certainly, if we have seen God's transcendence expressed in texts such as Genesis 1, then other texts, such as those mentioned earlier in this subsection, portray God in a more intimate relationship, consonant with the idea of God's immanence. This is certainly true of the following passage, for instance, which pictures God in such intimacy with the psalmist that it is hard to deny its contribution to a biblical picture of *creatio continua*:

> My frame was not hidden from you, when I was being made in
>   secret,
>   intricately woven in the depths of the earth.
> Your eyes beheld my unformed substance.
> In your book were written
>   all the days that were formed for me,
>   when none of them as yet existed.
>   (Ps. 139:15-16)

Other passages combine a sense of God's transcendence with immanence, consonant with the *creatio continua* picture. For instance, Psalm 33 describes God looking down from heaven on the earth, but at the same time fashioning human hearts and understanding them intimately.

> The LORD looks down from heaven;
>   he sees all humankind.
> From where he sits enthroned he watches
>   all the inhabitants of the earth –
> he who fashions the hearts of them all,
>   and observes all their deeds.
>   (Ps. 33:13-15)

And the New Testament also includes at least one passage that describes God's intimacy with humans in a way which may be used to support the idea of *creatio continua*:

> The God who made the world and everything in it, he who
> is Lord of heaven and earth, does not live in shrines made by

> human hands ... though indeed he is not far from each one of
> us. For "In him we live and move and have our being" ...
>
> (Acts 17:24-28)

It is fair to say though that the New Testament is more concerned with God's immanence in the work of *new* creation (i.e. eschatology). Texts describing the creative work of the Spirit provide the bridge. We have already seen the important role of the Spirit in this creation, especially through maintaining biological life, its "breath" (§ "Creation and Christ" in Chapter 4). The Spirit has a crucial role in the new creation too. This idea had been mooted as early as the Old Testament prophet Joel, that the outpouring of the Holy Spirit upon God's people would be a sign of the new creation (Joel 2:28-32). And this idea is developed in many places in the New Testament, for instance in the Pentecost narrative (Acts 2), in Paul's ethics (which rely on the idea that the Christian believer is the site of new creation by the power of the Spirit; Gal. 6:15), and pre-eminently in Romans 8, where the same Spirit who works in individual believers is implicated in bringing the whole cosmos to re-birth. Hence, the Spirit is recognized as a foretaste of the new creation (Joel 2:28-32; Acts 2:17-21; Rom. 8:23; 2 Cor. 1:22; 5:5; Eph. 1:13-14). We therefore find that the category of *creatio continua* goes beyond talk of continuous "preservation" or "conservation" (which is more appropriately described by *ex nihilo* in any case), and beyond the intimate making of new human lives as well, to embrace entirely new kinds of creative work.

In the light of this material, Westermann's (1984: 42) assertion that "there can be no *creatio continua*" in the Bible is too sweeping. If the presence of passages portraying God's *transcendence* in the act of making is taken as justification for identifying a *creatio ex nihilo* component, then the presence of texts speaking of God's creative *immanence* in history should be taken into account under the heading of *creatio continua*. Admittedly, such passages are not as numerous as those that speak of God's transcendent work, but there is enough of a sense of God's immanent creative activity to justify the claim that there is a *continua* component in the biblical creation motif. And certainly, we find that we are moving towards Fretheim's more inclusive view, with the important distinction that our approach emphasizes the different kinds of creative activity in the Bible by speaking of it in terms of God's relational being. Fretheim's view is rooted in the Old Testament, but ours, which includes the New Testament, is able to take the most inclusive view of all: once we broaden our outlook to take in a Trinitarian view of God – and especially one that sees the work of the Spirit in bringing creation to its fulfilment – then we find that there is new scope for the *continua* category beyond the predominantly Old Testament views of Westermann and Fretheim.

CONCLUSIONS

We must be careful not to impose anachronistic theological distinctions upon the biblical texts, since these categories arise from theological thinking which is hundreds of years later. Nevertheless, by discussing how the categories of *creatio ex nihilo* and *creatio continua* might be applied, we have been able to extract several important theological characteristics of biblical ideas of creation, characteristics which inform the theistic view of God. In particular, we have found biblical texts which suggest God's transcendent work in creation as well as texts which suggest God's immanent work. Some even suggest both modes of activity together. It may seem paradoxical to affirm God's transcendence alongside immanence, but this is a basic feature of the biblical picture of God which cannot be passed over. As Rogerson (1974: 160–61) has said, "the Old Testament language about the immanence and transcendence of God is deliberately contradictory, for only so can it describe the reality to which it points".

We have also noted that, although it might be tempting to identify the *ex nihilo* and *continua* categories with specific scientific models, yet it should be born in mind that the categories are fundamentally theological and cannot easily be reduced to scientific explanations, although they may analogize and parallel each other. In the same way, the biblical narratives have resisted scientific "explanation", although we have noted that they contain traces of scientific thought of their day, and especially mythological ideas of creation which were widespread in the ANE.

There is one final point connected with this: the *ex nihilo* and *continua* categories are useful for thinking through the various types of contingency. *Creatio ex nihilo* declares the total dependency of creation upon God against a fall into nothingness. This is the most basic theological form of contingency. On the other hand, in Chapter 2 we described a further form of contingency which is more accurately said to be scientific, since it takes into account the evolutionary nature of the world as seen by science, the fact that it is in a state of continuously coming-into-being. This form of contingency is often identified with the *creatio continua* category. However, we have expressed reserve about attempts to identify the theological categories too closely with scientific models. There are certainly analogies and parallels between *creatio continua* and scientific evolutionary models, but since *continua* is a fundamentally theological idea it has more to say. In particular, if *ex nihilo* affirms the contingency of the world against a return to nothingness, then *continua* affirms the contingency of newness in the world upon God, the ineluctable but fragile drive towards novel opportunities. In that sense, it has an unpredictable and eschatological dimension, expressed succinctly in the Bible by texts such as the parables and sayings of Jesus. It is the same contingency as that of the kingdom of God, which is discovered unexpectedly like a treasure hidden in a field (Mt. 13:44), or which grows like a great tree from the tiniest of seeds (Mk 4:30-32; Nichols 2002: 202). It is the same kind of contingency summed up by the words of Jesus, seated on the heavenly throne, as the last things become real: "See, I am making all things new" (Rev. 21:5). If the *creatio continua* category has been likened to the chance and contingency of scientific models of the world then it can also be connected with the uncertainty and contingency of the new creation upon God. If the new scientific models of the world are no longer deterministic, then *creatio continua* makes the same point about the new creation: it is the ultimate of all fresh possibilities, undetermined by all but God: "But about that day or hour no one knows, neither the angels in heaven, nor the Son, but only the Father" (Mk 13:32). We will explore the eschatological dimension of the Bible's creation material more fully in Chapter 9, where we will introduce a third category – *creatio ex vetere* (from the old) – but for the time being we will simply note that this idea of God's newness continuously entering the world (*creatio continua*) is transformed into something new in the eschatological end to this creation and the beginning of the next.

Chapter 7

THE FALL

SCIENTIFIC CHALLENGES

The previous two chapters have explored the scientific and theological frameworks of the biblical creation texts. In this we have said very little about J, the Yahwist's creation story (Gen. 2:4b-3:24). But such has been the importance of this text in the relationship between science and religion since Darwin's *Origin of Species* that it deserves its own chapter.

It is commonplace to hear biblical scholars and theologians refer to the story of Adam and Eve in the garden as "myth" (see, for example, Deane-Drummond 2009: 221). Certainly, modern evolutionary biology sees no historical credence in J's teaching that the first man emerged fully formed at the very beginning, even before the creation of other animals and plants. The modern scientific view of humans sees their appearance on earth as extremely recent, coming at the end of a tortuous evolutionary chain of developing life spanning hundreds of millions of years. On the other hand, many conservative Christians insist that it is vital to retain a basic historicity: "A historical Fall is a non-negotiable article of faith" (Blocher 2009: 169).

Such an uncompromising statement arises from the significance of the Fall in traditional Western theologies of redemption. If Darwinism indicates that the Fall cannot be affirmed historically, then two theological problems are seen to arise.

First there is the problem of evil. Darwinism implies that competition, struggle, suffering and death have always been integral to the world. Theologically, they must therefore arise from God's initial creative act (and continuing creative actions); they are "necessary evils", part of what has made the world what it is. The same might even be said of human sin, since it can be construed as inherent to the original created order if it is seen as the inevitable outcome of the selfishness which arises from the struggle for existence implanted in the evolutionary process. Without a historical Fall, humans must always have been sinful and "fallen"; they were made that way by God. And so we find that one of the earliest and most foundational controversies of the Church is revived: the Gnostic debate.

Christian gnosticizing teachings in the second and third centuries CE worked with a dualistic worldview which saw the created world as the evil product of a dubious under-deity. Salvation was liberation from the material world so as to gain the spiritual domain. But pioneers like Irenaeus established the orthodox Christian view of creation by pointing out that the initial creation was "good" (Gen. 1:31), and went on to deduce that it was made *ex nihilo*, and reflected the nature of the one God who made it. This is an important corollary of monotheism: if there is only one God and this God is good, then creation must be good too, since such a God cannot be the source of evil. And so the basic "goodness" of creation was enshrined as one of the foundational propositions of the doctrine of creation. The pronouncement of the Priestly God that creation was "very good" (Gen. 1:31) may have originally meant something more like "fit for purpose" (§ "Genesis 1 and God" in Chapter 3), but in the face of such later gnosticizing debates "goodness" came to take on a moral dimension, as the trenchant opposite of the evil and sin introduced by the Fall. "Good" became *morally* good.

But Darwinism challenges all of this. By casting doubt on the historicity of J and the idea of the Fall it revives the old Gnostic debate. Berry and Noble (2009: 12) put it succinctly from an evangelical perspective:

> Like the doctrine of creation *ex nihilo*, the doctrines of sin and the Fall are integral to Christian theology. Since the Creator cannot be the source of sin and evil, somehow it is because the human race is "fallen" that there is sin in the world. But many Christian thinkers, particularly since Darwin, have wanted to retain "fallenness", while dispensing with any event called "the Fall". Is that an option for Christian theology?

It will become clear in this and the next chapter that the situation is of such complexity that a simple "yes" or "no" answer to this question will not suffice.

The second theological problem raised by Darwinism concerns Christ:

> The resurrection of Jesus Christ makes Neo-Darwinism incompatible with Christianity. Accommodating Neo-Darwinism leaves the biblical story, centred on the resurrection, incoherent, as it creates a story in which the hero Jesus, through his resurrection defeats an enemy (1 Cor. 15:26) of his own making.
>
> (Lloyd 2009: 1)

Here we have, in a nutshell, the concern shared by many conservative Christians about Darwinism: that it is incompatible with Christian faith because Darwinism appears to make Christ's achievement pointless. Clearly, this concern introduces something of a "cart before the horse" syndrome: the authenticity of the Fall is important, but only in so far as Christ must have something to reverse. And such is the non-negotiable status of this view of Christ's work that Lloyd's solution is to reject Darwinism altogether (Lloyd 2009: 24–5).

It hardly needs saying that this entire debate would have been totally alien to the author of J, living perhaps a thousand years before the time of Jesus. And yet we cannot approach the scholarly literature and debates on Genesis 2–3 without flagging-up the Christian debate on redemption. It is a highly convoluted issue, and one which, more than 150 years after Darwin's *Origin of Species*, still arouses passions in Christian circles. This is illustrated by a recent volume of essays by evangelical scholars, entitled *Should Christians Embrace Evolution?* The answer is a resounding "no!", evolution must be rejected according to the authors, although they offer little by way of a replacement (Hills & Nevin 2009: 210).

Scepticism of Darwin is not confined to evangelical Christianity: the Roman Catholic Church's magisterial statement on evolution, *Humani Generis* (1950), also expresses considerable reserve. Here, evolution is not condemned, but neither is it accepted wholeheartedly. It is conceded that evolution is of value to scientific research, as long as it is clearly understood that: (a) evolution only has concern for the human body and not for the soul (since the soul is the concern of the Church), and (b) evolution should not be seen to jeopardize the primal position of Adam as the very first human, so that the doctrine of original sin (i.e. the idea that the original guilt of Adam is transmitted down the generations to all humans) might be safeguarded. In 1950 this stance represented a significant opening-up towards evolution in Catholic theology, but its emphasis on the historical Adam (who still appears in the more recent *Catechism of the Catholic Church*, 1994) has become harder to sustain in recent years, as evolutionary research gathers pace. While continuing to respect the authority of *Humani Generis*, recent popes such as John Paul II have expressed a more positive acceptance of evolution.

THE HISTORICAL ADAM

Notwithstanding the challenges, many interpreters continue to maintain that the J account describes a genuine human fall from grace which took place in authentic human history. It is pointed out, for instance, that Adam is regarded as a historical individual in a number of biblical passages outside of Genesis, especially genealogies which extend into recorded history:

Genesis 5; 1 Chronicles 1; Luke 3:38 (Berry 1999: 35). A number of scholars have looked to research into the evolution of humankind for scientific
support, asking the question of whether there is scientific evidence of a
single individual who is a common human ancestor of us all.

The earliest known hominid fossils date back some six or seven million
years and come from Africa (Ayala 2009: 91–4). Various kinds of more
developed and more recent forms have been found, but it was not until
Homo erectus around 1.8 million years ago that hominids appear to have
spread far beyond Africa. Modern humans (*Homo sapiens*) probably first
arose in Africa around 200,000 years ago and spread from there, gradually
replacing the already-dispersed populations of *Homo erectus* and *Homo
neanderthalensis*. In this, it has been claimed that all modern humans can
be traced back through their mitochondrial DNA to an individual *Homo
sapiens* woman living in Africa perhaps 200,000 years ago (which is why
she is often known as "African Eve" or "Mitochondrial Eve"). Every human
cell contains mitochondria: they are small organelles which provide energy
for the cell, and they contain some DNA of their own. Crucially, mitochondrial DNA is transmitted only through the mother, which is why it is unaf-
fected by the sexual process, and can be traced back so far.

It would be easy to misunderstand the claim of African/Mitochondrial
Eve, and to believe that scientists have found genetic evidence for the historical Eve, the first female *Homo sapiens* to walk the earth; indeed, the
very name "African/Mitochondrial *Eve*" suggests this conclusion. However,
this is not the case, and there were most likely many other women alive at
the time of African/Mitochondrial Eve who, like her, have many descendants living today. It is just that their *mitochondrial* DNA has not survived,
because at some point in the intervening thousands of generations between
them and us, their link passed through a male. For instance, if a mother
has only male children, then her mitochondrial DNA is lost to the generation of her grandchildren. African/Mitochondrial Eve is therefore by no
means the first woman, but rather the most recent common ancestor of all
currently living humans down the exclusively female line. This is a rather
different claim from saying that evidence for the historical Eve has been
discovered (Dawkins 1995: 44–57). A similar point may be made about the
male human who lived in Africa some 100,000–150,000 years ago who is
thought to have been the source for all current male genetic material (D. R.
Alexander 2008: 224). This individual is not the father of all humans since,
like African/Mitochondrial Eve, many others were alive at the time. And
a related point may be made about the idea of evolutionary "bottlenecks":
it has been suggested that *Homo sapiens* almost became extinct early on,
passing through a literal "Adam and Eve" situation where only a handful
of individuals – perhaps a couple – were alive in one generation (Berry
[1988] 2001: 72). However, while it seems likely that modern humans are
descended ultimately from African humans who then dispersed around

the globe, and that there have been quite drastic fluctuations in population numbers at times, genetic studies suggest that we are probably talking of an early human population that was never smaller than tens of thousands, which makes it unlikely that a historical Adam and Eve can be sought among early humans (Ayala 2009: 94).

On the other hand, some scholars suggest that the historical Adam should be not be sought in the first physical *Homo sapiens*, but in the first *spiritually aware Homo sapiens*. A popular version of this idea places the historical Adam in the Neolithic Age, some 6,000 years ago perhaps, and in much more recent times than Mitochondrial Eve or our African ancestors (Berry 1999: 38–9; Alexander 2008: 241). Such a "Neolithic Adam", it is pointed out, is consistent with the biblical accounts of Adam and his immediate descendants in Genesis 2–4, where they are placed in an early agrarian and pastoral context which suits the Neolithic Age. Indeed, Pearce ([1969] 1976: 63), from whom the initial idea of the Neolithic Adam largely derives, went so far as to suggest that Adam was the inventor of agriculture, acting under divine guidance. But apart from suppositions such as this, we have no way of knowing who this first spiritually aware Adam was, nor where and when he lived. All we can say is that Neolithic Adam would not then be the literal genetic father of all modern humans, since by this stage *Homo sapiens* was dispersed all over the globe. Rather, the suggestion is that he was the *spiritual* ancestor of modern humans – the first *Homo sapiens* to receive God's Spirit breathed into him, and therefore the first to be (theologically) made in God's image – which is why he is sometimes referred to as the first of a new type of human, *Homo divinus*. There is therefore nothing scientific or genetic which marks Neolithic Adam out from other humans of the time: it is an entirely theological distinction.

Ingenious as the Neolithic Adam explanation might be – avoiding the scientific difficulties of a historical Adam by moving his primacy into the spiritual dimension where science cannot get at it – it is not without its theological problems (Bimson 2009: 115; Blocher 2009: 171–2). First among these is the fact that it is a dualistic reading akin to Gnosticism. Neolithic Adam's forebears and contemporaries – as fully human as he was, and with plentiful religious awareness (as archaeological research shows) – were nevertheless not "spiritual", and they were therefore not capable of being open to God in the way that Adam was. And this means that, despite their no-doubt numerous acts of violence, murder, selfishness and wickedness, Neolithic Adam's forebears and contemporaries did not commit "sins" like that of Neolithic Adam. His act of disobedience was somehow far more serious than his peers', to the extent that modern humans have inherited Neolithic Adam's "original sin" and not theirs. This is hardly a credible reading of J, which indicates that sin, suffering and the struggle for life have been ubiquitous since the first humans. And neither does it account realistically for what has become the most important feature of the Fall for Christian theology, that suffering, death and the struggle for life (i.e. natural evil) are connected with human sin by the fact they all entered God's "good" created world *together*.

As we have said, the wish by conservatives to retain Adam's historicity is often rooted, not in a desire to be true to J, so much as to Christian theologies of atonement, especially those influenced by Paul and by Augustine. Blocher's comment is typical: "Whatever the tensions, the non-historical interpretation of Genesis 3 is no option for a *consistent* Christian believer ... It conflicts openly with Paul's comments in Romans 5 – as many acknowledge who deny historicity for themselves" (Blocher 2009: 155–6). If Blocher is to be believed, everything rests on Paul and on what he thought of Adam. The question at stake therefore is not primarily whether we interpret Genesis 3 historically; nor is it whether we regard Adam as a historical individual, and nor is it whether we regard the Fall as a historical event. Rather, the key interpretative question (in Blocher's view), is whether *Paul* regards Adam and the Fall as historical or not, and whether his theology of atonement requires it. We shall look at this shortly, after setting the scene by looking at the problem of death.

J AND DEATH

Adam is important in Paul's argument because it was his sin which brought death into the world. Death spread to every human being who sins like Adam (Rom. 5:12), but through a dramatic reversal Christ's life now spreads to all (Rom. 5:18; 1 Cor. 15:22). Adam stands for all people in the present age, and Christ stands for those in the new age, by virtue of his resurrection. Adam's act of sin leads to death; Christ's act of righteousness leads to life. The logic is impeccable, except for the niggling inconsistency that J – which was presumably Paul's source for the Adam tradition – does not say that Adam's sin introduced death into the world.

Let us look at J again. This is the crucial passage: "And the LORD God commanded the man, 'You may freely eat of every tree of the garden; but of the tree of the knowledge of good and evil you shall not eat, for in the day that you eat of it you shall die'" (Gen. 2:16-17). It is perhaps this passage – and this passage alone – which has led to the fact that Paul, and generations of later interpreters, associated the story of the disobedience in the garden with the introduction of death into the world, since God makes the connection plain. However, as we follow the story, it is clear that this does not actually happen – the man and woman do not die. Of course, Adam and Eve are tempted by the serpent to disobey the command. The serpent reveals that God has misled them; they will not die (Gen. 3:4-5). Sure enough, the man and the woman follow the serpent's advice and disobey God. Exactly as the serpent predicted, instead of dying they find that their awareness is drastically heightened. Indeed, not only does Adam not die for many years, but we are later told that he goes on to live to the extremely ripe old age (almost uniquely so) of 930 (Gen. 5:5). This leads to intriguing theological questions about the character of God (§ "J and God" in Chapter 3): God appears to threaten the man and woman with what turns out to be an untruth, while the serpent leads them into enlightenment by telling them the truth. That this was a theological problem was recognized early on, since we find ingenious attempts to resolve it even in the inter-testamental period (e.g. Jubilees 4:29-30; see Kugel 1997: 68–9).

All the same, God imposes three punishments on the couple for their disobedience (Gen. 3:16-24), and none of them appears to be death (unless we interpret Gen. 3:19 as the introduction of death): (1) God curses the ground so that the man must work hard to grow crops for food; (2) God increases the woman's pain in childbirth; (3) God expels them from the garden. The first two punishments are not arbitrary; they are meted out to the man and the woman in their traditional roles: the man is the "breadwinner" while the woman is the home maker. But it is the third punishment which has the most bearing upon the question of death. The rationale behind the expulsion from the garden seems to be that, if the man and the woman remain, they will be able to eat from the tree of life which is in the garden, and "live forever" (Gen. 3:22).

We have already noted the strange and mythological characteristics of the two trees (§ "J and God" in Chapter 3), that one is linked with death and the other with life. The tree of the knowledge of good and evil, that which God had said would cause the man and the woman to die, actually appears to make them like God (Gen. 3:22). We have here a sort of counterpart to P, where humankind was blessed and *made in God's image* (Gen. 1:26-27). Rather than a blessing, they receive a curse. Moreover, the implication of Gen. 3:22 is that if they were to remain in the garden and eat of the tree of life and live forever, then they would become *exactly* like God, an eventuality clearly unpalatable to J's God, which is why the man and woman are expelled. But in all this, we are not told that the man and woman were immortal beforehand (Bimson 2009: 113), nor that death is introduced to humankind at this point; instead, the text seems to operate on the assumption that the man and woman were *always* mortal (Wenham 1987: 85). Indeed, if they had been created immortal, the tree of life would seem to be an irrelevance (Fretheim 2005: 77).

On the other hand, some early interpretations of the story, again from the last few centuries BCE, suggest that Adam and Eve were originally created immortal, but that God punished them by making them mortal, and thereby the whole human race (e.g. Wisdom 1:13; 2:23-24; Sir. 25:24; 4 Ezra 3:7; 1 Enoch 69:11). These approaches appear to interpret God's statement that "in the day that you eat of it you shall die" (Gen. 2:17), as meaning

something more like "in the day that you eat of it you shall become someone who can die" (Kugel 1997: 69–71). However, Westermann (1984: 225)
maintains that such a translation of the Hebrew is "quite impossible". Quite
so, but this reading does have the advantage that God is no longer seen
to tell a lie, and it agrees with Paul's assessment of the story, that death
entered the world at this critical point in time. For instance, a passage from
Wisdom which takes this approach offers a striking parallel with one of
Paul's key passages:

> ... through the devil's envy death entered the world,
> and those who belong to his company experience it.
>
> (Wisdom 2:24)

> Therefore, just as sin came into the world through one man,
> and death came through sin, and so death spread to all because
> all have sinned   (Rom. 5:12)

We will look at Paul's approach shortly but for now we will simply note
that, unlike these later readings, the text of Genesis 2–3 makes no such
statement about Adam and Eve's putative original immortality, but is
instead consistent with the idea that they were always mortal.

What is perhaps more revealing at this point is to look at the story in
the light of the narrative which follows it (Gen. 4–11). What we find here
is a sequence of stories which connect very closely with the event in the
garden, since they explore the complex and devastating outcomes of further acts of disobedience: the onset of murder in human society (Gen. 4),
the wholesale wickedness of humankind which leads to the flood (Gen.
6–9), and the failure of the tower of Babel (Gen. 11). In every case humankind is seen to overstep the mark, and God responds, as in the garden, by
re-asserting divine domination and by underscoring the limits of humankind. But as Westermann points out,

> The narrative certainly shows the connection between man's
> guilt and his limitation through suffering, toil, and death. But it
> is not said that "the wages of sin is death". The penalty of death,
> the threat which accompanies the prohibition, does not follow;
> man, despite his disobedience, is guaranteed the freedom of a
> full life.   (Westermann 1974: 109)

Westermann touches on something important here, a significant feature of
both the story of the garden in Genesis 2–3 and the further acts of disobedience in Genesis 4–11. We see that humankind is punished consistently
for every act of disobedience, but only ever in passing. God may threaten,
but God never abandons humankind altogether: in various concrete ways

God still protects, cares for, and blesses them. The genealogies of Genesis 5 and 11 point to the fact that God's blessing in the act of originally creating humankind continues for generation after generation. And the various stories of human defectiveness in between show that it belongs to human nature to be defective with respect to God and each other, not just in a single act in history at the beginning, but continually. Westermann's point (1974: 120–21) is that the narrative explores the dynamic divine–human relationship in ways which cannot easily be compressed into once-for-all doctrinal statements about beginnings, but is best expressed through the subtlety of extended story. Humankind is stricken by guilt and death throughout, by the inevitable finitude of existence, but simultaneously enjoys freedom and God's blessing.

Hence, although the J story of the garden has become inextricably linked in Christian theology with a single decisive Fall and the introduction of death into the world, this is a not altogether fair reading of the text, especially when seen in the wider context of Genesis 4–11.

PAUL AND DEATH

Outside of Genesis 1–11, the Old Testament shows rather little awareness of Adam and Eve, and especially of the motif immortalized by Paul, that this story tells of the momentous entry of sin and death into the world. On the other hand, there are Jewish texts from the last few centuries BCE that seem to be aware of this motif, and which introduce the idea that the story of the garden tells of a once-for-all fall from grace: "O Adam, what have you done? For though it was you who sinned, the fall was not yours alone, but ours also who are your descendants. For what good is it to us, if an immortal time has been promised to us, but we have done deeds that bring death?" (4 Ezra 7:118-119). This passage, which possibly dates from the first century CE, roughly contemporaneous with Paul, shows two interesting features (cf. 4 Ezra 3:21-22). First, it uses the terminology of "the fall" explicitly (which does not appear in the New Testament). Second, there is an interesting ambiguity in this text about the historicity of Adam. In the opening question Adam is addressed as though he were someone who might actually have lived ("O Adam"). But in the third sentence, he stands more as a symbol of the human race, the "we" who "have done deeds that bring death". Likewise we see in the second sentence that although it was "Adam" who sinned, "the fall" also belongs to his descendants. In other words, this passage does not appear to know the idea of original sin, but suggests that all are guilty by their own deeds in something of the same way that "Adam" was guilty.

The idea of original sin, so basic to Western theologies of redemption, arose largely through Augustine's response to Pelagius in the early fifth century CE. Pelagius taught that sin arises entirely from human free will. It is morally reprehensible, but it is deliberate and conscious. One can choose to follow the example of Adam's disobedience, or one can choose to follow the example of Christ. In other words, one can in principle remain sinless. So, while sin is widespread, it is not a universal condition, according to Pelagius. Augustine could not agree with such an optimistic assessment of the human condition, believing that humans are incapable of living without sin, and that we must rely entirely on God's grace. Augustine insisted that all humans alike possess original sin due to Adam's first act of disobedience, which corrupted the entirety of humankind through no fault of their own other than being Adam's descendants. Crucially, Augustine relied on a faulty Latin translation of Romans 5:12 for support (Kelly [1960] 1977: 354, 363). Augustine read it as saying that Adam was the one "*in whom* all sinned" – that all humans inherit Adam's original act of sin because it is somehow passed down from generation to generation – whereas the Greek text indicates that this phrase should be read as "*because* all sinned". We all experience death, suggests Paul in the Greek text, because like Adam we all sin. Paul therefore does not appear to maintain Augustine's problematic idea that sin is somehow passed down genetically from our ancestor Adam, but he still maintains the causal connection between our sin and our death. It hardly needs saying that this flies in the face of all modern biological accounts of death, that death is entirely a natural and inevitable consequence of life.

But what does Paul mean when he speaks of "death"? On the face of it this may seem obvious – it refers to basic human mortality, the fact that we will all literally die one day. But some interpreters (e.g. Berry 2009: 67–8) have sought to escape the challenge of science by interpreting Paul's talk of "death" as *spiritual* death. Just as sin is always a theological category – it is that which rebels against God, that which breaks down the human–divine relationship – so "death" in this reading also becomes a theological category unrelated to physical death: it denotes eternal separation from God, and relates to the separation which Adam and Eve experienced figuratively when they were banished from the garden. Likewise, Finlay and Pattemore (2009: 61–3) point out that in 1 Corinthians 15, where Paul contrasts "death" with "life", the life he speaks of here is actually a theological category, since he means *resurrection* life and not ordinary life as we know it (1 Cor. 15:20-26). Therefore, they conclude, Paul must be speaking of theological death not physical death. And Alexander (2008: 250–76) relates this to the Neolithic Adam model – if the historical Adam is said to be the first *spiritually aware* human (although he was by no means the first *Homo sapiens*, nor the first to die physically), then his Fall can be described as the first *spiritual* death.

This "spiritual death" reading of Paul may conveniently sidestep the challenge from modern biology, but it is not without its theological difficulties.

There is the basic problem that it leads to a dualism similar to the Neo-lithic Adam model, a dualism which is very unlike Paul but very like that of classic gnosticism (Anderson 2009: 89). Here, we find that it is only *spir-itual* awakening and *spiritual* death which are counted as important in the redemption stakes, not what happens in our ordinary material realm. In other words, natural evil and the suffering of our material world cannot be redeemed; the new creation – to which the resurrection of Christ is usually said to point – must be either an entirely spiritual realm (pure gnosticism) or else one in which the material suffering and evolutionary struggle of this world continue unchecked.

It is highly unlikely that Paul would have operated with such a dualistic view. For one, Paul's exploration of the new creation in Romans 8 makes it clear that he sees it as the redemption of the whole material cosmos, not just human souls (Rom. 8:19-21). Now it is true that Paul was certainly capable of using "death" as a metaphor for the separation between God and humankind (Berry 2009: 67–8), and this appears in various places in the New Testament (e.g. Lk. 15:32; Rom. 6:2-11; Eph. 2:1, 5; Col. 2:13). But it is always clear from the context when "death" is meant as a metaphor, and this is emphatically not the case in Romans 5, since Paul introduces "death" by referring to Christ's very literal death (vv. 8-10).

Likewise, in 1 Corinthians 15 Paul may juxtapose "death" with *theologi-cal* life (i.e. resurrection), but the whole logic of the passage rests on the fact that Jesus died *physically* before he was raised. If Paul has *spiritual* death in mind here then it is simultaneously a *physical* death. For Paul, death is both the end of earthly existence, and separation from God, in common with much Jewish thinking of the time, as is illustrated by frequent refer-ences to Sheol and the "Pit" in the Old Testament (e.g. Ps. 143:7). In this way of thinking, death – both spiritual and physical – can only be escaped by resurrection in the pattern of Jesus, where resurrection is also both a physical and a spiritual transformation, albeit one shrouded in mystery (1 Cor. 15:35-51).

Therefore, the "spiritual death" interpretation of Paul might avoid the difficulties raised by science, but it is theologically problematic. Hence, we are forced back to the conclusion that when Paul speaks of "death" in Romans 5:12 he really does think that physical death is caused by sin. But note that Paul does not appear to believe in "original sin" transmitted down the generations from Adam. His point appears to be that all humans sin in the same way as Adam, and that therefore all die in the same way as Adam. This may stem from a rather loose reading of J, but it is not clear that Paul is offering us a reading of it as such. Rather, Paul is using Adam in a loose, figurative way: Adam is the representative symbol of all that Christ redeemed and reversed, in every generation of humans.

We may now return to the question about the historicity of Adam. Con-servatives such as Lloyd (2009: 5) may claim that Paul's crucial argument in

Romans 5 requires a historical Adam, but our view is that this misunderstands Paul's point. Paul may well have believed that Adam was a historical individual, but Paul's argument rests on the *representational* importance of Adam; Adam represents the *sin and death* which all humans experience, in contrast to the *obedience and life* which Christ offers (Rom. 5:17-19). This reading of Adam-as-archetype has come to prominence in recent work (e.g. Walton 2012); even a traditionalist such as C. J Collins (2011: 130–31), who attempts to hold fast to a historical Adam and Eve, puts forward a model that in fact emphasizes their *representative* and *symbolic* significance for humankind over historical details such as whether they were truly the first humans or not.

Hence, even though many conservative Christians regard it as an important issue, Paul's attitude to the historicity of Adam is not actually at the heart of what he was trying to say. In short, debating the historical Adam and Eve does little to help us appreciate Paul's point (Enns 2012: 121). Importantly, Paul refers to Adam explicitly as a "symbol" (a *type*; Rom. 5:14). In common with other Jewish interpretations of the time, Paul uses Adam as "Everyman" (or Everywoman) – each of us has become our own Adam (2 Baruch 54:19; Ziesler 1989: 147) – and therefore we all alike need Christ's salvation. For sure, Paul sees Adam as the originator of sin and death (Rom. 5:12), but every succeeding generation has shared fully and without exception in sin by means of their own deeds. Therefore, in setting Adam up as a *type* in contrast to Christ, Paul is seeking to draw out the significance of Christ as a universal, not to historicize Adam as a particular. As Dunn points out (1988: 290), ancient writers had a more sophisticated and subtle understanding of symbols and myths from their primeval past than we give them credit for; we are too ready to brand them with a "primitive mentality' (Chapter 5) where everything must be taken literally.

If we are right that Paul's atonement theology uses Adam largely as a *symbol* to illustrate the importance of Christ, then the issues begin to change, and we may begin to develop evolutionary theologies that respect the biblical traditions *without being bound to a historical reading of J.* Augustine's model of original sin, on the other hand, *does* require Adam to be historical, and we may surmise that conservative interpreters who are concerned to preserve the historicity of Adam are reading Romans 5 from a perspective which is more Augustinian than it is Pauline.

This important point does much to weaken the traditional Christian argument for a historical Fall. But it by no means resolves all of the difficulties, since Paul's tying-together of sin and physical death flies in the face of Darwinism every bit as much as Augustine's. And we are still faced with the need to explain theologically how evil and sin came to be a part of God's "good" world. We therefore need to explore the idea of the Fall more thoroughly.

THE HISTORICAL FALL?

The story of Adam and Eve's disobedience might be significant to Christian theology as the historical source of sin and evil, but the Old Testament shows little or no interest. It is almost as though the problem of the source of evil was not seen to be a problem until Christ did away with it. The Old Testament also does not appear to contain the idea (widespread in Christian treatments of the Fall) that sin and evil are a kind of cosmic infection ("fallenness") introduced into God's "good" creation by the Devil and/or humans. Supernatural evil forces very occasionally appear in the Old Testament, but are often sent by God (e.g. the "lying spirit" of 1 Kgs 22:21-23, or the evil spirit which torments Saul in 1 Sam. 16:15-16).

The New Testament is a more fertile ground for the metaphysical speculation of evil. In the Synoptic Gospels, for instance, which are infused with an apocalyptic atmosphere almost unknown in the Old Testament, we find Jesus repeatedly battling against Satan and evil spirits. Likewise, Paul's letters and other parts of the New Testament, especially the book of Revelation, warn against spiritual powers and forces which are opposed to God (e.g. Eph. 6:12), and which work to enslave humans (e.g. Gal. 4:3; Col. 2:8). Sin is itself spoken of as a cosmic force whose tendency it is to enslave and to rule (Rom. 6:12-23; Heb. 3:13). There is a basic good/evil dualism which sets out two spiritual domains: God in the one and evil powers in the other. Christians have been transferred to the former while they effectively live their daily lives in the presence of the latter, and so they are in constant danger (e.g. 1 Cor. 6:9-20; Eph. 2:1-3; Col. 1:13).

This kind of apocalyptic dualism is not specifically Christian, and we find related sentiments expressed in the Dead Sea Scrolls and in other Jewish apocalyptic literature. An interesting feature of this worldview, which parallels the modern conservative desire to maintain a *historical* Fall, is the suggestion that evil is the result of a *supernatural* fall of angels who disobey God. Thus 1 Enoch 6–36, for instance, develops the enigmatic passage at the beginning of the flood story (Gen. 6:1-4) into the legend of the "Watchers", the fallen angels who married human women and produced a race of malign giants. Christian tradition has tended to see this supernatural fall in terms of the "fall of Lucifer" (Isa. 14:12-15), whereby Satan – once a good angel in the service of God – attempted to usurp divine authority and was cast down, taking other evil angels with him. This story appears in the New Testament in the guise of the battle between Michael and the dragon in heaven: Michael wins and the dragon and his angels are thrown down to earth (Jude 6, 9; Rev. 12:3-4, 7-9). Of course, such stories of a supernatural fall have exactly the same theological purpose as the historical Fall: to preserve God's goodness. The historical Fall means that God is not the source of historical evil, and the fall of the angels means that God is not the source of supernatural evil either.

In light of the New Testament's widespread treatment of evil and sin as *metaphysical* realities, it is interesting to reflect on the desire of modern conservative Christians to make them *historical* realities, that is, stemming from a historical Fall. It is not that the categories of *metaphysical* and *historical* are exclusive, since they can be understood to complement each other, and both have the effect of distinguishing the source of evil in the world from God, thus retaining the divine holiness. But if conservative Christians are apt to make rather too much of evil and sin as *historical* realities, then it is worth remembering that the New Testament shows little or no awareness of this outside of the difficult territory of Romans 5.

The relative indifference of the Old and New Testaments to the idea of a historical Fall might lead us to ask whether Christian theology really needs to assert it so strongly. Before addressing this question directly, we shall look at two possible attempts to modify the historical Fall model to take account of the problems.

There is a way of expressing the complementarity of the metaphysical and the historical approaches to sin and evil which also attempts to avoid the scientific problems of the Fall. This is achieved by looking at the Fall from an *eschatological* perspective which is, after all, the temporal location towards which all of Christian theology attempts to point. Noble explains that the time and conditions of the End, the *eschaton*, cannot be known from the perspective of *secular* scientific enquiry, since by definition science is engaged with this age (*saeculum*); it cannot by definition see into the next (Noble 2009: 116–20). Instead, the new creation must be known by revelation. The same is true of the Fall, Noble claims. Secular scientific and historical enquiry can only look back into the past, and project forward into the future, by assuming that things have always been, and always will be, what they are in "the present evil age" (Gal. 1:4). This means that science and history are methodologically unable to predict the *eschaton* in the future nor to detect the Fall in the past, because they tacitly assume that the present conditions of fallenness and subjection to evil powers are the norm. Therefore, the Fall will only be apparent as a historical reality from the perspective of the End, and for now it can only be known by revelation, according to Noble.

There is undoubtedly something to be said for this. The Fall must be affirmed by faith, however much conservative believers may insist that it is a historical fact. But it must be admitted that this ingenious way of avoiding the scientific and historical difficulties of the Fall, while also making use of its theological opportunities, is something of a sleight of hand. If the Neolithic Adam and "spiritual death" explanations moved the difficulties into the *spiritual* domain where science cannot touch them, then Noble's eschatological explanation of the Fall moves them into a *temporal* domain where science cannot reach. There is also the question as to whether this interpretation actually offers any explanatory value, other than to preserve the idea of the Fall at all costs. After all, it entirely precludes us from saying anything concrete about what happened at the Fall, or when it happened, other than to say that it *somehow* happened, as long as we rely on revelation. Might it not be simpler just to say that all humans have sinned since their beginnings? In which case, a second possibility presents itself. Here, we simply say that the Fall is the theological name for the onset of consciousness (and especially of *conscience*) in humankind. The higher apes show evidence of remorse, but we assume that it is only hominids (and perhaps only humans) who have the well-developed sense of sin and shame which we connect with conscience. This must have developed at some point in history during the process of human evolution. The biological sciences may not be able to pinpoint the genesis of the conscience, but we can safely conclude that it has been a psychological – and, we could say, spiritual – reality in the human condition for many thousands of years. From that point of view, the story of Adam and Eve could be seen quite simply as an aetiology of the human conscience, where their symbolic eating of the tree of the knowledge of good and evil is the moment of awakening. Although humans (or their hominid ancestors) must have committed many acts of selfishness and violence beforehand, the Fall came at the stage in evolution when they first began to experience guilt and shame at their actions, the spark of conscience.

Straightforward as this model of the Fall may be, and possessing the added advantage that it does not clash with evolutionary biology, it still suffers from a number of disadvantages. First, the fact that the Fall is seen as an entirely human affair means that its redemption can hardly be seen to alleviate the problem of "fallenness", of natural evil and suffering, either in the animal or human kingdoms. Human evil may be reversed by Christ, but not natural evil. Second, it is a "subjective" Fall – an awakening of the individual conscience – not an "objective" Fall which changes the nature of the universe. And third, this model of the Fall runs counter to the traditional interpretation which sees the disobedience of the first humans as a grave and fatal mistake which can only be redeemed by God's initiative of sending Christ. But in this model of the Fall, it is a positive evolutionary step forward, a vital advancement in human self-awareness and intellectual capacity, not a wholesale mistake which must be reversed at all costs. It is a "fall upwards" rather than a fall downwards. Hence, while this evolutionary model of a historical Fall solves the scientific problems of the traditional picture, it appears to make Christ rather superfluous (Berry 2009: 67).

SUMMARY

The doctrine of the historical Fall is problematic on many counts, especially evolutionary science, but it has been deemed essential by many traditionalist Christians, not least in order to preserve the significance of Christ. However, we have seen that the writers of the Old and New Testaments were able to exist without asserting the historical Fall strongly (if at all), although they were certain that sin and failure are universal features of the human condition. In fact, much of the reliance on the Fall stems from the dominance of Augustinian thought in Western theology, and especially from Augustine's insistence (against Pelagius) on the corrupting presence of original sin. But for those who find modern attempts to shore up Augustine's view of the Fall unsatisfactory, especially in the face of the challenges from evolutionary biology, there is a case to be made for re-evaluating the idea of the Fall, especially since our examination of the Old and New Testaments reveals it to be marginal to the biblical witness.

The importance of the Fall lies in its connecting human free will with the historical beginnings of suffering, evil and death, which is why Romans 5 is so significant, not least because it offers the possibility of redemption. Any re-evaluation of this causal connection must provide a transparent account of the scientific difficulties involved, but must by no means paint over the talent of human free will to commit appalling evil, as the history of the twentieth century illustrates all too well. It turns out that there are some solutions, but they require a lateral approach, tackling the problem of *natural* evil alongside human evil. We therefore carry this discussion straight through into the next chapter.

Chapter 8

SUFFERING AND EVIL

THE PROBLEMS OF PAIN AND DEATH

In the previous chapter we observed that the idea of a historical Fall – fundamental to so much Christian thought on sin, death and salvation – is not only problematic from a scientific perspective, but also finds rather less support in the Bible than might be supposed. We now turn to consider whether a suitable *evolutionary* theology can be framed: one without strong reliance on a Fall but which nevertheless can answer the challenge of human evil and death, and of evolutionary suffering in the natural world.

A note is in order at this point. The theological response to sin and death which takes account of the evolutionary context is often known as "theistic evolution". My own tendency is to speak instead of "evolutionary theologies" because, besides the fact that there is a plurality of such responses, they offer ways to understand *God* in the light of *evolution* rather than the reverse; that is, they are incorrigibly theological rather than biological. For that reason, I consider that the term "evolutionary theologies" is more transparent than "theistic evolution".

The problems of pain and death are highly significant in forming a successful evolutionary theology. It is difficult to see the cosmos as the loving work of a munificent Creator who cares for every bird, lily and grass of the field (Mt. 6:26-31) when it is also haphazard, and impersonally disregarding of suffering; full of sickness, destruction and death. Traditionally, these have been identified as signs of "fallenness", a consequence of the Fall of humankind. But the fact that humans are a very late development of life on earth makes it difficult to sustain such an explanation.

In any case, suffering and death are not unmitigated evils; there are subtleties to account for. To begin with, the biblical picture of natural suffering is complex. It does not appear to consider suffering in the animal kingdom to be evil or a manifestation of "fallenness", and we find passages which express praise to God for providing prey for carnivorous animals to eat (Gen. 49:27; Job 38:39-41; Pss. 104:21; 147:9). On the other hand, we also find the recognition (Horrell 2010: 90–95) that there will be a divine eschatological solution to predation in the future, which will mean that "the wolf shall live with the lamb ... they will not hurt or destroy on all my holy mountain" (Isa. 11:6-9; cf. 65:25). By implication, meat-eating and predation were not originally ordained of God. Indeed, according to the Priestly author, humans and animals were originally herbivorous until after the flood (Gen. 1:29-30; 9:1-4). Perhaps Isaiah's eschatological visions suggest a hope to return to such an idyllic situation. All the same, the fact that predators currently need to kill in order to survive – and that death is paradoxically a fact of life – is not expressed as an evil. And neither are natural disasters or disease in the human world spoken of as evils, nor results of "fallenness", but instead as judgements from God, sent to underscore the ways of holiness and obedience (e.g. Exod. 23:28; 32:35; Lev. 26:21; Num. 14:37; 16; 25; Rev. 15-16).

Another point to consider is that suffering and death are necessary to life as we know it. Southgate (2008: 40) explains that pain need not be seen as an out-and-out theological evil but as an inevitable hurdle in the experience of life, the overcoming of which can lead to richness and maturity. This is true whether we are thinking in terms of the story of an individual human life which prevails over adversity, or of the evolution of whole biological species into higher forms. Likewise, death is not necessarily an evil if it is the peaceful and natural end to a fulfilled life, and there are biblical passages which reflect this sentiment (e.g. Lk. 2:25-32). In any case, the natural food resources of our planet would quickly be exhausted if creatures did not die to replenish them.

In this sense, Darwin did not introduce a totally new problem: the theological difficulties that arise from pain, suffering and death have been reflected upon since the dawn of human culture, and positive outlooks have been found. It is when pain is unrewarded, when it offers no apparent gain and appears undeserved, that the theological problem of the futility of existence becomes acute, and this is something which Darwinism emphasizes through the immense wastage of life inherent to the process. There is a balance to be made then: it is not that suffering and death need be seen as evils in themselves, but rather that particular *qualities* of suffering and death are problematic, and that modern science sharpens the problematic by suggesting that they are inherent to the world as God made it. This is the reason why they are often referred to under the umbrella term "natural evil".

NATURAL EVIL AND FALLENNESS

How to justify a good God in the face of natural evil is an age-old problem, and features prominently in the Bible (e.g. Gen. 18:22-33; Job).

For that reason, the modern solutions to it are not necessarily novel. However, they bring to the fore the difficulties which stand behind the terms "natural evil" and "fallenness". To speak of natural evil is effectively to gather up the destructive and dangerous aspects of the natural world, label them with the theologically emotive category of evil, and pin the blame for them on God. After all, nature cannot be blamed for doing what comes naturally. But we should not forget that there is an ambiguity here. Those very laws of nature which precipitate an unexpected earthquake killing thousands are the same laws which have provided stable, temperate and fertile landmasses for the flourishing of land creatures over millions of years. These processes are not obviously "evil" in the sense that freely willed human action can be evil, and if we were to look for a biblical perspective we would have to conclude that they are in fact "good" (Gen. 1:10). "Natural evil" is a category best avoided.

And what of "fallenness"? One of the key biblical texts is Paul's discussion in Romans 8:18-23, which sees the whole of "creation" waiting eagerly for the revelation of Christ's redemption. The creation was "subjected to futility" (v. 20), he says, and it is groaning for release from its "bondage to decay" (v. 21). Paul's earlier discussion in Romans was pre-occupied with human death (Chapter 7), but here the focus is dramatically altered to take a cosmic perspective, where "futility" and "decay" (or "corruption") have been woven into the fabric of the whole world. Paul does not say, but traditional interpretations assume, that this corruption was precipitated by the man and woman's sin in the garden (Murray [2008] 2011: 74). The suffering and death which all creatures experience is therefore a direct result of the Fall in this reading; all exists in a state of "fallenness".

Not only does Paul not say this, but the modern evolutionary picture of the world makes it very difficult to accept such a view. If we can no longer assert a historical Fall unreservedly, it then becomes incoherent to speak of the natural world existing in a state of "fallenness" arising from the spread of human sin. Science sees "bondage to [the] decay" of the second law of thermodynamics as part of the fabric of the world from the beginning, as well as evolutionary competition and "survival of the fittest". We are left with a fundamentally ambiguous view of creation, and we may concur with Darwin's famously vivid assessment (in a letter to J. D. Hooker on 13 July 1856, available at www.darwinproject.ac.uk/entry-1924): "What a book a Devil's chaplain might write on the clumsy, wasteful, blundering, low & horridly cruel works of nature!" Darwin had realized that his proposal of evolution by means of natural selection effectively codifies suffering, cruelty, waste and decay as intrinsic to the development of life on earth. It may be problematic to speak of "fallenness", but we must admit that there is *ambiguity* in God's "good" creation; or better, a "shadow side" (Southgate 2011: 384).

THE "SHADOW SIDE"

Much of the sin and brokenness we humans experience arises from self-ishness which can be related to the same struggle for dominance we see in the world of nature. Ruse suggests that we understand original sin in evolutionary terms:

> Richard Dawkins ... speaks metaphorically of selfish genes, meaning that features had better serve their owner's ends or the owners will be biological failures. However, today we real-ize that major adaptations, especially for intelligent beings like humans, are directed towards co-operation with fellows. Getting together to hunt or to forage or to fight attackers pays big dividends. Helping others can lead to help for ourselves – when we are young or old or sick we need help and the best way to obtain this is to be prepared to help others in their hours of need. You scratch my back and I will scratch yours. So, thanks to our evolution, we are a rather tense melange of selfishness and of friendliness or altruism. And this is surely close to what religious people mean by original sin. We are made in the image of God, so we are naturally good. But we are fallen – this is now part of our nature – and so we are also bad. An uneasy hotch-potch of selfishness and altruism.   (Ruse 2010: 234)

Non-human animals display both selfishness and altruism too, and it has been argued that there are signs of moral awareness in animals such as dol-phins. But whether or not animal immorality constitutes sin as such is less clear (Deane-Drummond 2009: 166–7). Ruse's argument does, however, support the point that sin in humans can be connected with our evolution-ary background, and that it constitutes a kind of *original* sin – a tendency to sin which is common to all humans because it predates us (Peters 2010: 930).

This evolutionary approach has the advantage that it does not call upon the traditional idea of the Fall, with its accompanying difficulties. There is, however, the problem which we have repeatedly highlighted, that such a view jeopardizes the goodness of God, for it suggests that God intended to make humans this way, with original sin an inevitable part of our evolution-ary makeup. There is also the difficulty with this view that it gives humans something of an excuse for their sin: it is in our genes. But when we remem-ber the truly appalling and radical evil of which humans are capable – and the Holocaust always serves as a sobering reminder of this point – then such an apology for the human tendency to sin hardly seems adequate.

Ruse (2001: 205) has attempted to address these problems by suggesting that, just as God *chose* to make creation, so God makes beings that are free to *choose* at every point, "to evaluate and decide between courses of action, and to act on our own decisions". But it is in the nature of freedom that it can be abused, and a selfish course of action will result in greed and sin. Ruse's point is that God should not be blamed for this, because it may have been the only way that such a world of freedom could be made. In Ruse's words, "It is not His [God's] direct fault that we are sinful or that this is a tendency which we inherited" (*ibid.*: 210).

Peacocke has made a similar point, about the inevitability of suffering in an evolutionary world characterized by freedom, and we see the paradox that the creation of *free* creatures entailed a self-imposed *limitation* on God's part:

> This is one of those unanswerable metaphysical questions in theodicy...[T]here are inherent constraints on how even an omnipotent Creator could bring about the existence of a law-like creation that is to be a cosmos not a chaos, and thus an arena for the free action of the self-conscious, reproducing complex entities and for the coming to be of the fecund variety of living organisms whose existence the Creator delights in.
> (Peacocke 2001: 37)

This limitation on God's part is significant, and Peacocke suggests that God makes a further step of self-limitation by sharing in creation's suffering, by analogy with the ways in which the human creative process – from childbirth to artistic creation – is laborious and painful. If Peacocke is right, then there is a sense in which such suffering becomes hallowed, and it becomes even more difficult to speak of it as a type of natural evil if it is voluntarily shared by God.

On the other hand, there are difficulties with seeing evolution as the "only way" in which God could have made a free world like ours (Southgate 2011: 388). The "only way" approach might seem to preserve God's goodness in the face of evolutionary suffering and death, but it is no comfort to the individual who is undergoing suffering. Indeed, the "only way" argument is related to Leibniz's famously optimistic answer made in 1710 to the problem of evil, that we live in "the best of all possible worlds". Such a position was savaged by Voltaire in his 1759 novel *Candide*, and Voltaire's criticism of the "only way" theodicy – that such optimism rings hollow in the face of enormous suffering – still retains its force.

In the face of these difficulties, Southgate (2008; 2011) urges a more subtle approach. He concedes that evolutionary suffering and death seem to be necessary to our world; we should start with an "only way" argument, but we cannot end there. We must also affirm God's care for every creature. God is not only the God of whole systems of blind, indifferent suffering, but also the God who experiences joy when creatures flourish, and who grieves alongside those who hurt. Moreover, there is an over-arching divine plan, which in the eschatological future will perfect the "shadow side" of creation. For the moment though, we live in a state of ambiguity: creation is "very good" (Gen. 1:31), but it is also "groaning in labour pains" (Rom. 8:22; see Southgate 2011: 391).

One of the attractions of Southgate's evolutionary theology is his emphasis on the non-human world, and especially on his belief that the evolutionary suffering of every creature will be addressed by God. His is therefore not a human-oriented account, although he points out that humans should take full responsibility for their own contribution to the suffering of the world, which has arisen because of greed for the world's natural resources (Southgate 2008: 100). Southgate suggests that humans, made in the divine image (Gen. 1:26-27), should respect their special status as God's co-creators. Just as God bore the pain of evolution and of human sin through Christ's death on the cross, so humans should be ready to take on a more sacrificial role in their stewardship of the natural world (Southgate 2008: 113–15).

The cross of Christ is often invoked in evolutionary theologies. As Ruse (2001: 134) points out, the fact that Christianity is a cross-centred religion means that it draws suffering to its heart, making it an attractive theological solution to Darwinism. This is a crucial point, and one worth exploring. Note though, that a different kind of theological move is being made here from traditional theologies of the cross. In the traditional Christian view, God suffers on the cross through the humanity of Christ, and so atones for the sins of the human world. But in modern evolutionary theologies, Christ *additionally* takes on the evolutionary suffering and death of the *entire* living world, suffering and death that are not clearly a result of human sin and so do not require "atonement" as such. The cross is therefore being utilized in a markedly different way from traditional atonement theologies. We shall turn now to consider how such an evolutionary theology might be put together.

THE REDEMPTION OF CREATION

The starting point is inevitably the evolutionary vision of Teilhard de Chardin. In his *The Phenomenon of Man* (1959), Teilhard saw Christ as the pinnacle of evolutionary progress, the "Omega Point" towards which all of creation was tending. For Teilhard (*ibid.*: 293–4, 297–8), this is not true in a spiritual or metaphorical sense, but in a very literal physical sense: the process of biological evolution is moving towards Christ, as its consummation. Widely influential but also highly controversial, Teilhard's thought has been questioned on a number of grounds (Barbour 1997: 247–9; Southgate 2008: 25–7, 36; Deane-Drummond 2009: 36–40). One of the foremost criticisms is that his sense of the unerring evolutionary movement of the universe towards Christ requires a view of progress which Darwinism simply does not support. And on theological grounds, it is not clear how Teilhard's Christ, as Omega Point, is to be connected with the historical Jesus and the narrative of cross and resurrection. In short, Teilhard seems to conflate evolution with salvation. It is therefore hard to see how Teilhard's solution can be an adequate answer to the problem of theodicy. For one thing, since evolution inevitably spells *death* for all creatures, it cannot itself fulfil the Christian hope for resurrection into *life*.

Teilhard's solution has not been taken up widely, and more recent evolutionary theologies have tended to highlight a number of issues which Teilhard did not address. There has been a re-emphasis of the traditional stress on (a) the redemptive suffering of Christ in order to redeem both the non-human and human worlds, and (b) the eschatological dimension, in which redemption will be consummated as a work of God (rather than of evolution). Also, (c) it has been considered important to re-assert the challenge of theodicy, to the extent that God is seen to enter into the suffering of the world:

> the ubiquity of pain, predation, suffering, and death as the means of creation through biological evolution entails, for any concept of God to be morally acceptable and coherent, that we cannot but tentatively propose that *God* suffers in, with, and under the creative processes of the world with their costly unfolding in time. (Peacocke 2001: 37)

Whether or not this is indeed a moral problem, there is a clearly a need to stress God's intimate presence with suffering creation. This goes hand-in-hand with the realization brought about by Darwinism that the initial creation is still ongoing and unfinished. This has meant that evolutionary theologies have also focused on (d) the *immanence* of God in creation, and on (e) God's *continual* work of creation.

This is a complex set of components for any theological view of creation to balance, and the first of these – the suffering of Christ – has been pivotal. This itself has become a complex discussion, veering between subjective views of Christ's sacrifice (he is an example to follow), and objective (his suffering achieves an objective work of redemption in itself). Rolston, for instance, points to the value of redemptive suffering to make sense of nature and of human history. It is transformative, and evolution teaches us that throughout the long history of the earth creatures have given up their lives for the benefit of others: "The story is a passion play long before it reaches the Christ. Since the beginning, the myriad creatures have been giving up their lives as a ransom for many. In that sense, Jesus is not the exception to the natural order, but a chief exemplification of it" (Rolston

2001: 60). In this way, Rolston develops the cross of Christ chiefly as a subjective *representation* to all creation of the value of sacrificial self-giving. Rolston has not been alone in this, and a number of theologians have spoken of the cross of Christ as God's pre-eminent act of solidarity with suffering creatures (Peters 2010: 929–33). God is said to redeem suffering largely by sharing in it.

Southgate (2008: 76), on the other hand, insists that the atoning work of Christ must be viewed objectively. It cannot rest on the free and subjective decision of creatures whether to accept it or not, since the New Testament witnesses to the fact that it will transform the cosmos objectively in the new creation – it is for *all things* (Rom. 8:19-22; Col. 1:20; Eph. 1:8-10). Through Christ, God "takes responsibility" for all of the human sin and non-human suffering of the world (Southgate 2008: 76).

Note Southgate's careful choice of phrase – "takes responsibility". This reveals one of the chief difficulties that beset evolutionary theologies of the cross, namely the highly suggestive nature of the metaphors commonly used, such as "redemption", "atonement", "sacrifice" and "reconciliation". Traditionally, Christian thought has focused on the cross's role in putting right *human* sin, and all that arises from this breakdown of the human–divine relationship. Sin is a thoroughly theological concept which must be addressed theologically, of which "redemption", "atonement", "sacrifice" and "reconciliation" are four common metaphors speaking of brokenness, healing of wrongs, and a price to be paid. But when we speak of the suffering and death which arise from evolution – from entirely *natural* causes – it makes little sense to speak in terms of such metaphors. If evolutionary suffering and death are part and parcel of God's "good" creation – part of the way God intended things to be – there is no broken relationship to heal, or price to be paid. In short, such metaphors are empty, and probably cause more problems than they solve.

From that point of view, Southgate's judicious phrase that God "takes responsibility" for human sin and non-human suffering is wise, if rather vague. But it is appropriate, in that he sees the taking-of-responsibility in wider terms than the cross and its difficult metaphors. The cross atones for human sin, but it is the whole incarnate life of Christ that secures a transformed existence for suffering creation. At the heart of Southgate's vision is the crucial passage of Romans 8:19-22. The "futility" to which the creation was subjected (v. 20) is, for Southgate (2008: 94), the futility of the evolutionary process. But out of the deaths of untold billions of creatures there eventually came God's incarnation in Jesus, a shared solidarity in suffering, and a precarious but eventual hope for the whole of creation which will be realized in a new creation. Christ's dying and rising again point to new possibilities for the world: atonement for human sin, and transformation for the whole of creation in the eschatological future. Southgate proposes (*ibid.*: 94–5) that we see the evolutionary struggle of the world as the "groaning in labour pains" (Rom. 8:22), so that complex and free beings like us might be born. It is from humans that the greatest danger to the world arises, but also the greatest hope, in the incarnate Christ.

Southgate's account is attractive because he explores the biblical traditions thoroughly, and he is honest about the difficulties that beset evolutionary theologies. But the difficulties are not inconsiderable. Like all evolutionary theologies that call upon Christ's incarnation as the solution to suffering (so that God is seen to enter into the condition of fellow sufferers), Southgate's approach (2008: 94) effectively has to introduce a teleology into evolution (§ "Chance and law, contingency and emergence" in Chapter 2, above), such that creatures of sufficient self-consciousness and complexity would one day emerge in order for the Son of God to be incarnated as Christ. Not only is this idea of upwards progress highly contentious in evolutionary biology, it is also a metaphysical claim made in the language of science, with the inevitable difficulties that arise when theological developments are tied closely to science (Chapter 6); as with approaches that speak of the cross "redeeming" evolutionary suffering, there is a danger of confusing theological categories with scientific categories. If there is indeed such a "purpose" behind the evolutionary process, it can probably only be apprehended eschatologically, that is, looking back from the perspective of the *new* creation: "It is omega that determines alpha" (Peters 2010: 929).

Therefore, the difficulties of developing an evolutionary theology are best solved by recourse to the theological future, which is, in any case, the approach of the New Testament. We must recognize that there is a divine work of perfection still to be finished, of which we know little and understand even less. Any adequate evolutionary theology must recognize this fact and underscore its own provisionality. And this is not a new realization: it was originally made by Irenaeus some 1800 years ago.

THE ESCHATOLOGICAL PERSPECTIVE

Irenaeus' vision of creation is one of the earliest in Christian theology. Long overlooked on account of the Augustinian paradigm adopted by Western Christianity, it has become increasingly valued in the science–religion dialogue because of its evolutionary overtones. It is fully incarnational, and against the development of Gnostic dualism in his time Irenaeus asserts the importance and "goodness" of material creation in God's purposes. In a brief and innovative passage (*Against Heresies* IV: 38), Irenaeus describes how God originally created humans deliberately short of perfection, because in their immaturity they were incapable of bearing it. The initial creation was "good" in so far as it was "destined for perfection" (Gunton 1998: 56). God's plan was that humans would grow into maturity and perfection, as children grow into adults. But like children, Adam and Eve were easily led astray in the garden, disobeying God. For Irenaeus, this is not so much a fall as a "failure to ascend" (Bimson 2009: 119). Through the work of Christ and the Spirit, Irenaeus believes that humans can recover from sin and grow towards perfection in God.

But what is "perfection"? At one point Irenaeus connects it with immortality and imperishability, like that of the risen Christ (*Against Heresies* IV: 38.4). In an earlier passage (*ibid.*: III: 23.1), Irenaeus had implied that Adam and Eve were immortal before their disobedience. But here, he says clearly that humans were always mortal (i.e. imperfect) and subject to death, because they are unable to "sustain the power of divinity" in their immaturity. According to this passage then, death is a consequence of the "created nature" of humankind. R. P. Brown (1975: 21) summarizes Irenaeus here: "Death is not a punishment, but the natural end of imperfect creatures. Immortality is not something they lost, for it was never possessed." Irenaeus offers a startlingly effective solution to many of the problems we have seen with the Augustinian model of the Fall. If we assume, with Irenaeus, that the original creation was not meant to be perfect, but to grow towards God through Christ who completes ("recapitulates") all things in himself, then we have no need to preserve a historical Fall at all costs, nor to insist upon the initial perfection of creation, in order to preserve God's goodness. Creation will be perfect, and will reflect God's perfect goodness, but it will be so at the end of the process not the beginning.

Notice though, that Irenaeus' vision of creation is not evolutionary in the sense of physical or biological evolution (Gunton 1998: 201). It suggests that the "shadow side" of creation is entirely natural and intended by God, but will become unnecessary in the fullness of time because of the miraculous and eschatological process of resurrection, and not through any kind of biological teleology. Christ completes creation and brings about perfection by first experiencing its imperfect "shadow side" (i.e. death), and then by passing through it into a new kind of eschatological life where there is no shadow side. We must die in order to live, appears to be the point: we must accept evolutionary suffering but hope for the future.

This is entirely consonant with the pervading apocalypticism of the New Testament: creation can only be understood from the perspective of its eschatological fulfilment (Fergusson 1998: 87). And here we underline one of Southgate's strongest points, his certainty that the ambiguities of evolution can only be assuaged by a firm vision of future consummation, confirmed by Paul's visionary passage in Romans 8. Hence, if it is said of Christ's life (which, of course, includes his suffering on the cross) that it is God's answer to suffering creation, then it should be emphasized that this will only become fully realized from a perspective in the future, which is essentially the perspective provided by Christ's risen life. Resurrection is the key for the whole cosmos, not just for humans. For the time being though, it can only be said in a loose and metaphorical sense that there is a theological answer to the "shadow side" of creation, not least because all theological statements made in the present age are metaphorical of the future consummation (Chapter 9).

Returning to the outstanding problem of the previous chapter – how to understand Paul's causal connection between human sin and death in his atonement theology of Romans 5 – we must concede that, scientifically, these are two things which cannot be connected clearly at present. There is one tentative possibility, which involves postulating that the evolutionary awakening of human consciousness in our distant past was bound up with an awakening of conscience and a sharpening of the awareness of personal finitude (i.e. death). In such a way, the "Fall upwards" (§ "The historical Fall?" in Chapter 7, above) became the awareness both of morality and of mortality. In support, it is said that our sophisticated cognitive perception of ourselves as freely willed causal agents, and our unique awareness of our own mortality, sets humans apart from other animals (W. S. Brown 1998: 119–20). And both of these factors play an important part in our moral and spiritual development: we become aware that our freely chosen actions have had abiding consequences for ourselves and for others, and that they are an inescapable component of the finite human condition (sin), a condition which is summed-up by the inescapably finite fact of death. Our sin is bound up with our death; they are part of a package, and if we are prone to one then we must also suffer the other, simply because we are human. And if we return to considering the "heresy" of Pelagianism which began this discussion (for Augustine at least; see § "Paul and death" in Chapter 7), we see that there is perhaps little need for anxiety on this count, since we are suggesting that conscience (awareness of sin) and the abstract awareness of death are inescapable factors of our evolutionary history. In other words, there is no way in this view that I might fall into the error of Pelagianism, believing that I could be sinless through effort of my will. Instead, I am inescapably born with "original sin" just as I am born with awareness of my death; they are both a consequence of my human evolutionary past.

Admittedly, what we are suggesting here is a rather vague and subjective way to connect sin and death, and it is not a causal connection. The problem we face in trying to think through the issue is that there is simply no easy way to affirm with Paul that "death came through sin" (Rom. 5:12), unless we read him as "*knowledge* of death came *along with* sin". For us, sin is a theological category, but death is largely a scientific (natural) category. For Paul, they could be both; but then Paul was thinking eschatologically, "in hope in the glory of God" (Rom. 5:2), when sin and death will be problems of the past.

THE ECOLOGICAL CHALLENGE

There is one final aspect to our theme of suffering and evil, namely the extra suffering and evil which has arisen upon the earth due to human-kind's mis-management of the planet's resources – the ecological crisis.

An important idea, often cited in ecological theologies, derives from Lynn White Jr's suggestion (1967) that the current environmental crisis stems from the Christian doctrine of creation. In this view, the impending global catastrophe arose from a biblical (mis)interpretation, where Western Christians fulfilled the injunction in P to "fill the earth and subdue it" (Gen. 1:28) so comprehensively that they have brought the planet to the brink of disaster. While supporting White's overall point, Peter Harrison has made a significant modification, pointing out that the rise of science (and its attempts to conquer nature) began in the seventeenth century at a crucial time when the medieval biblical hermeneutic of symbol and allegory was being replaced by a more literal approach, thanks to the European Refor-mation. This meant that the natural world, as well as the Bible, was being interpreted differently: no longer seen in terms of a cosmos of signs and metaphors of a deeper spiritual reality, its significance began to be appre-hended as a literal, physical reality, and utilized as such. As Harrison puts it:

> When the world could no longer be interpreted for its transcen-dental meanings, it was actively exploited solely for its mate-rial utility ... Literalism thus contributes to the emergence of natural science in two distinct ways: first, by evacuating nature of its symbolic significance; second, by restricting the possible meanings of the biblical narratives of creation and Fall, in that they cannot be read other than as enjoining upon the human race the necessity of re-establishing its dominion over nature.
> (Harrison 1998: 206, 208)

Harrison's point is that it is not so much the Christian doctrine of crea-tion that is to blame for the looming ecological crisis. Rather, the crisis has arisen from a much more complex pattern of intellectual development in the West, which allowed for the rise of science by promoting a more literal reading of the world and the Genesis creation narratives.

It is, of course, highly ironic that the very same intellectual trend of liter-alism which made the development of modern science possible has crystal-lized into Creationism, which rejects much modern science. It is also ironic that Creationism rejects much mainstream biblical scholarship, another product of the literalizing Reformation. Biblical scholarship has though, been important in re-discovering ecological perspectives in the Bible, and a comprehensive treatment of ecological views of the Bible already exists in this series of volumes (Horrell 2010).

Ellen Davis (2009), for instance, sets out an agrarian view of Old Testament texts by focusing on the ethics of land use in biblical times in comparison with our own. For her, the ecological catastrophe of our present times – especially as it is worked out agriculturally – is a moral and theological crisis that presents a key hermeneutical context for understanding the Hebrew Bible. Such a hermeneutic highlights the "land-centeredness of the Bible" (*ibid.*: 9), and the human vocation to serve the "land", all the more.

One of the best illustrations of an ecological perspective in the creation motif is in its regard for eschatological hope for all living creatures, and modern theologians who have developed evolutionary theologies have not been slow to point this out (e.g. Edwards 2009: 184–9). If "all things" have been reconciled to God through Christ (Col. 1:20), or have been "recapitulated"/"gathered up" in Christ (Eph. 1:10), and are even being made "new" (Rev. 21:5), and if "every creature" (Rev. 5:13) will one day give praise to God because of Christ, then humans cannot afford to ignore their place in the *wider* scope of God's creation now. In such ways, an ecological consciousness may be said to fall straight out of the eschatological texts of the Bible, if it is not already "latent" in its wider creation motif (Brueggemann 1997: 163, n. 35).

In the next chapter we will discuss some of the biblical visions of the end of the world, and we will suggest that there is a chance they were never meant to be taken as literal predictions. However, our contemporary environmental crisis raises the possibility that some of these apocalyptic predictions might actually be fulfilled in our crippled natural world rather more literally, and rather sooner, than we might think, if we are not more attentive to the future of the planet in our present day. If the ecological challenge (and the fact of the "shadow side" of creation) warn us to think eschatologically, it is clear that there are implications here for our present behaviour too.

CONCLUSIONS

In the last two chapters, we have examined the challenges from evolutionary biology for a historical understanding of the Fall, and the various attempts that have been made to defend it. In every case, we have argued that they are inadequate as interpretations of the biblical witness, in both the Old and New Testaments. We have also pointed out that they are, unwittingly, not motivated by a desire to be true to Genesis 2–3 so much as Paul, and an Augustinian perspective on sin and death. A closer examination reveals that the idea of a historical Fall is rather less important to the biblical texts than conservatives often suppose. By questioning the status of the Fall we are able to move towards an understanding of evil, sin and death in the world that is both more true to the Bible, and makes more sense in the context of modern evolutionary science.

This means that we must understand evolutionary suffering and death less as a result of the "fallenness" of the world, and more as an integral feature of its original creation at the hands of God. For sure, suffering and death are not explained away any more easily in this view. We cannot explain their original entry into the world as a consequence of human free will, and must see them as the "shadow side" of God's "good" creation instead; they may not be evil of themselves, but they possess a difficult ambiguity. A number of modern evolutionary theologies have considered this "shadow side" to represent such an insurmountable problem that it can only be faced by asserting the suffering of God alongside and in creation, especially through the cross of Christ. This, however, is problematic itself on closer examination, since it is not clear what are the wrongs that such a view "redeems", nor how it offers creatures hope for release from suffering, if even God must be said to suffer alongside them. On the other hand, we introduced an Irenaean theodicy as a possible solution, one that removes many of the difficulties of the Fall by suggesting that the original creation was never "good" in the sense of perfect, but "good" in the sense of "fit for purpose", and ready to grow towards perfection in the eschatological future. Such a theodicy de-emphasizes the Fall by emphasizing the future consummation. It is therefore clear that hope for the future must form the main answer to both human brokenness and the "shadow side" of crea-tion, and the Bible's eschatological texts form the strongest basis for such a hope. It is to these that we now turn.

Chapter 9

SCIENTIFIC ESCHATOLOGY AND NEW CREATION

The creation motif in the Bible is not complete until we have considered its complement, the "new creation". The beginning of the world will only find its true meaning in its end, and its consummation in the new beginning (Pannenberg 1994: 142–6). That is, the evolution of the physical universe – highly contingent from our perspective – has a theological significance which will only be apparent from the perspective of its end point. But there is an important question here: to what extent do the Bible's eschatological texts predict the *literal* fate of the physical world? Could its apocalyptic predictions instead be meant metaphorically for social, political or religious transformation in history? Two thousand years of Christian tradition have tended to assume that these texts are meant to be taken literally, but we will question this, after reviewing "scientific eschatologies".

The end of human civilization and the end of the earth

There have long been those who have warned that "the end is nigh". Not only is this a theme of perennial fascination for some religious believers, but it has been a popular subject matter for countless novels and films of the twentieth century in the science fiction and horror genres, many inspired by H. G. Wells's *The War of the Worlds* (1898). To some extent, this cultural pre-occupation with future apocalypse took the place of seventeenth and eighteenth century "catastrophism", the belief that the form of the earth as we see it today had been formed largely by huge catastrophes of the relatively recent past, pre-eminently Noah's flood. The new science of geology made belief in catastrophism largely redundant, when it became clear through research at the end of the eighteenth and first half of the nineteenth centuries that the earth was inconceivably older than the

6,000 or so years calculated by Ussher, and that it had in fact been formed largely by very slow and uniform processes throughout that vast history, not catastrophes. This philosophy came to be known as "uniformitarian- ism", and it has by and large dominated scientific thought ever since, over and against forms of catastrophism. And this is true not only in geology: Darwinism is an obvious example of a scientific model in biology which borrows much from uniformitarianism.

However, in recent decades there has been a revival of scientific interest in catastrophist ideas, together with anxiety about potential catastrophe from space, inspired by the discovery that the extinction of the dinosaurs some sixty-five million years ago might have been precipitated by the impact of a monumental asteroid some six miles in diameter. This would be unusually large, but a comet or asteroid only a hundred metres wide could cause immense destruction today and possibly millions of human deaths. It is known that mass extinctions have occurred throughout the history of life on earth, on average every thirty million years, and it is pos- sible that a number of these were caused by comet or asteroid impact. This has led to political discussion about how to protect the earth against such dangers from space. There is growing awareness of the fragility of life on this planet, which inevitably leads to theological questions.

In addition to the danger of impact from space, the sun, our source of light, heat (and thereby life) will one day make life on earth impossible. Comet and asteroid impact can be predicted in advance to some extent, but it is absolutely certain that one day the sun will extinguish all life on earth. The sun is slowly expanding, and roughly five billion years from now it will reach its maximum size as a "red giant", by which time its radius will have increased so far that it will practically have swallowed up the earth. Long before this though, the earth's seas and atmosphere will have boiled away. If humankind is to survive into the very far future, we must find an alternative home in the universe.

The end of the universe

As well as the earth, physicists have long suspected that the universe itself only has a finite lifespan. Early conjectures, beginning in the nineteenth century, were based on the second law of thermodynamics, which indi- cates that all physical processes will tend to increase the amount of entropy (a measure of randomness) in a thermally isolated system. The upshot is that in time, energy comes to be distributed more and more evenly (i.e. randomly) through a system until the maximum possible entropy of the system is reached. If the universe is one such isolated system, then this would suggest that the energy and matter currently localized in stars, planets (and in our case, life forms), will slowly become distributed evenly throughout the universe, leading to "heat death". At which point, it will be impossible for new stars, planets or life forms to be born. As James Jeans put it:

> there can be but one end to the universe – a "heat death" in which the total energy of the universe is uniformly distributed, and all the substance of the universe is at the same temperature. This temperature will be so low as to make life impossible. It matters little by what particular road this final state is reached; all roads lead to Rome, and the end of the journey cannot be other than universal death. (Jeans 1937: 11)

However, despite Jeans's rhetoric, this is by no means a foregone conclusion, and the issue remains debated in modern cosmology. Is it the case that the entire universe can really be considered as a simple isolated system of the kind governed by the second law? And if the universe is expanding, as is suggested by the Big Bang model, then surely its maximum possible entropy will be increasing too, perhaps faster than its actual entropy is growing, suggesting that heat death might never be reached. There is consequently some uncertainty, although it seems safe to conclude that, as the universe continues to expand, it will become colder and colder, perhaps making it totally inhospitable one day. This also turns out to be a consequence of the most likely solution for the Big Bang model.

Although the Big Bang model has been highly successful in providing a consistent scientific picture for the broad evolution of the universe up to its present state, its ability to predict the long-term future of the universe is severely hampered by a number of factors, not least of which is our ignorance of the total amount of matter in the universe, and therefore its density. The problem is that all of the matter that can be observed by astronomers only accounts for less than twenty per cent of the total anticipated. It is therefore supposed that most of the matter in the universe is unseen, or "dark", although in quite what forms this "dark matter" resides is unknown. Highly mysterious, and so far resistant to direct experimental observation, dark matter's existence is inferred from the otherwise-inexplicable shapes of many galaxies and their spatial distribution across the sky (Dobson 2005: 309–10).

And what of the future of the universe? The universe has been expanding up to the present time, but Friedmann's and Lemaître's classic solutions to Einstein's theory of general relativity, made in the 1920s, indicate that there are three possible scenarios for its future expansion, all of which depend critically upon the density of the universe. The whole issue relates the density of the universe to the force of gravity which works against the expansion from the Big Bang, seeking to pull the universe back together again. The models therefore arise from estimates of how strong is this gravitational pull compared to the headlong rush of out-wards momentum.

Since general relativity indicates that mass makes space curve, the greater the density of the universe, the more curved will be spacetime. The first type of model describes the situation where the universe is denser than the critical value. In this case, the force of gravity will one day overcome the expansion, pulling it back together again. This type of universe is said to be "closed", that is, it is of finite size, and its boundaries are like the surface of a sphere. If you leave your home and follow a straight line you will eventually return to your starting point (Jastrow 1992: 49). The universe will continue to expand for perhaps 500 billion years from now, before it contracts upon itself in a dramatic reversal of the original Big Bang, aptly called the "Big Crunch". It is possible that a new universe will be re-born from the ashes of our present one; nevertheless, all life as we know it will have ceased by then, since in the process of collapsing in on itself the universe will have shrunk to microscopic size and heated up to unfeasibly high temperatures even before the possibility of a new Big Bang.

The second scenario is where the density of the universe is less than the critical value. This model describes an "open" universe, which is infinite in size. If you leave your home and travel in a straight line you will never return to your starting point. Equally, the universe will continue to expand indefinitely, much as it has done for the past fourteen billion years or so, but forever. If this is the case, the temperature of the universe will gradually decrease (as it has been decreasing since the Big Bang), until life as we know it becomes impossible; this is the so-called "Big Freeze".

In the third type of model, the density is exactly equal to the critical value, and the universe is said to be "flat". It is on the cusp between being "closed" and "open" but it is also infinite; this type of universe also results in a "Big Freeze".

It is difficult to be certain which of these three models best describes reality, since so little is understood about the total mass of the universe, but it appears to be very close to being flat. Many cosmologists suspect that our universe will actually turn out to be exactly flat, probably because of a deeper underlying reason as yet unknown (Penrose 2010: 66; Krauss 2012). If so, the universe will keep expanding indefinitely into a cold, dark future in billions of years.

However, these three scenarios are now understood to be somewhat simplistic (Penrose 2010: 59–67). It is becoming clear that the universe is expanding at an increasing rate, which cannot be accounted for in these three solutions without including an extra term into the equations of general relativity, the infamous "cosmological constant". Einstein had initially incorporated this constant in order to contrive a static universe, but then discarded it when the weight of observational evidence began to make it clear that the universe is not static after all. Indeed, he described the cosmological constant as the greatest blunder of his life. Ironically, cosmologists are now re-introducing it to account for the increased expansion over that predicted by Friedmann's three solutions. The physical basis underlying the cosmological constant is unclear at present, and it is usually interpreted in terms of the hypothetical presence of "dark energy" in the universe, energy which is invisible and mysterious (matching the presence of "dark matter"), but may constitute as much as seventy per cent of the mass-energy of the universe (Krauss 2012: 55).

But, dark energy or no, a bleak future is in store. On the face of it, life will be unlikely to survive indefinitely, according to each of these models, with or without the dark energy and Einstein's cosmological constant. It should not be forgotten though, that life on earth will become impossible a good deal sooner than any of these models suggest. The earth will be engulfed perhaps five billion years from now as the sun expands to become a red giant. To survive in the medium term of the universe, humans will therefore need to find another home, and that before the problems of the long term are even considered. In fact, finding another home might be a solution to the longer-term problem too. Current work in cosmology and particle physics operates with the supposition that there could be many other universes in addition to our own, and it has been suggested that black holes in our universe might work as gateways ("wormholes") into some of these other, younger, universes before ours becomes inhospitable (Wilkinson 2010: 17).

However, there have been several scientific suggestions for the far, far future which point to other novel ways of surviving even when biological life has become impossible in this universe. This scenario arises from a claim made by Freeman Dyson in an influential paper of 1979, that "life" could continue forever in an open universe, if it was possible to replace *biological* life by an equivalent form of synthetic but conscious existence able to process information. One possibility he suggests is that of a self-organizing dust cloud (Dyson [1979] 2002: 122). If such a form of "life" was able to maintain itself at very low temperatures then it may be possible, Dyson argues, for such "life" to continue indefinitely. This is an intriguing suggestion, and raises many questions. The assumption that life may be reduced to information-processing has striking parallels with the gnostic idea that material reality is illusory compared to the spiritual reality of the soul. If material reality is the source of doom (as the three cosmological models predict), then escape is sought in the spiritual (information-processing) realm.

Dyson preferred to think in terms of an "open" universe, simply because he believed this offers the most congenial future for life in the long term. On the other hand, Frank Tipler has produced an optimistic scientific eschatology assuming a closed universe (Tipler [1994] 1996). All carbon-based life will become impossible near to the Big Crunch due to the high temperatures, explains Tipler. However, there is a special significance about the end point, which is why Tipler refers to it as the "Omega Point"; it is equivalent to God in Tipler's scheme. Tipler explains that, as human technological ability improves, it will be possible one day to replace biological life by more-resilient computer emulations which will be, to all intents and purposes, alive. Close to the Omega Point, it will be possible for "life", so defined, to expand and fill the universe, and therefore to experience its entirety. It will become omnipresent, omniscient and omnipotent, or in other words, God. Moreover, every life form which has ever lived can be resurrected at the Omega Point as a computer emulation, since full knowledge of the universe's past will be available. The upshot is that, according to Tipler, even though the universe will be ending, yet as the Omega Point is approached time will be experienced as effectively stretching out indefinitely, and life here will be to all intents and purposes "life forever".

Tipler's suggestions are highly speculative, and have aroused a great deal of criticism and disbelief from both scientists and theologians, being branded as "science fiction" by some (Barbour 1997: 218–19; Fergusson 1998: 90; Jackelén 2006: 961). Ironically, scientists are able, using the methods and discoveries of science, to formulate hypotheses every bit as high-blown and ultimately optimistic as are the traditional claims of faith. Indeed, studies of miracles such as the crossing of the Red Sea indicate that scientists are also capable of explaining some of the most challenging of biblical miracles using science (Harris 2007). There appears to be little that is beyond their grasp when it comes to explaining the claims of faith, an observation that raises interesting questions about the nature and definition of miracle as a scientific/theological problem. These questions are beyond the scope of this present book, but suffice it to say that scientific eschatologies like Tipler's, which propose natural explanations for the most seemingly impossible and bizarre scenarios (in human terms), are as theological in their claims as they are scientific.

It is notable that Tipler's suggestions have been met with scepticism, especially from theologians, who live and work alongside equally bizarre and outlandish claims for the future made in the Bible and the Creeds. The difference in understanding appears to concern that of metaphor. Tipler develops his model using scientific ideas, believing that this is how reality *might really turn out*. Theologians and biblical scholars, on the other hand, are aware that the eschatological narratives of faith are by their nature metaphorical, a point to which we shall return shortly. And yet, Tipler's approach cannot be so easily dismissed if we hope to look through the metaphors to understand better what might really be in store for the universe (Hardy 1996: 156–7). Tipler's account might best be judged as another metaphor of the possible future – an unlikely one for sure, given that we now believe our universe to be flat rather than closed – but still a metaphor. In which case, scepticism of it should be matched with an open-ness to the breadth of what cosmology and theology might have to say to each other, since in the eschatological future they will become one and the same discipline. At present, though, theological work on the future of the universe is "quite disappointing" (Wilkinson 2010: 52), due to a limited engagement with cosmology and a limited understanding of it. Perhaps most importantly of all, when we take the biblical perspectives on escha-tology into account, we see that it is of direct relevance to the *present time* (not just the far future), indicating that there is a biblical imperative to engage with eschatology and its consequences in the present. As we shall see though, this calls for a far more subtle and far-reaching view of escha-tology than simply what science might have to say about the end of the world.

ESCHATOLOGY IN THE BIBLE

New creation

The idea of the ultimately fresh start is extremely rich in the Bible, espe-cially in the Old Testament. It is expressed in many ways, sometimes using mythological language, sometimes metaphors and allusions to highpoints in Israel's past (e.g. the Exodus, or David as King), and sometimes using very familiar imagery from the natural and social worlds. In the Hebrew prophets, the predictions of new creation, renewal and redemption are particularly vivid, and the sense is that the fresh start combines concrete deliverance for God's people together with a new society (and sometimes a new natural world too). Deliverance is described in different ways: it is the fulfilment and completion of God's work in the history of Israel, the final setting-to-right of Israel's mistakes, an end to foreign oppression, a time of unrivalled prosperity and harmony in Israel, and the definitive offering of worship to Yahweh on Mount Zion in Jerusalem (e.g. Amos 9:11-15; Hos. 14; Isa. 2; 11; 35; Jer. 31–32; Ezek. 40–48; Joel 3; Zech. 8). Even though it is often spoken of using images from this world, redemption is always a divine action. This probably explains why it becomes linked with ideas of creation (the first divine action in the world) especially in the later proph-ets: Second Isaiah (Isa. 40–55) and Third Isaiah (Isa. 56–66). It reaches its apotheosis in the language of "new creation":

> I am about to do a new thing;
> now it springs forth, do you not perceive it?
> I will make a way in the wilderness
> and rivers in the desert.
>
> (Isa. 43:19)

> For I am about to create new heavens and a new earth;
> the former things shall not be remembered
> or come to mind.
>
> (Isa. 65:17)

Second Isaiah, written during the Exile, makes frequent connections between creation and redemption, often through mixing natural and mythological metaphors of creation with metaphors of the Exodus (Isa. 40:3-5, 27-31; 41:17-20; 42:5-9, 16; 43:1-2, 5-7, 14-21; 44:1-5; 45:11-13; 48:20-21; 49:8-13; 51:9-11; 55:10-13). Third Isaiah, written probably after the return to Jerusalem, makes the idea of new creation most explicit of all, describing the future redemption as the fashioning of a new physical world ("new heavens" and a "new earth"; Isa. 65:17; 66:22).

Although the idea of "new creation" as the re-formation of the heavens and earth (i.e. the physical universe) is only articulated explicitly in Third Isaiah, it is continuous with the wider language of redemption in the prophets, and also with the language of judgement, which is sometimes expressed in similarly cosmic terms, even if it is probably meant metaphorically of political (rather than cosmic) disaster (e.g. Isa. 2:5-22). The Hebrew prophets tend to juxtapose messages of judgement with messages of redemption; with criticism on the one hand, and with hope for new creation on the other, whether they are speaking in terms of the physical, social, political, or religious worlds. And because the message of hope for redemption is (a) *uniform*, in the sense that it always speaks of renewal, and (b) *metaphorical*, in the sense that it involves many different images from the human and natural worlds, we will therefore group it together under the umbrella of "new creation". We must remember though that, if the term "new creation" brings to mind thoughts of the literal end of this world, then it is not clear that the Hebrew prophets thought so literally. Third Isaiah might have recorded the prediction that God is "about to create new heavens and a new earth" (Isa. 65:17), suggesting a new physical universe, but it is entirely possible that he meant it as a metaphor for political transformation in this world (Wilkinson 2010: 63). We shall explore this idea shortly.

Apocalyptic

Before describing how the language of redemption and new creation was taken up by the New Testament, we must take account of an important trend in between times. It is not understood exactly how this happened, but it seems that, in the centuries soon after the return from Exile (described in Ezra and Nehemiah), the genre of written prophecy either ceased or was transformed into a new type of vision for the future: "apocalyptic".

There has been much discussion about how to define this genre, and much disagreement too, but it is generally said to contain an interest in describing visions of heavenly scenes and terrible future events, often accompanied by angelic intermediaries, of heavenly journeys, coded symbols and bizarre images. And it is also thought that the genre of apocalyptic arose particularly in communities which felt isolated and threatened in some way, perhaps because of religious persecution. If the classical Hebrew prophets of the eighth century BCE (Amos, Hosea, Micah and First Isaiah) tended to frame their hopes for the future in terms of social and political renewal in *this* world, then the apocalyptic communities often described their hopes in more cosmic terms, articulating a new divine beginning which first necessitates a dramatic end to this world order, followed by divine judgement and an affirmation of the ethical purity of the apocalyptic community (Hanson 1975: 11–12). Taken literally then, their "new creation" became not a symbol for renewal in this world, but for a completely "new heavens" and a "new earth" (Isa. 66:22). Whether they intended it to be read literally though, is an important question to which we shall keep returning.

There are relatively few examples of apocalyptic texts in the Old Testament (largely Dan. 7–12, and perhaps Isa. 24–27 and Zech. 9–14), but many more after it. The New Testament uses several of the concepts and images of apocalyptic as its *lingua franca*. The Christian hope for the resurrection of the dead probably derives ultimately from the vision of resurrection first described in Daniel 12, where "many of those who sleep in the dust of the earth shall awake, some to everlasting life, and some to shame and everlasting contempt" (v. 2). Paul sees Christ as the "first fruits" (1 Cor. 15:20, 23) of this vision, and much of the hope for redemption and new creation which was expressed in the Hebrew prophets and apocalyptic literature becomes in the New Testament especially focussed on the person and work of Christ, and has therefore already been realized to some extent in him.

In a similar way, Paul teaches that believers are living simultaneously in the old world and the new, and much of his ethical teaching assumes this tension (e.g. 1 Cor. 5–7). Indeed, it is in Paul that the phrase "new creation" explicitly surfaces, but he uses it more to describe the altogether-new spiritual state of believers rather than a new physical universe (2 Cor. 5:17; Gal. 6:15). So although Paul can speak of his hope for the future transformation of the entire creation (Rom. 8:18-25), it is clear that it has already been partially realized in the life of the Christian community, especially through its experience of the Holy Spirit (2 Cor. 1:22).

And yet, alongside the sense that eschatological hopes have been partially realized through the life and work of Christ, and through the presence of the Holy Spirit with believers, there is also a clear future hope, often expressed in terms which evoke cataclysmic physical changes, and perhaps even the end of the world (e.g. Mk 13; Heb. 1:10-12; Rev. 15–19). The second coming of Christ features prominently in such visions in the Synoptic Gospels, and in one very significant place in Paul (1 Thess. 4:13-18). Matthew's Gospel in particular also links these events with the day of judgement, which will result in damnation for some and salvation for others (e.g. Mt. 25:31-*end*). The book of Revelation is a full-blown apocalypse which predicts earth-shattering (literally) events in the future, as redemption is brought about for the faithful. The "new heaven" and the "new earth" in Revelation 21 describe a vision of future redemption which is entirely universal in scope, since "the first heaven and the first earth had passed away" (v. 1). Likewise, in the picture of 2 Peter 3, the "present heavens and earth" (v. 7) will be burnt up and consumed by fire on the "day of the Lord" (v. 10), when judgement for all will take place. These pictures represent a synthesis of a number of images from the Old Testament (e.g. Isa. 66; Mal. 3 [ET 4]), worked into a sobering message of coming destruction and judgement. This message has been upheld relatively literally in the traditional Christian expectation of judgement and hell for the unrepentant, and heaven for the blessed. But was it meant to be taken literally?

The question of reality

Several scholars have argued forcefully that the eschatological and apocalyptic language of the Bible, especially where it appears to predict the end of the world, was always meant metaphorically (e.g. Caird 1980; Wright 1992, 1996). On the other hand, the dominant trend in twentieth-century scholarship has been to interpret this hope literally, largely since Albert Schweitzer's ground-breaking study of the historical Jesus in 1906, which put forward the idea that Jesus was motivated by the imminent expectation of a literal apocalypse, the end of the world. In the face of traditional Christian belief, which also tends to interpret such language literally, it is an interesting exercise to question these tacit assumptions of faith. After all, the poetic and prophetic literature of the Bible is replete with metaphorical imagery, and in many cases no one would ever think to take it literally, such as with the famous statement "The Lord is my shepherd" (Ps. 23). Much of the language clearly comprises metaphorical descriptions of God's nature and present work in the world, which, since they concern the divine, almost by definition can only be meant metaphorically. It becomes more difficult when the text speaks of events in the future though. For instance, when Isaiah predicted that "the host of heaven shall rot away, and the skies roll up like a scroll" (Isa. 34:4), was he speaking of the end of the world, or of something more subtle? In this case, the text gives us clues which make this image fairly straightforward to interpret, and Caird (1980: 115) points out that it should not be taken as a literal expectation that the physical world would end, but rather as a vivid evocation of the political setting-to-rights of the rival nation of Edom (Isa. 34:5).

In this light, the eschatological teachings of Jesus have been particularly controversial in modern scholarship. Should they be taken literally or metaphorically? And if metaphorically, metaphorical of what? For instance, when Jesus is quoted as predicting that the sun and moon would be darkened, the stars fall from the skies, and that the Son of Man would come again in the clouds (Mk 13:24-26), was this a literal expectation that the world would end at the bodily advent of the Son of Man from the sky? Or was it entirely coded language, using stock images derived from the Old Testament, for a social, political or religious transformation of Israel in real time and in this world? Some scholars sidestep this difficult question by arguing that Jesus never actually said these things in the first place, but that they were placed on his lips by early Christians who had an intense desire for his bodily return (e.g. Allison 1998 argues against Wright 1996; see Allison *et al.* 2001). The Jesus Seminar, for instance, as a body of scholars, has largely rejected as inauthentic the apocalyptic sayings associated with Jesus, believing them to be later traditions from the early church (Funk *et al.* 1993). On the other hand, some other scholars (e.g. Sanders 1985), working in the spirit of Albert Schweitzer, believe that the apocalyptic sayings are not only authentic to the historical Jesus but even give us the core content of his teaching. Still other scholars (notably N. T. Wright 1992, 1996) believe the sayings to be authentic but argue that they should be interpreted metaphorically. In Wright's reconstruction of the historical Jesus, the apocalyptic sayings function as Jesus' coded warning of imminent socio-political judgement upon Israel (1996: 96–7). Read literally, they may appear to describe the end of the world, but Jesus meant them (and they were understood by his listeners, according to Wright) as metaphors of political disaster. Of course, this disaster came true in 70 CE at the hands of the Romans.

Along the way, Wright (1992: 298–9) makes a point which is particularly important for our purposes, arguing that the reason modern scholars have been so ready to interpret the apocalyptic sayings of Jesus literally since Schweitzer is because of the pervasive but subtle influence of Deism in modern times, whereby the world is conceived of as a self-sufficient system largely closed to divine influence; God is normally absent but might intervene occasionally, in radical discontinuity with the world order. If Wright is right, then scholars have tended to think in deistic terms, assuming that, when apocalyptic discourse speaks of the end of the world, it can only mean it literally: that God simply does not act in the world except to end it and start all over again with a whole new space-time universe (a literal new creation). If so, it is hardly surprising that some scholars question the authenticity of Jesus' apocalyptic sayings: what they are really doing is questioning a deistic reading of biblical eschatology. In which case, we need to attend to the question of the implied reality underlying the apocalyptic sayings attributed to Jesus, not so much their authenticity.

The question of the reality underlying Jesus' apocalyptic language raises important issues. In our time, science is regarded as the pre-eminent yardstick of what constitutes reality in the physical world, and yet it has revealed many counter-intuitive surprises and persistent mysteries about the nature of reality (Chapter 2). Moreover, philosophers of science have pointed out that, methodologically, science does not uncover reality in any straightforward way. Detailed discussion of this point is beyond the scope of this book, but suffice it to say that there are various schools of thought ranging from "naïve realism" at one end of the spectrum, which holds that scientific models tell us what is truly going on in the world, to "instrumentalism", which holds instead that they are useful tools ("instruments") for predicting the results of observations and experiments, but do not reveal the underlying reality in itself (Barbour [1974] 1976: 34–8). A popular kind of "middle" position is that of "critical realism". Like naïve realism, critical realism takes scientific models to be representations of reality, but recognizes that they are also human constructs, and are therefore incomplete and provisional. A number of prominent scientist–theologians (Barbour, Hodgson, Peacocke, Polkinghorne) have professed support of critical realism in their own thinking, as have some New Testament scholars (e.g. N. T. Wright and J. D. G. Dunn), who see it as a useful analogy for their approach to the subtleties of trying to extract historical reality from biblical texts.

This spectrum of approaches raises the question of what exactly is reality in the first place, and how we might be able to tell. A similar point can be made about the biblical text and our ability to uncover the true reality to which it refers, especially when it speaks of the otherworldly in terms of this world. For that reason, the interpretation of miracles, divine revelations, and of course, the nature of God in biblical texts, is fraught with complex interpretative questions.

Jesus' predictions of the future

The debate about whether the apocalyptic language of Jesus was ever intended to be taken literally or metaphorically is a good example of the hermeneutical difficulty involved in determining the reality underlying a text. Predicting the future in any arena is always fraught with high levels of uncertainty at best. But in principle, we usually believe that we ought to be able to understand the reality to which the prediction points, whether or not it will come to pass. This is not the case here.

Let us take a specific example, that of Jesus' apocalyptic discourse (Mk 13; Mt. 24–25; Lk. 21), and especially his prediction of "earthquakes in various places" (Mk 13:8). This functions as a sign of the impending end of the world, culminating in the return of the Son of Man "coming in the clouds with power and great glory" (Mk 13:26). Since earthquakes are relatively well understood geologically, we could apply the discoveries of modern science to this image. If so, we would quickly find that this image derives ultimately from the fact that the land of Israel is prone to earthquakes due to the presence of the Dead Sea Rift. It is perhaps not surprising then that the earthquake is a widespread image in the prophetic, poetic, and apocalyptic literature of the Bible, usually functioning as an image either of divine revelation or of divine judgement (e.g. Judg. 5:5; Job 9:6; Isa. 5:25; Zech. 14). Science is able to shed light on the image, and to explain how personal experience would probably make it more vivid for those who live in the area. It is entirely possible, of course, that it was also widely understood by listeners and readers of the time that talk of earthquakes in certain contexts was actually code for something entirely different, political upheaval perhaps. But unless the text indicates that this was the reality underlying the image, we have almost no way of knowing.

There is, in fact, one place in Jesus' apocalyptic predictions where the evangelists *do* give a clear indication that there is a coded reality standing behind at least one of the images used, that of the "desolating sacrilege": "But when you see the desolating sacrilege set up where it ought not to be (let the reader understand), then those in Judea must flee to the mountains" (Mk 13:14). Mark's cryptic editorial comment, "let the reader understand", indicates that there is more here than meets the eye, and Matthew's later version attempts further clarity by adding that it will be in "the holy place" (the Jerusalem temple?) and that it "was spoken of by the prophet Daniel" (Mt. 24:15). Given the undoubtedly high degree of familiarity with the book of Daniel which the early Christian communities must have enjoyed, Matthew's insertion hardly seems necessary, because the "desolating sacrilege" (or "abomination that desolates") is a recurring motif there (Dan. 9:27; 11:31; 12:11), probably referring back to the desecration of the Jerusalem Temple at the time of the Maccabean revolt of the second century BCE (1 Macc. 1:54). Matthew's additions were presumably made in order to ensure that his readers understood without a shadow of a doubt that these words of Jesus were to be read with reference to the cataclysmic destruction of the Jerusalem Temple in 70 CE at the hands of the Romans, which had presumably already happened by the time Matthew was writing (but was still in the future for Jesus). Mark's "let the reader understand" – although clearly a coded hint – simply was not explicit enough for Matthew. The fact that the evangelists give these mysterious clues without explaining them more clearly (from our perspective) suggests that they regard this text as a cipher for a socio-political reality played-out in their time, that is, *not* the end of the world.

However, there is a degree of uncertainty here. We might deduce that in Matthew's case the "desolating sacrilege" refers to the destruction of the Jerusalem Temple, but it is uncertain, and we are even less sure that this is what Mark is referring to (A. Y. Collins 2007: 608–12; Marcus 2009: 889–91). And if this is the case with the single saying in Jesus' apocalyptic discourse which is deliberately decoded by the evangelists, we face an even greater difficulty in trying to uncover the reality behind the other signs in the apocalyptic discourse. Little wonder then, that modern readers tend to either interpret the discourse literally, or else dismiss it as a bizarre parable of little relevance to modern life. We therefore have something of a parallel with the Genesis creation stories which, as we pointed out in § "Genesis 1 and modern science" in Chapter 3, tend to be read either literally, or else as "poetry", but without attending to deeper underlying realities. Like the Genesis texts, the apocalyptic sayings may point to many different under-lying realities, but we have little way of knowing. This is both the prob-lem and the opportunity of metaphor, which may stand in the place of the thing to which it refers so successfully that in the re-telling it inadvertently becomes the reality to which it refers.

There is a further difficulty, to do with the fact that any description of divine action must be metaphorical by definition. This is true whether we are speaking of eschatological events in the future, or those in the historical past, such as the miracle traditions of the Bible. They speak of a divine real-ity in terms of the material reality of this world; they are inherently meta-phorical. And this is true even before we begin to ask the difficult question of a miracle story concerning "what really happened". We have no clear access to the objective reality underlying the text beyond what the text tells us literally which, as we have said, is actually a metaphor for a divine reality.

On the other hand, there are many places in the Bible where historical study can establish that it is speaking of historical and material realities we can understand from our own experience, some of which may even be verified independently. Accounts of kings and military campaigns are good examples (§ "Dates and numbers" in Chapter 5), and the critical realism we mentioned previously is a perfectly sound approach to use in historical study *of these kinds of texts*. There is, however, a profound difference when we are seeking to understand a biblical text which describes something *entirely out of our experience*, such as a miracle, or a divine action, even one of creation. And the prophecies of new creation, by their very nature, concern divine action, and *new* action at that. Clearly, all talk of contact between the divine and the earthly must then be inherently metaphorical, an attempt to explain the otherworldly in terms of our world. But this is all that we can do: speak of the new creation using the language of our crea-tion, images from our world which refer to a reality coming from another world.

New creation is, by its very nature, then, an unknown. We simply do not have a handle on its reality (what it will be like), since it is fundamentally *new*, and is a *divine* act of *creation*. There are three layers of metaphor here straightaway, and we must add the further complication that we do not have the key to unlock the code behind many of the apocalyptic images associated with Jesus.

If it seems as though we are all at sea in trying to understand the reality underlying new creation, there is one theological fixed point (Fergusson 1998: 93–4). The image of the second coming of Christ, descending on the clouds with angels, is one that has tended to divide fundamentalist Christians – who argue over the nature of the "Rapture" and pre-millennialist versus amillennialist and post-millennialist interpretations of Revelation 20 – from many other Christians, who are apt to a degree of agnosticism concerning it, no doubt because of its outlandish and mythological overtones. But at root, the idea of the second coming articulates an important theological point about the Christian slant on the new creation. Just as God chose to be revealed as a human being in the incarnation, in order to redeem creation, so God will do so again at its completion. This is the reason why the New Testament is able to place Christ both at the foundation of the world and at its final fulfilment and setting to rights on the Last Day: his resurrection demonstrates his role in the past of creation, provides believers with hope and purpose in the present creation, indicates that his ethical teachings are to be taken seriously, and points to the reality of the future in the new creation. His resurrection is the key.

Resurrection, and a third category of creation: creation "from the old" (ex vetere)

It is helpful at this point to sharpen the theological categories of creation. Does new creation correspond to *creatio ex nihilo* or *creatio continua*? A little thought indicates that we need a third category, since a creation which is a redemption of the old must in some sense be a transformation of the old while also offering a clean break with it; it is neither a creation "from nothing", nor a "continuous" act of creation. Polkinghorne (1994: 167) has helpfully suggested *creatio ex vetere* – "creation from the old".

The foremost biblical example demonstrating that the new creation is a transformation "from the old" is the resurrection of Jesus. The empty tomb tradition (Mt. 28; Mk 16; Lk. 24; Jn 20) indicates that the evangelists believed the resurrection of Jesus to be bodily (i.e. the risen Jesus is not a purely spiritual being), and yet, taken literally, they also appear to have believed that it was more than the resuscitation of a corpse, since they describe him as capable of impossible feats, such as the ability to appear and disappear at will, to walk through walls, and to ascend to God for eternity. Likewise, Paul's celebrated description of the resurrection body in 1 Corinthians 15 may be highly allusive, using assorted images from the heavenly and earthly worlds, yet it clearly anticipates a new kind of reality which is somehow

related inextricably to the old (1 Cor. 15:35-57). He might describe the resurrection body as a "spiritual body", but it is still a "body" (1 Cor. 15:44), and
one which is "imperishable" and "immortal" to boot.

Much of this language, in both the Gospels and Paul, is highly metaphorical; nevertheless, taken together, it suggests a state of existence which
is recognizably human and physical, and yet represents a transformation
into something new and unknown. And since the Christian church has
always maintained that the resurrection state of Jesus is the precursor for
what believers can expect in the new creation, then it is fundamentally a
redemptive transformation: it redeemed Christ's death on the cross, and is
also caught up in his redemptive activity for the "sin of the world" (Jn 1:29).
This is a message of profound hope: the old creation is not rejected, but it is
the raw material of what is to come. Whatever is the Christian idea of new
creation, it must hold the resurrection of Jesus at its heart.

And yet, many Christians, faced with the difficulty of believing in the
miraculous on this scale, have preferred to think of Jesus' resurrection in
spiritual terms, and of heaven as a spiritual reality, where the non-physical
souls of the blessed reside for eternity. In this case, "resurrection" becomes
a dualistic metaphor for the freeing of the soul from the material body at
death, so that it can unite with God. This may avoid the challenge of mate-
riality, but it is also a manifestation of Gnostic belief. For this reason, many
modern theologians resist speaking of the soul as a separate entity from the
human body, and are inclined to speak of the human being as a psychoso-
matic unity instead. Mascall points out that Christianity has attempted to
maintain persistently – often against the odds, and often with some embarrassment – that our final condition is not just spiritual immortality but
bodily resurrection, as demonstrated by Jesus. This has profound consequences for the whole cosmos:

> Because we are by nature physical beings linked by our bodily
> metabolism both with one another and with the rest of the
> material world ("Whatever Miss T. eats", Mr de la Mare has
> reminded us, "turns into Miss T."), our resurrection will involve
> nothing less than the transformation of the whole material
> order.   (Mascall 1956: 17)

To be precise, bodily resurrection implies transformation of the whole
cosmos, including all creatures which currently suffer in subjection to the
"shadow side" of evolution. It potentially offers salvation for all of creation
which is currently in "bondage to decay" (Rom. 8:21), and is "perishable"
(1 Cor. 15:42).

Attempting to understand what is behind these predictions – which
must be metaphorical to a greater or lesser extent – tests our imagination
to the extreme. The Bible predicts that "death will be no more ... pain will

be no more" (Rev. 21:4), but it is hard to imagine how such a dream could be a truly biological possibility given our present scientific knowledge. We know that decay and perishability – together with suffering, pain and death – are (paradoxically) essential for the flourishing of biological life in this world of finite resources. And the facility to feel physical pain, for instance, is an important protective biological function (in humans at least), without which we would unwittingly inflict terrible injuries upon ourselves in the course of everyday life – "the gift of pain" (Murray [2008] 2011: 112–21). And yet, we hope that suffering and death will be things of the past in the life to come. How, we do not know. But the more science we learn, the more outlandish and impossible such a transformed world seems. We should not forget though, that the biblical predictions are metaphorical of an unimaginable hope which should not be read or imagined too literally, or else the whole genre will be misunderstood.

Still, to grasp the mind-blowing nature of such metaphors in our modern world we must speak fundamentally of the laws of nature – how might they change in order to attain such a transformation? – can they change in the first place? – and to what extent can present-day science contribute to such a discussion? (Note that cosmologists already speculate that the laws of physics may be different in different parts of the multiverse). And we must also speak of our own identity and continuity. If we are to speak literally of resurrection and transformation, will I be raised in the body in which I died, or in the body I had as a 21-year old? I must hope that the resurrection existence must involve some discontinuity with my present existence for it to become "immortal". But what will that discontinuity be? What needs to remain in continuity for me to remain "me", and what can be transformed? The questions rapidly proliferate and rapidly become absurd, but they are by no means new. Augustine considered them in depth (*Enchiridion* 84–92; see Mascall 1956: 19), as did Paul centuries before him (1 Cor. 15:35-54).

The answer to this conundrum seems to be *hope*, pure and simple. Hope must remain in God's purposes, a great "mystery", namely that "we will all be changed" (1 Cor. 15:51). And Jackelén (2005: 215) has wisely pointed out that the more we hope for personal continuity between the form of our present existence and the world to come, the less freedom we grant to God to achieve transformation of the "shadow side" of this creation. Therefore, by giving ourselves up to *unconditional* hope in God's purposes, we might find our true selves.

In this way, we find a new understanding of the picture of Romans 8, where the whole of creation waits eagerly for something which is currently unclear, "the revealing of God's children" (v. 19). It is unclear to us too. Christ's resurrection *ex vetere* demonstrates the pattern for its transformation, and it is the only fixed point, but it is a fixed point about which we know practically nothing except what the biblical texts tell us.

It is vital, therefore, both to maintain the mysterious and divine nature of the future eschatological transformation, and to maintain a certain degree of critical circumspection regarding the biblical texts. They must not be constrained too closely.

However, we must note that several studies have already attempted to provide scientific perspectives on the resurrection of Jesus, in order to investigate what can be said physically about the new creation. One suggestion, for instance, is that the new creation exists as a new dimension, or a parallel universe that somehow intersects with ours (Polkinghorne 2011: 107). These ideas are at an early stage, largely just beginning to map out some of the potential issues (Polkinghorne 1994, 2002, 2005; Russell 2002a, 2002b), and apart from Wilkinson (2010), the biblical texts are barely considered. But this is a crucial oversight, because the resurrection texts contain many pertinent interpretative problems. We cannot simply assume that the risen Jesus as described in the New Testament may be taken as data for reconstructing physical features of the new creation, when actually *it is the New Testament texts which are the data, not the risen Jesus*. Not only are we necessarily at one remove from the object of enquiry (the risen Jesus), but it is a remove that is both highly significant and highly complex from a hermeneutical perspective. There is sufficient diversity in the various biblical resurrection traditions to indicate that we cannot simply harmonize across them. While Luke, for instance, goes to some lengths to emphasize the *earthliness* of the risen Jesus (e.g. Lk. 24:39-43), Paul emphasizes the *otherworldliness* of the resurrection body (1 Cor. 15:50), and we find straightaway that we have two highly relevant observations that are not easily cohered. Therefore, if the diversity of the texts is to be respected, then any conclusions we draw from the resurrection traditions will be more complex and more tentative than has so far been the case.

Further difficulties arise from these points. As with the apocalyptic sayings of Jesus, the resurrection traditions concern a reality that is literally out of this world, an attempt to describe divine eschatological redemption in the terms of our present world. This means that any conclusions we take from them are theological allusions, and not physical evidence which can be treated scientifically. This is emphatically not a denial of the resurrection, nor of the Gospel accounts, but rather a methodological warning about the limitations of science, and of the kinds of texts with which we are dealing. Any scientific conclusions made from such a study are analogical at best, and moreover they are *interpretations* of the text, not objective statements about a reality which exists apart from it. This may be a simple point, but it is one that is often not appreciated in the science–theology field, as is the all-important context of the resurrection traditions in the New Testament: they are described in order to provide ethical guidance and pastoral support for the lives of Christians *in the present age*; they only describe life in the far-off future insofar as it is relevant for how to live life now (e.g. 1 Cor. 6:9-20; 15:58).

New creation and the possibility of cyclical creation

Consideration of the eschatological outlook of the Bible leads us to think more deeply about its views of time. We have already pointed out (§ "The end of time?" in Chapter 5) that, if we take the longest view, from beginning to end, there is a sense in which a linear view of time must be modified to take on a more cyclical character. This is also evident to some extent on a smaller scale too. The famous passage in Ecclesiastes 3 suggests that time is endlessly cyclical on a small (seasonal) scale: "For everything there is a season, and a time for every matter under heaven: a time to be born, and a time to die; a time to plant, and a time to pluck up what is planted" (Eccl. 3:1-2). Certainly, the rhythms of the seasons and of nature are cyclical, and when they interact with linear time then evolutionary novelty can arise (Wilkinson 2010: 35). This can be further modified by an eschatological outlook, and we find the prediction that the cycles of light and dark, heat and cold, planting and harvest will become one uniform summer day in the eschatological future:

> On that day there shall not be either cold nor frost. And there shall be continuous day (it is known to the LORD), not day and not night, for at evening time there shall be light. On that day living waters shall flow out from Jerusalem, half of them to the eastern sea and half of them to the western sea; it shall continue in summer as in winter.   (Zech. 14:6-8)

This is a good example of the subtlety which can be found in the Old Testament's eschatological expressions of time. Written hundreds of years before Jesus, the more uniform Christian view of time – focussed on Christ's cross and resurrection at one point and his second coming at the other – is not in view. The Old Testament is more diverse in its eschatological expressions of time, although they are still, of course, linked closely with redemption. And since redemption is often thought of in material terms in the Old Testament, as Yahweh's deliverance from adversity in this life, there is a sense in which we see more than one final, definitive act of new creation. There is a sense in some texts that divine acts of new creation occur through cycles of creation, fall, and then redemption, where the old is redeemed in unforeseen ways which can be likened with the original act of creation. Particularly good examples occur in Second Isaiah (43:14-19; 51:9-11), where the redemption of the original Exodus is linked with mythological creation motifs, but due to a "fall" (the Babylonian exile), a new creation is anticipated which will involve a new redemption. Likewise, in several psalms (Pss. 74; 77; 89), the psalmist prays for God's present deliverance in terms which recall creation and sometimes the Exodus. In this way, hope is effectively expressed for a metaphorical new creation in whichever situation of oppression the writer is experiencing at the time of writing.

So it is interesting to note that the new creation which is born of the Exodus, namely the settlement in the land of Canaan, was by no means the final redemption. Instead, it soon led to many further such cycles of creation, fall, and then redemption. These are described in the book of Judges. The people of Israel turn away from Yahweh and worship other gods (fall). Consequently, the people suffer at the hands of their enemies, so call upon Yahweh, and a judge is raised up to deliver them and lead them into a time of new prosperity (new creation). This pattern occurs over and over again. For instance, a complete cycle is given in just the few verses describing Othniel's career as a judge (Judg. 3:7-11).

A scientific analogy

There exist interesting scientific analogies to such an idea of cyclical time, many of which are connected with the idea of "emergence", of a new and unexpected reality emerging from disorder (Chapter 2). Indeed, W. P. Brown (2010: 210–20) has already suggested emergence as a scientific analogy to Second Isaiah's prophecies of new creation from bleak situations of despair.

It is now well known that many aspects of nature operate through cycles of creation which necessitate catastrophe (fall) first. We might view this as a regrettably inefficient situation to be in; and yet it appears to be characteristic of much of the natural world. A well-known example in physics is the phenomenon of "self-organized criticality", where the idea of creation is matched by its destruction and renewal (Bak 1997). Essentially, it describes a state where a system of some kind (be it animal, vegetable, or mineral), is perpetually teetering on the brink of transforming into a new type of existence; it is in a "critical" state which can hardly be said to be stable, yet it retains a kind of stability and creativity by virtue of its perpetual teetering. One of the simplest examples is the behaviour of a simple pile of dry sand. As sand is steadily dropped onto a flat surface, it slowly builds into a conical pile where the sides become steeper and steeper until a certain critical angle is reached. No matter how much more sand is added, the pile retains this critical angle, because avalanches of all sizes occur down the side of the pile. As more sand is added to the top of the pile, so avalanches preserve the balance by taking sand lower down; the critical angle is retained. But the avalanches are random in both size and frequency. Sometimes, even the addition of just a few grains of sand causes a much larger avalanche which spans the whole pile; the pile is therefore said to be in a critical state, and it remains there.

It is not just sand piles which follow self-organized critical behaviour; the examples are many and varied, from animal extinctions preserved in the fossil record, through the frequency and size of earthquakes and volcanic eruptions, the distribution of rivers and streams, the development of fjords in the coastline of Norway, to examples in the human world such as traffic jams and stock market fluctuations. The point is that the critical state, where the system seems to be at its most turbulent, experiencing one avalanche after another on all scales, is often the most favourable state to be in. Not only are the avalanches unavoidable, but they allow the system to explore every corner of its critical state, and to settle into a kind of positive medium of creation matched by destruction. It is annoying to sit in a traffic jam, but ironically, it turns out that this probably allows for a greater flow of traffic than a tightly regulated system where everyone drives at a steady speed. Clearly, examples like this point towards the emergence of new types of dynamic (turbulent) order built through disorder.

The conclusion we can reach from this example is that self-organized criticality is a rather good illustration of a diverse suite of natural phenomena which are perpetually renewed by cycles of destruction and catastrophe. In that sense, we have found a scientific analogy which matches the biblical examples of cycles of creation, fall, and then redemption.

We have found an analogy, but does it provide any new insights? It certainly cannot add any ontological depth to the potential realities behind the biblical texts, since the analogy is drawn from the world of nature, while the texts mostly describe the human world. If there is an insight to be drawn from the analogy, it is perhaps the point that the critical state is by no means an unfortunate state to be in: it may be turbulent, it may bring loss as well as profit, and yet it is quite simply the most favourable state for progress. In our very human, imperfect world, we may likewise welcome the turbulence of cycles of new creation. Fall is regrettable and painful, but virtually inevitable in our broken world, and if redemption comes out of it, then not only have we re-forged our bonds with the divine, but we have also learnt a new lesson, and hopefully grown stronger. All of this is not meant to sermonize, but to give one possible example of how an analogy from science might be developed in a positive theological direction, making clear that it is no more than an analogy, a chance perhaps to acquire a new perspective on old texts.

There is a further theological point which comes out of this. In putting forward my example of self-organized criticality, I have clearly not uncovered an "explanation" of biblical texts, but an analogy which says that cycles we see in the Bible of creation, fall and redemption, resemble in a figurative sense some aspects of the natural world. But since the biblical texts mostly describe the cycles in very *human* situations (deliverance from exile, war, oppression), we do not need a scientific illustration to explain the reality underlying them; they are already part and parcel of human experience. As a result, it would never occur to us that my example of self-organized criticality offers anything deeper than a loose analogy.

But let us now consider other types of texts which describe new creation, texts which use imagery from the *natural* world (such as apocalyptic predictions of the end of the world). We might be inclined to compare the texts with scientific eschatologies, such as those of Tipler and Dyson. But if so, we should remember that the comparisons are operating on the level of analogy just as much as my analogy of self-organized criticality: analogy of texts which are *metaphorical* by their very nature.

If it seems that I am labouring this point concerning analogy and metaphor, it is because it is so under-appreciated in the science–theology field. We have seen that the language of new creation contains many of the motifs of hope in the Bible, and becomes especially focussed on the work and teaching of Jesus in the New Testament, and the hope for a potentially new world after this. We have discussed extensively the question of the potential reality behind the language of new creation, and suggested that, since it always springs from a divine source, it is metaphorical in nature, since it expresses a hope for *divine* redemption. This means that, although many of the images may be attractive to interpretation using the methods of science, there is a real need to take into account both the analogical nature of scientific explanations, and the metaphorical nature of biblical language. Only an integrated *theological* approach is able to form the bridge between them.

CONCLUSIONS

We began this chapter by reviewing scientific perspectives of the end of life on earth and the end of the universe. We saw that the far future appears bleak. On the other hand, in reviewing the biblical material on the theme of new creation, we found a diverse expression of hope in God's purposes. Apocalyptic texts in particular appeared to cast this in terms of the end of this physical world and hope for a new. However, we highlighted the fact that biblical scholarship has debated the extent to which this was ever meant literally. Added to which there is the consideration that eschatological predictions are by their very nature metaphorical at best. Recent work has focussed especially on the resurrection of Jesus as the key component of the new creation, but our preliminary discussion suggested that more sensitive hermeneutical work needs to be done before the resurrection narratives of the Gospels can be read as blueprints for the future. As a way of illustrating the metaphorical dimension in which science might aid interpretation of biblical eschatology we looked – not at models of the end of the world, but at a different area of science altogether – at the cycles of creation and destruction known as "self-organized criticality". We suggested that this might offer a more appropriate scientific analogy for some of the rich new creation material in the Bible than models of the end of the universe, and stressed its role as analogical.

Theological work on eschatology that takes science into account has been relatively scarce, and has not engaged closely with the biblical materials (Jackelén 2006: 959; Wilkinson 2010: 52). Such discussion as there has been has tended to assume that the Bible's apocalyptic texts can be read relatively literally as predicting something of a physical cessation of this world. For this reason, discussion has automatically referred to the predictions of science about the possible fate of our universe. It should be clear by now that I believe that a number of category mistakes appear in this way of thinking. First, the full diversity and subtlety of the new creation motif is not taken into account, and second, the question of whether it was ever meant to be taken so literally as to predict the real end of the world is overlooked. Clearly, this reflects a lack of attention to the kinds of reality the texts might be invoking, and of the many interpretative issues which are raised by biblical scholarship.

If we found in Chapter 6 that science has relatively little to say directly to the Bible's creation motif when the initial and continuing creation is in view, then we have found here that science also has relatively little to say to the eschatological dimension of the creation motif. As we have repeatedly emphasized, the reality of biblical eschatology is considerably more subtle than that spoken to by scientific models of the far future. In the Old Testament it is more prophetic of present-day hopes and concerns, of social and political realities, than it is of the form of the physical universe (although we should not rule the latter option out of court altogether). And although the New Testament suggests a future salvation for the entire cosmos – every stick and stone – it does so in terms of the everyday life of the Christian believer, lived in the experience of the Spirit. The balance can be seen in Trinitarian terms: while the resurrection of Christ points to a *future* universal work of new creation, the eschatological work of the Spirit in every believer points simultaneously to a *present* reality.

Fundamentally, biblical eschatology is an expression of hope first and foremost, a confession of a relationship of faith existing between creature and Creator. Therefore, like any relationship of trust and fidelity, it necessitates a moral dimension which science cannot share. As Jackelén (2006: 962) puts it, it is "the difference between *is* and *ought* ... Biblical eschatology is concerned less with the end of the world than with the end of evil". And as Gunton (1998: 225–6) has pointed out: "The acid test of any cosmological theory ... is the ethic it generates." And so while Tipler's view of the end of the world is an ethic of "technological domination", and while other scientific cosmologies can only offer unremitting pessimism, the New Testament's cosmological theory promotes an eschatological ethic of purity and hope which is lived in the here and now. It is a reality which is, at least at present, largely opaque to science, but no less meaningful for that.

Chapter 10

CONCLUSIONS

SCIENCE AND CREATION: A COMPLEX RELATIONSHIP

Creation is a major theological theme in the Bible, with many diverse strands and layers of meaning, but we have seen that modern science only impacts them on a surprisingly superficial level. While we can pinpoint traces of an ancient scientific view in the texts which is clearly superseded in our modern perspective, yet it serves wider theological aims that are still relevant. In other words, the fact that the Bible's creation texts are drastically outdated from a scientific point of view has not invalidated their various portraits of the relationship between God and creation; indeed, modern science can say very little directly about this relationship. Furthermore, against the reductionist tendencies of science, we found that the Bible takes a much more expansive approach. Its creation texts can rarely be pinned down to a single level of meaning, a single interpretation, or a single explanation, and certainly not an explanation in terms of physical reality alone. The fact that we described a number of very different types of creation text existing alongside each other, some of which, for instance, spoke of creation in mythological terms while others spoke of divine Wisdom, points to the Bible's basic "multiculturalism".

On the other hand, modern science has rendered a service to the Bible's creation texts by indicating that some long-standing interpretations need to be re-assessed. The obvious case in point is the traditional Western Christian reading of Genesis 2–3, which sees it as the story of the Fall (Chapter 7). Evolutionary biology creates severe difficulties for this reading, but at the same time it has inspired fresh modern theologies of creation and redemption which have led to a better appreciation of the subtleties of the biblical texts. Also, the fact that modern cosmology and biology highlight evolutionary views of the universe has led to a fresh appreciation of the idea of *creatio continua*, as a supplement to the consensus theological view of *creatio ex nihilo* (Chapter 6). In a similar way, the scientific predictions of the far future of our universe have led to interest in the apocalyptic texts of the Bible, and in its idea of new creation, which we interpreted in terms of a third category of creation, *creatio ex vetere* (Chapter 9). So we can see that science has played an important part in renewing appreciation of biblical ideas of creation, even if it is unable to shed much direct light on these ideas themselves. Ultimately the texts say rather little about the physical makeup of the world, but much about God's creative relationship with it, and about who God is.

WHO IS GOD-THE-CREATOR?

Unitary yet diverse

An appealing consistency has begun to surface between the categories of creation *ex nihilo*, *continua* and *ex vetere*. Each has shown resonances with the biblical motif of creation, and each has been subjected to scientific "explanations", but each has revealed theological depths which go beyond what a physical explanation might provide. Furthermore, although each category has ostensibly described an idea of how creation comes about, yet in reality, each describes an idea about God's relationship with the world.

- The category of *creatio ex nihilo* has been linked with the Big Bang model, but we saw that it was best expressed as a statement of God's transcendence. This was the main evidence which allowed us to link this category with biblical theologies of creation, which otherwise do not show explicit awareness of the idea that creation might come "from nothing". They do, however, frequently express God's transcendent relationship with the world, and Genesis 1 is a good example.
- The category of *creatio continua* has attractive links with cosmological and biological evolution, and with the scientific idea of "emergence", but it is most clearly an expression of God's immanence. Biblical texts which paint God in intimate relationship with humans and animals are the best illustration of this view.
- Finally, the category of *creatio ex vetere* has been connected with physical cosmologies, and especially with discussion of the end of the universe. However, it is fundamentally a descriptive term for God's redemptive activity in creation, and this is how it is best connected with the resurrection of Jesus, the supreme redemptive action in Christian belief. There are numerous examples of other biblical texts which fall into the category of "new creation", especially in the Hebrew prophets, which may be said to describe a kind of creation

"from the old" for social and political realities, but not necessarily meaning a literal end to this physical world.

Convenient as they are, these categories are simplifications for what are sometimes very subtle and complex portraits of God in the biblical texts. They are also anachronisms, but then so are key divine attributes such as "transcendent" and "immanent". These later categories and terms can be identified with various biblical texts, but the Bible develops no equivalent convenient terminology itself. Biblical talk is of God as unitary, but its portraits of God and of God's works in creation are subtle and diverse. The tension between these two observations has important implications for the way we understand creation language.

We have noticed that it is inaccurate to speak of a single theology of creation in the Bible, but rather biblical theologies of creation, and biblical views of creation. This is yet another element of the Bible's paradoxical presentation of God, since we have seen that the biblical talk of creation is another way of speaking of God's nature. If the Bible is capable of speaking of God's transcendent creative actions one moment, it is equally capable of speaking of God's immanent creative actions the next, and of God's redemptive actions a little later. The paradox cannot be faced unless we acknowledge that our natural tendency is to try to explain diversity by simplifying – to provide simplified models for the complex and the baffling. The biblical portraits of God, however, are highly resistant to such simplifying, just as they are resistant to the explanatory powers of science. The God of the Bible may be unitary, but may not be unified or simplified in any straightforward way, without flattening or misrepresenting the biblical witness. Therefore, the biblical God is both unitary and diverse, just as biblical talk of creation may be seen as both unitary and diverse.

The message is that the three categories of creation are not different types of creative work that God does. As far as the Bible seems to be concerned, God does one single job of work, but paradoxically it appears to take on different dimensions, or to be separable into quite different, incompatible compartments in our perception. From that point of view, God's work of creation *ex nihilo*, *continua* and *ex vetere* are not three different actions, but one creative action, while at the same time they point to the diversity of the unitary God. It is no accident that this is reminiscent of Trinitarian language of God – three in one and one in three – for it was through observations such as these, of God's diverse work in the theatres of creation and redemption, that the three persons of the Trinity came to be recognized and distinguished as such. But the three categories of creative work are not to be identified with the three persons of the Trinity; rather, it is distinctions such as these which have been important in the development of Trinitarian thinking. And modern theological scholarship tends to underscore this point by highlighting the centrality of the doctrine of the

Trinity, asserting that it is within the doctrine of the Trinity that all other theological ideas find their home, that they are all various applications of faith in God as Trinity (e.g. Webster 2003: 43). With this all-embracing claim in mind, we turn now to consider how the idea of God as Trinity can take up what we have said about creation, science and the Bible.

The Trinity, science and creation

In § "Creation and the beginnings of the idea of God as Trinity" in Chapter 4 we argued that, in spite of the problem of anachronism, it makes good hermeneutical sense to develop a Trinitarian reading of the Bible's creation material. Not only does this respect the canonical context in which the texts are read as the foundational basis of Christianity, but it also holds the paradox of divine immanence and transcendence in balance. It therefore allows us to maintain the Bible's theistic stance over and against the pervasive spirit of Deism of our modern world.

Two advantages arise straightaway from a Trinitarian view of creation.

First, it highlights the simultaneously creative and redemptive roles of the Son (Col. 1:14-15), so that creation cannot be understood apart from its completion and perfection. The problem of theodicy is not neglected, but it is caught up in an eschatological resolution, where "pain will be no more" (Rev. 21:4).

Second, in Christ, God has become visible and physical; by no means an intangible and impersonal power, nor an abstract philosophical concept, but a human being like us (Wilkinson 2009b). The Creator has therefore become intimately connected with creation at its most basic level, that of material and "flesh". As has often been emphasized in eastern Orthodox theologies, this leads to a sense in which ordinary matter and ordinary creatures might be "deified" or "divinized", that is, mysteriously glorified and perfected: taken up into God's real being, where we become "participants of the divine nature" (2 Pet. 1:4). The transfiguration of Christ (e.g. Mk 9:1-10, cf. 2 Pet. 1:16-18) and his resurrection illustrate that his material flesh, this small part of our universe, has already taken part in the eschatological process (Edwards 2009: 181).

Adopting a Trinitarian view can also bring a more subtle understanding of the created world. The "social doctrine of the Trinity", which emphasizes the three divine persons existing in dynamic relational terms with each other, has achieved great theological currency in recent decades, but it is arguably a re-discovery of Patristic ways of thinking. One of its strong points is that it has the effect of enlivening all of creation, not only humans. By emphasizing the relationships (perhaps even to the point of interdependence, § "Creation and narrative" in Chapter 4) between the three persons who are God, and also between God and the created universe, we emphasize the fact that the non-human creation has its own creational responsibilities with respect to God, but also its own freedom. Such an emphasis on freedom is necessary if, for instance, we wish to uphold the biblical texts which speak of the whole of creation joining in praise of God (e.g. Isa. 55:12). In this way, we give the entire cosmos a worshipping life of its own, simply by virtue of its being; it is no longer to be seen as a bare physicality to be explained by science, nor exploited by technology. And this leads to another crucial point: the Bible's creation texts cannot be fully understood for what they are outside of the dimension of praise and worship, a dimension which those who treat this as a purely cerebral debate often fail to grasp (§ "Conclusions" in Chapter 4).

Therefore, if humans have been made as free creatures existing in relationship with God, and they respond with worship, then the same must be said of the rest of the universe: God has given it *freedom* and autonomy to be what God has created it to be, but God also *supports* it, not least by continuously creating and renewing it. These are relational terms, and they do not translate well into the language of science. Indeed, this is probably an advantage, because attempts to articulate divine work in the world using scientific language have a tendency to fall into "god of the gaps" approaches, or into a subtle deism, especially when we speak of divine action as an "intervention". And when we remember that all descriptions of divine work are metaphorical in any case, it is clear that scientific descriptions have no inbuilt authority over relational descriptions; it is simply a case of using whichever type of metaphor is most successful. And certainly, when faith in God as Trinity is in view relational metaphors lend themselves more easily to a description of God's interaction with the world than scientific metaphors.

But this does not mean that we should speak only in relational terms when we describe God's work. Speaking in scientific terms can complement the age-old theological conviction that God is faithful, abiding and dependable: full of "steadfast love", and delighting in law and order (e.g. Exod. 34:6-7). An affinity with law is an enduring component of God's personality expressed through much of the Bible, enshrined especially in the "Law of Moses" (§"Creation and narrative" in Chapter 4), but also in the covenants with Noah, Abraham and David. It is hardly surprising that, given such a picture, the laws of nature might be said to flow from God's being. The laws of nature themselves are credited with practically divine status in some branches of physics (§"The laws of nature" in Chapter 2), and it is argued that the empirical methodology of modern science arose from the Christian doctrine of creation, which holds that creation is orderly and "good", reflecting God's nature. In short, there is a more than passing resemblance between the presuppositions of modern science and the divine law-giver of Judaism and Christianity. The laws of nature are not necessarily a created theoretical construct apart from

God, but might be manifestations of God's very nature (McGrath [2002] 2006a: 225–32).

Chance, law and contingency revisited

As we saw in Chapter 2, there are many subtleties contained within the umbrella term "laws of nature", including the paradoxical importance of random events, which might approach law-like behaviour when a statistical (i.e. probabilistic) approach is taken. The modern sciences see a complex interplay of both chance and necessity at work in the natural world, and different sciences discern their significance differently.

This has consequences for models of God (Clayton 2008: 41–2). If we emphasize the importance of law over chance in shaping the world, we emphasize a deterministic view of the world which sees a theological parallel in the picture of the transcendent law-giver, and possibly even the absent God of deism. If, on the other hand, we highlight the importance of chance and emergence over law we emphasize freshness and novelty at the heart of creation, and our view of God changes accordingly. This latter view accorded by chance has not, however, been met with ready acceptance in theological circles, and there has been some concern to downplay the key role allotted to chance in evolutionary biology, by interpreting evolution in more-or-less teleological terms (Fergusson 2009: 78). However, this anxiety is probably misplaced, because chance in creation can be likened to the *creatio continua* model of God, and to the immanent work of the Spirit. Then, we find that the created world may be seen as gifted with a fundamental creative liberty which the deterministic view otherwise squashes. That humans and other creatures possess free will is no longer the philosophical conundrum that it is in a determined universe, but a marker of God's grace in creating and supporting the world to grow to fruition in freedom.

These two angles need not be incompatible. They can be brought together in a view where the world is seen to develop by chance within the limits of the laws imposed upon it. Such a world is able to explore its full potentialities without being "controlled" (Carr 2004: 939). And it is made possible by a Creator-creation relationship not unlike that of a parent and child, a metaphor used frequently by the Bible (e.g. Isa. 66:13; Lk. 11:11-13). A God who makes the world by allowing it to make itself is like a parent who allows her child to learn and mature through free and creative play. There are boundaries, but they encourage rather than limit creativity; they are adaptive.

Taking all of this together, it would seem important therefore to keep these diverse models of God in mind simultaneously, something which the idea of God as Trinity does straightforwardly.

Furthermore, contrary to the widespread view that chance is difficult to integrate into theologies of creation, it can be seen to promote a strong view of the contingency of the creative process. We outlined two types of contingency in Chapter 2: that which arises theologically from the fact the cosmos exists in the first place, and that which arises scientifically, from the fact that the universe is continuously evolving into being. In Chapter 6 we explored the category of *creatio continua* and pointed out that, although it resembles this second (evolutionary) contingency, it is theological, and therefore makes a different kind of statement. Theological contingency and evolutionary contingency are not identical, although they can be related to each other analogously. But it is apparent that the anxiety which some feel about incorporating chance into theologies of creation arises because these two forms of contingency are easily confused. A similar confusion arises in the tendency of many theologians to look for "purpose" and teleology in evolution. In doing so, they misunderstand the science, which is staunchly resistant to applying such "from above" theological explanations when there is no scientific warrant to do so (Peters 2010: 925–9). A belief in teleology is wormwood to many scientists who, by contrast, point to the dominant force of chance driving biological evolution, such that there can be no purposive direction to it whatsoever (Rolston 2005: 222). And although it is often said that evolution shows signs of progress towards life forms of greater complexity and diversity (Nichols 2002: 193–5), even this is debatable (Schloss 2002: 72–6). In any case, talk of progress or "purpose" in evolution raises theological difficulties of its own, because it implies divine "guidance" behind evolutionary processes, and raises the problems which flow from deistic talk of divine "intervention". After all, why should some aspects of nature be seen as more guided than others? Why should evolution be seen as more directed than another chance physical process, such as the falling of a leaf?

A more studiously theistic view would be open to evolutionary contingency and the role of chance in evolution, seeing it theologically as an expression of God's gift of *freedom* to the world, rather than a problem to be avoided. The chance which is so crucial to the operation of evolution is something of the same chance which decides the falling of a leaf. They are both contingent processes in a *scientific* sense, and are only *theologically* contingent in the sense that all created processes are theologically contingent upon God. In other words, evolutionary chance is no more theologically "creative" than the chance which decides the falling of a leaf. The theological contingency of the *creatio continua* viewpoint, on the other hand, makes a very different kind of statement: it points to the novelty and freshness of *divine action* in creation, and only relates to the scientific idea of chance by means of analogy. In short, *creatio continua* is not the same as evolution.

The logos *and the laws of physics*

A Trinitarian perspective can make further sense of the ways in which sci-entific and divine contingencies complement each other, especially if we consider Christ, who forms the bridge by means of his incarnation.

Divine Wisdom, a key component of the creation motif in the Old Tes-tament, was taken up by the New Testament and expressed particularly through the person of Jesus of Nazareth (§"Creation and Christ" in Chapter 4). This is clear in John's device of the *logos*. And so we see the paradoxical claim that a human being who died as a common criminal was also respon-sible for making the world "In the beginning" (Jn 1:1). The Redeemer must also be the Creator. The association between Christ and Wisdom means that he in some sense embodies divine principles of organization and law, including that which is recorded in Scripture (i.e. Torah). Indeed, Mat-thew's Jesus makes this very point: "Do not think that I have come to abol-ish the law or the prophets; I have come not to abolish but to fulfill" (Mt. 5:17). It is just a small step from saying that Jesus embodies scriptural law (and prophecy) to saying that he embodies all divine Wisdom, including that which has been discerned in the natural world by science. Indeed, we have already begun to make the point that Old Testament expressions of the creation motif can see law (Torah) and creation (natural law) in some-thing of a holistic symbiosis (§"Creation and narrative", in Chapter 4). And there is a venerable tradition going back to medieval times that the natural world constitutes a "book" revealing God's creative work, in parallel with the book of Scripture (Harrison 1998: 3). A similar connection can be made between Christ and science through the *logos* concept which, whether we trace it into John's Gospel through Stoic thought or the Jewish Wisdom tra-dition, still encapsulates the idea that "all things came into being through him" (Jn 1:3). Therefore, by virtue of his role in creation as the *logos* and the embodiment of divine Wisdom, it makes sense to affirm Christ as contain-ing "all the treasures of wisdom and knowledge" (Col. 2:3; cf. Col. 1:15-20 and Heb. 1:3). This means that he must also contain the laws of nature as sought by scientists, and not only the predictive, mathematically regular laws, but also those which give birth to complex and emergent properties. In short, Christ as *logos* must embody both chance and necessity, the prin-ciples behind all creative processes in the universe. And if this is the case, then the Spirit can be seen as the divine communicator of these principles to the creatures of the world, the divine spark which actuates and breathes life into all creative processes. This is what lies behind Pannenberg's idea of the Spirit as a divine creative field, by analogy with the electric, magnetic and gravitational fields of physics (Pannenberg 1994: 209–10).

Of course, it is one thing to speak of the Spirit – the invisible, intangible divine presence – as the mediator of the laws of nature (especially if the Spirit can be likened to a physical field), but it is quite another to speak of the incarnate Christ – a physical being like us – as *embodying* the laws of nature. In what sense can this be true? Although the term "incarnation" is later than the New Testament, it is a handy codeword for the New Testament's insistence that Christ is a human being exactly like us, made of "flesh and bones" (e.g. Lk. 24:39; Jn 1:14; 1 Jn 4:2; 2 Jn 1:7). Therefore, in whatever sense we affirm that Christ embodies the laws of nature, the doctrine of the incarnation means that we must affirm it in his very human flesh and bones.

One way of understanding this is to turn to the anthropic principle, and the idea that the physical constants and laws of physics have been deliberately "finely tuned" to produce intelligent human life like us. If so, Christ embodies these laws because they were purposely designed to produce him in his flesh and bones (G. L. Murphy 1994: 111). However, this is a highly controversial claim, and few philosophers or theologians (let alone scientists) would interpret the anthropic principle so strongly (Ward 2008: 236–9), nor posit Christ as the *telos* of science in such a Teilhardian way.

Another possibility for understanding how Christ might be said to embody the laws of nature is hinted at by one important biblical text: "Then God said, 'Let us make humankind in our image, according to our likeness'" (Gen. 1:26). How exactly this text is to be understood has been endlessly debated. One important interpretation, due to Augustine, sees the "image of God" based in human rationality, an intimation of the divine mind implanted into humans (McGrath [2002] 2006a: 200–204). Therefore, if the incarnate Christ is truly the embodiment of divine Wisdom then it would be reasonable to expect that his human nature is a reflection of this – that he is most certainly in God's image by virtue of his rationality – and that therefore other humans who share his image and his human nature might also be able to probe the depths of divine Wisdom through rational enquiry.

In this way, we have the basis for constructing a theology of science (cf. the "scientific theology" of McGrath [2002] 2006b: 297–313). It has often been wondered by more philosophically minded scientists just why it is that science in general, and mathematics in particular, are so well-suited to the act of describing the physical world. Humanly speaking, this success has remained something of a mystery; the world need not have been so amenable to our rationality, unless there is deep reason behind it all, and that "we have the mind of Christ" (1 Cor. 2:16). The Bible's creation texts therefore supply us with an explanation for the miracle of modern science, namely its unstoppable success in understanding the physical world: it is because science taps directly into the mind which made it all.

THE BIBLE AND SCIENCE

In this book, we have attempted to demonstrate a way to bring the Bible into sustained focus in the science–religion dialogue.

In this, we have steered a course between two clashing rocks: a creation faith expressed in terms of biblical literalism on the one hand, and a position that holds scant regard to the form and relevance of the Bible's creation texts on the other. We have held the creaturely but hallowed nature of the Bible as central. And we have argued that our course is best steered by engaging with both modern critical biblical scholarship and with modern science, within the context of a Trinitarian theological framework. In this way, we have argued that a living faith finds a means to appropriate the Bible's creation theologies and to engage constructively with science.

Along the way, we have explored many of the ways in which science speaks to the biblical creation texts. By and large, we have discovered that the biblical texts are remarkably resilient to the imperialistic tendencies of science. They have consistently pointed to a reality beyond that revealed by modern science, and to a creation faith that is not constrained by scientific discoveries, but is in many ways enriched by them. This is a message clearly at odds with the popular conception that science has disproved the Bible. But it is apparent that, as far as the nature of creation is concerned, science can only get us so far.

BIBLIOGRAPHY

Albright, John R. 2009. "Time and Eternity: Hymnic, Biblical, Scientific, and Theological Views". *Zygon* 44: 989–96

Alexander, Denis R. 2008. *Creation or Evolution? Do We Have to Choose?* Oxford: Monarch.

Alexander, Philip S. 1992. "Early Jewish Geography". In *The Anchor Bible Dictionary*, D. N. Freedman (ed.), II: 977–88. New York: Doubleday.

Allison, Dale C. 1998. *Jesus of Nazareth: Millenarian Prophet*. Minneapolis, MN: Fortress.

Allison, Dale C., Marcus J. Borg, John Dominic Crossan, Stephen J. Patterson & Robert J. Miller (eds) 2001. *The Apocalyptic Jesus: A Debate*. Santa Rosa, CA: Polebridge.

Anderson, David 2009. "Creation, Redemption and Eschatology". In *Should Christians Embrace Evolution? Biblical and Scientific Responses*, Norman C. Nevin (ed.), 73–92. Nottingham: IVP.

Averbeck, Richard E. 2004. "Ancient Near Eastern Mythography as It Relates to Historiography in the Hebrew Bible: Genesis 3 and the Cosmic Battle". In *The Future of Biblical Archaeology: Reassessing Methodologies and Assumptions*, James K. Hoffmeier & Alan Millard (eds), 328–56. Grand Rapids, MI: Eerdmans.

Ayala, Francisco J. 2009. "Being Human after Darwin". In *Theology After Darwin*, Michael S. Northcott & R. J. Berry (eds), 89–105. Milton Keynes: Paternoster.

Bailey, Lloyd R. 1989. *Noah: The Person and the Story in History and Tradition*. Columbia, SC: University of South Carolina Press.

Bak, Per 1997. *How Nature Works: The Science of Self-Organized Criticality*. Oxford: Oxford University Press.

Barbour, Ian G. [1974] 1976. *Myth, Models and Paradigms: A Comparative Study in Science and Religion*. New York: HarperSanFrancisco.

Barbour, Ian G. 1997. *Religion and Science: Historical and Contemporary Issues*. New York: HarperOne.

Barker, Margaret 2010. *Creation: A Biblical Vision for the Environment*. London: T. & T. Clark.

Barr, James [1977] 1981. *Fundamentalism*. London: SCM.

Barr, James 1984. *Escaping from Fundamentalism*. London: SCM.

Bartlett, Robert 2008. *The Natural and the Supernatural in the Middle Ages: The Wiles Lectures given at the Queen's University of Belfast, 2006*. Cambridge: Cambridge University Press.

Barton, Stephen C. 2009. "'Male and Female He Created Them' (Genesis 1:27): Interpreting Gender after Darwin". In *Reading Genesis after Darwin*, Stephen C. Barton & David Wilkinson (eds), 181–201. Oxford: Oxford University Press.

Barton, Stephen C. & David Wilkinson 2009. "Introduction". In *Reading Genesis after Darwin*, Stephen C. Barton & David Wilkinson (eds), xi–xiv. Oxford: Oxford University Press.

Bentor, Y. K. 1989. "Geological Events in the Bible". *Terra Nova* 1: 326–38.

Berry, R. J. [1988] 2001. *God and Evolution: Creation, Evolution and the Bible*. Vancouver: Regent College Publishing.

Berry, R. J. 1999. "This Cursed Earth: Is 'the Fall' Credible?". *Science and Christian Belief* 11: 29–49.

Berry, R. J. 2009. "Did Darwin Dethrone Humankind?". In *Darwin, Creation and the Fall: Theological Challenges*, R. J. Berry & T. A. Noble (eds), 30–74. Nottingham: Apollos.

Berry, R. J. & T. A. Noble 2009. "Foreword". In *Darwin, Creation and the Fall: Theological Challenges*, R. J. Berry & T. A. Noble (eds), 11–14. Nottingham: Apollos.

Bimson, John J. 2009. "Doctrines of the Fall and Sin After Darwin". In *Theology After Darwin*, Michael S. Northcott & R. J. Berry (eds), 106–22. Milton Keynes: Paternoster.

Blocher, Henri 2009. "The Theology of the Fall and the Origins of Evil". In *Darwin, Creation and the Fall: Theological Challenges*, R. J. Berry & T. A. Noble (eds), 149–72. Nottingham: Apollos.

Briggs, Richard S. 2009. "The Hermeneutics of Reading Genesis after Darwin". In *Reading Genesis after Darwin*, Stephen C. Barton & David Wilkinson (eds), 57–71. Oxford: Oxford University Press.

Brooke, John Hedley 1991. *Science and Religion: Some Historical Perspectives*. Cambridge: Cambridge University Press.

Brooke, John Hedley 1996. "Science and Theology in the Enlightenment". In *Religion and Science: History, Method, Dialogue*, W. Mark Richardson & Wesley J. Wildman (eds), 7–27. New York: Routledge.

Brown, Robert P. 1975. "On the Necessary Imperfection of Creation: Irenaeus' *Adversus Haereses* IV, 38". *Scottish Journal of Theology* 28: 17–25.

Brown, Warren S. 1998. "Cognitive Contributions to Soul". In *Whatever Happened to the Soul? Scientific and Theological Portraits of Human Nature*, Warren S. Brown, Nancey Murphy & H. Newton Malony (eds), 99–125. Minneapolis, MN: Fortress.

Brown, William P. 2010. *The Seven Pillars of Creation: The Bible, Science, and the Ecology of Wonder*. Oxford: Oxford University Press.

Brueggemann, Walter 1997. *Theology of the Old Testament: Testimony, Dispute, Advocacy*. Minneapolis, MN: Fortress.

Buckley, Michael J. 1987. *At the Origins of Modern Atheism*. New Haven, CT: Yale University Press.

Bultmann, Rudolf 1960. *Jesus Christ and Mythology*. London: SCM.

Burge, Ted 2005. *Science and the Bible: Evidence-Based Christian Belief*. Philadelphia, PA: Templeton Foundation Press.

Caird, G. B. 1980. *The Language and Imagery of the Bible*. London: Duckworth.

Carlson, Richard F. & Tremper Longman III 2010. *Science, Creation and the Bible: Reconciling Rival Theories of Origins*. Downers Grove, IL: IVP.

Carr, Paul. H. 2004. "Does God Play Dice? Insights from the Fractal Geometry of Nature". *Zygon* 39: 933–40.

Clayton, Philip 2008. "Contemporary Philosophical Concepts of Laws of Nature: The Quest for Broad Explanatory Consonance". In *Creation: Law and Probability*, Fraser Watts (ed.), 37–58. Aldershot: Ashgate.

Cogan, Mordecai 1992. "Chronology". In *The Anchor Bible Dictionary*, D. N. Freedman (ed.), I: 1002–11. New York: Doubleday.

Cohn, Norman 1996. *Noah's Flood: The Genesis Story in Western Thought*. New Haven, CT: Yale University Press.

Collins, Adela Yarbro 2007. *Mark: A Commentary*. Minneapolis, MN: Fortress.

Collins, C. John 2011. *Did Adam and Eve Really Exist? Who They Were and Why it Matters.* Nottingham: IVP.

Conway Morris, Simon 2003. *Life's Solution: Inevitable Humans in a Lonely Universe.* Cambridge: Cambridge University Press.

Copan, Paul & William Lane Craig 2004. *Creation out of Nothing: A Biblical, Philosophical, and Scientific Exploration.* Grand Rapids, MI: Baker Academic and Apollos.

Cormack, Lesley B. 2009. "That Medieval Christians Taught That the Earth Was Flat". In *Galileo Goes to Jail and Other Myths about Science and Religion*, Ronald L. Numbers (ed.), 28–34. Cambridge, MA: Harvard University Press.

Corner, Mark 2005. *Signs of God: Miracles and their Interpretation.* Aldershot: Ashgate.

Cross, Frank Moore 1973. *Canaanite Myth and Hebrew Epic: Essays in the History of the Religion of Israel.* Cambridge, MA: Harvard University Press.

Cullmann, Oscar 1951. *Christ and Time: The Primitive Christian Conception of Time and History.* London: SCM.

Davies, Eryl W. 1995. *Numbers.* New Century Bible Commentary. Grand Rapids, MI: Eerdmans.

Davis, Ellen F. 2009. *Scripture, Culture, and Agriculture: An Agrarian Reading of the Bible.* Cambridge: Cambridge University Press.

Dawkins, Richard 1995. *River out of Eden: A Darwinian View of Life.* London: Weidenfeld & Nicolson.

Day, John 1985. *God's Conflict with the Dragon and the Sea: Echoes of a Canaanite Myth in the Old Testament.* Cambridge: Cambridge University Press.

Day, John 1992. *Psalms.* Sheffield: Sheffield Academic Press.

Day, John 2000. *Yahweh and the Gods and Goddesses of Canaan.* Sheffield: Sheffield University Press.

Deane-Drummond, Celia 2009. *Christ and Evolution: Wonder and Wisdom.* Minneapolis, MN: Fortress.

Dell, Katharine 2000. *"Get Wisdom, Get Insight": An Introduction to Israel's Wisdom Literature.* London: Darton, Longman & Todd.

Dobson, Geoffrey P. 2005. *A Chaos of Delight: Science, Religion and Myth and the Shaping of Western Thought.* London: Equinox.

Douglas, Mary [1966] 2002. *Purity and Danger: An Analysis of Concept of Pollution and Taboo.* London: Routledge.

Dunn, James D. G. [1980] 1989 *Christology in the Making: A New Testament Inquiry into the Origins of the Doctrine of the Incarnation.* London: SCM.

Dunn, James D. G. 1988. *Romans 1–8.* Dallas, TX: Word.

Dunn, James D. G. 2011. *Jesus, Paul, and the Gospels.* Grand Rapids, MI: Eerdmans.

Dyson, Freeman J. [1979] 2002. "Time without End: Physics and Biology in an Open Universe". In *The Far-Future Universe: Eschatology from a Cosmic Perspective*, George F. R. Ellis (ed.), 103–39. Philadelphia, PA: Templeton Foundation Press.

Edwards, Denis 2009. "Hope for Creation After Darwin: The Redemption of 'All Things'". In *Theology After Darwin*, Michael S. Northcott & R. J. Berry (eds), 171–89. Milton Keynes: Paternoster.

Ellis, George F. R. 2008. "Multiverses and Ultimate Causation". In *Creation: Law and Probability*, Fraser Watts (ed.), 59–80. Aldershot: Ashgate.

Enns, Peter 2012. *The Evolution of Adam: What the Bible Does and Doesn't Say About Human Origins.* Grand Rapids, MI: Brazos.

Farrer, Austin [1966] 2009. *A Science of God?* London: SPCK.

Fatoorchi, Pirooz 2010. "Four Conceptions of *Creatio ex Nihilo* and the Compatibility Questions". In *Creation and the God of Abraham*, David B. Burrell, Carlo Cogliati & Janet M. Soskice (eds), 91–106. Cambridge: Cambridge University Press.

Fergusson, David A. S. 1998. *The Cosmos and the Creator: An Introduction to the Theology of Creation.* London: SPCK.

Fergusson, David 2009. "Darwin and Providence". In *Theology After Darwin*, Michael S. Northcott & R. J. Berry (eds), 73–88. Milton Keynes: Paternoster.

Finlay, Graeme & Stephen Pattemore 2009. "Christian Theology and Neo-Darwinism are Compatible". In *Debating Darwin. Two Debates: Is Darwinism True and Does it Matter?* Graeme Finlay, Stephen Lloyd, Stephen Pattemore & David Swift (eds), 31–67. Milton Keynes: Paternoster.

Frankfort, H., H. A. Frankfort, John A. Wilson & Thorkild Jacobsen [1946] 1949. *Before Philosophy: The Intellectual Adventure of Ancient Man. An Essay on Speculative Thought in the Ancient Near East*. Harmondsworth: Penguin.

Fretheim, Terence E. 2005. *God and World in the Old Testament: A Relational Theology of Creation*. Nashville, TN: Abingdon.

Funk, Robert W., Roy W. Hoover & the Jesus Seminar 1993. *The Five Gospels: The Search for the Authentic Words of Jesus*. New York: HarperSanFrancisco.

Garner, Mandy 2009. "To Infinities and Beyond ...". *Cam: Cambridge Alumni Magazine* 58: 30–33.

Ginzberg, Louis 2003. *Legends of the Jews. Volume One: Bible Times and Characters From the Creation to Moses in the Wilderness*. Philadelphia, PA: Jewish Publication Society.

Gould, Stephen Jay [1990] 2000. *Wonderful Life: The Burgess Shale and the Nature of History*. London: Vintage.

Graves, Robert & Raphael Patai [1963] 2005. *Hebrew Myths: The Book of Genesis*. Manchester: Carcanet.

Gunkel, Hermann 1997. *Genesis*, Mark E. Biddle (trans.). Macon, GA: Mercer University Press.

Gunton, Colin E. 1998. *The Triune Creator: A Historical and Systematic Study*. Grand Rapids, MI: Eerdmans.

Hamilton, Victor P. 1990. *The Book of Genesis Chapters 1–17*. Grand Rapids, MI: Eerdmans.

Hanson, Paul D. 1975. *The Dawn of Apocalyptic*. Philadelphia, PA: Fortress.

Hardy, Daniel W. 1996. *God's Ways with the World: Thinking and Practising Christian Faith*. Edinburgh: T. & T. Clark.

Harris, Mark J. 2007. "How did Moses Part the Red Sea? Science as Salvation in the Exodus Tradition". In *Moses in Biblical and Extra-Biblical Traditions*, Axel Graupner & Michael Wolter (eds), 5–31. Berlin: de Gruyter.

Harrison, Peter 1998. *The Bible, Protestantism, and the Rise of Natural Science*. Cambridge: Cambridge University Press.

Harrison, Peter 2008. "The Development of the Concept of Laws of Nature". In *Creation: Law and Probability*, Fraser Watts (ed.), 13–35. Aldershot: Ashgate.

Hawking, Stephen W. 1988. *A Brief History of Time: From the Big Bang to Black Holes*. London: Bantam.

Hawking, Stephen & Leonard Mlodinow 2010. *The Grand Design*. London: Bantam.

Heisenberg, Werner 1989. *Physics and Philosophy: The Revolution in Modern Science*. London: Penguin.

Hills, Phil & Norman Nevin 2009. "Conclusion: Should Christians Embrace Evolution?". In *Should Christians Embrace Evolution? Biblical and Scientific Responses*, Norman C. Nevin (ed.), 210–20. Nottingham: IVP.

Hodgson, Peter E. 2005. *Theology and Modern Physics*. Aldershot: Ashgate.

Horrell, David G. 2010. *The Bible and the Environment: Towards a Critical Ecological Biblical Theology*. London: Equinox.

Høyrup, Jens 1992. "Mathematics, Algebra, and Geometry". In *The Anchor Bible Dictionary*, D. N. Freedman (ed.), IV: 602–12. New York: Doubleday.

Hurtado, Larry W. 2003. *Lord Jesus Christ: Devotion to Jesus in Earliest Christianity*. Grand Rapids, MI: Eerdmans.

Hurtado, Larry W. 2005. *How on Earth Did Jesus Become a God? Historical Questions about Earliest Devotion to Jesus.* Grand Rapids, MI: Eerdmans.

Jackelén, Antje 2005. *Time and Eternity: The Question of Time in Church, Science, and Theology.* Philadelphia, PA: Templeton Foundation Press.

Jackelén, Antje 2006. "A Relativistic Eschatology: Time, Eternity, and Eschatology in Light of the Physics of Relativity". *Zygon* 41: 955–73.

Jaki, Stanley L. 1987. "The Universe In The Bible And In Modern Science". *Ex auditu* 3: 137–47.

Jastrow, Robert 1992. *God and the Astronomers.* New York: W. W. Norton.

Jeans, James 1937. *The Mysterious Universe.* Cambridge: Cambridge University Press.

Kelly, J. N. D. [1960] 1977. *Early Christian Doctrines.* London: A. & C. Black.

Kraus, Hans-Joachim 1989. *Psalms 60–150: A Commentary.* Minneapolis, MN: Augsburg.

Krauss, Lawrence M. 2012. *A Universe From Nothing: Why There Is Something Rather Than Nothing.* New York: Free Press.

Kugel, James L. 1997. *The Bible As It Was.* Cambridge, MA: Belknap Press.

Lamoureux, Denis O. 2008. *Evolutionary Creation: A Christian Approach to Evolution.* Cambridge: Lutterworth.

Lennox, John C. 2011. *Seven Days That Divide the World: The Beginning According to Genesis and Science.* Grand Rapids, MI: Zondervan.

Levenson, Jon D. 1985. *Sinai and Zion: An Entry into the Jewish Bible.* New York: HarperSanFrancisco.

Lévy-Bruhl, Lucien 1923. *Primitive Mentality.* London: George Allen & Unwin.

Lloyd, Stephen 2009. "Christian Theology and Neo-Darwinism are Incompatible: An Argument from the Resurrection". In *Debating Darwin. Two Debates: Is Darwinism True and Does it Matter?* Graeme Finlay, Stephen Lloyd, Stephen Pattemore & David Swift (eds), 1–29. Milton Keynes: Paternoster.

Louth, Andrew 2009. "The Six Days of Creation According to the Greek Fathers". In *Reading Genesis after Darwin*, Stephen C. Barton & David Wilkinson (eds), 39–55. Oxford: Oxford University Press.

Lucas, Ernest [1989] 2005. *Can We Believe Genesis Today? The Bible and the Questions of Science.* Nottingham: IVP.

Mackey, James P. 2006. *Christianity and Creation: The Essence of the Christian Faith and Its Future Among Religions. A Systematic Theology.* New York: Continuum.

Macquarrie, John 1990. *Jesus Christ in Modern Thought.* London: SCM.

Marcus, Joel 2009. *Mark 8-16: A New Translation with Introduction and Commentary.* The Anchor Yale Bible. New Haven, CT: Yale University Press.

Mascall, E. L. 1956. *Christian Theology and Natural Science: Some Questions on Their Relations.* London: Longmans, Green.

McCalla, Arthur 2006. *The Creationist Debate: The Encounter between the Bible and the Historical Mind.* London: Continuum.

McGrath, Alister E. [2002] 2006a. *A Scientific Theology: 1. Nature.* Edinburgh: T. & T. Clark.

McGrath, Alister E. [2002] 2006b. *A Scientific Theology: 2. Reality.* Edinburgh: T. & T. Clark.

McGrath, Alister E. [2003] 2006c. *A Scientific Theology: 3. Theory.* Edinburgh: T. & T. Clark.

Miller, J. Maxwell & John H. Hayes 1986. *A History of Ancient Israel and Judah.* London: SCM.

Moltmann, Jürgen 1985. *God in Creation: An Ecological Doctrine of Creation.* London: SCM.

Moore, Aubrey [1889] 1891. "The Christian Doctrine of God". In *Lux Mundi: A Series of Studies in the Religion of the Incarnation*, Charles Gore (ed.), 41–81. London: John Murray.

Morgan, Robert with John Barton 1988. *Biblical Interpretation.* Oxford: Oxford University Press.

Murphy, George L. 1994. "Cosmology and Christology". *Science and Christian Belief* 6: 101–11.

Murphy, Roland L. 1992. "Wisdom in the OT". In *The Anchor Bible Dictionary*, D. N. Freedman (ed.), VI: 920–31. New York: Doubleday,.

Murray, Michael J. [2008] 2011. *Nature Red in Tooth and Claw: Theism and the Problem of Animal Suffering*. Oxford: Oxford University Press.

Nash, Kathleen S. 2000. "Time". In *Eerdmans Dictionary of the Bible*, David Noel Freedman, Allen C. Myers & Astrid C. Beck (eds), 1309–12. Grand Rapids, MI: Eerdmans.

Nichols, Terence L. 2002. "Evolution: Journey or Random Walk?". *Zygon* 37: 193–210.

Noble, T. A. 2009. "Original Sin and the Fall: Definitions and a Proposal". In *Darwin, Creation and the Fall: Theological Challenges*, R. J. Berry & T. A. Noble (eds), 99-129. Nottingham: Apollos.

Norris, Richard A. Jr (ed.) 1980. *The Christological Controversy*. Philadelphia, PA: Fortress.

Oden, Robert A. Jr 1992a. "Cosmogony, Cosmology". In *The Anchor Bible Dictionary*, D. N. Freedman (ed.), I: 1162–71. New York: Doubleday.

Oden, Robert A. Jr 1992b. "Myth and Mythology". In *The Anchor Bible Dictionary*, D. N. Freedman (ed.), IV: 946–56. New York: Doubleday.

Pannenberg, Wolfhart 1968. *Jesus: God and Man*. London: SCM.

Pannenberg, Wolfhart 1994. *Systematic Theology: Volume 2*, Geoffrey W. Bromiley (trans.). Edinburgh: T. & T. Clark.

Pannenberg, Wolfhart 2005. "Eternity, Time, and Space". *Zygon* 40: 97–106.

Parker, Andrew 2009. *The Genesis Enigma*. London: Doubleday.

Peacocke, Arthur 1996a. *God and Science: A Quest for Christian Credibility*. London: SCM.

Peacocke, Arthur 1996b. "The Incarnation of the Informing Self-Expressive Word of God". In *Religion and Science: History, Method, Dialogue*, W. Mark Richardson & Wesley J. Wildman (eds), 321–39. New York: Routledge.

Peacocke, Arthur 2001. "The Cost of New Life". In *The Work of Love: Creation as Kenosis*, John Polkinghorne (ed.), 21–42. Grand Rapids, MI: Eerdmans.

Pearce, E. K. Victor [1969] 1976. *Who was Adam?* Exeter: Paternoster.

Penrose, Roger 2010. *Cycles of Time: An Extraordinary New View of the Universe*. London: Bodley Head.

Peters, Ted 1989. "Cosmos as Creation". In *Cosmos as Creation: Theology and Science in Consonance*, Ted Peters (ed.), 45–113. Nashville, TN: Abingdon.

Peters, Ted 2010. "Constructing a Theology of Evolution: Building on John Haught". *Zygon* 45: 921–37.

Pimenta, Leander R. 1984. *Fountains of the Great Deep*. Chichester: New Wine Press.

Polkinghorne, John 1994. *Science and Christian Belief: Theological Reflections of a Bottom-Up Thinker*. London: SPCK.

Polkinghorne, John 1998. *Science and Theology: An Introduction*. London: SPCK.

Polkinghorne, John 2002. *The God of Hope and the End of the World*. London: SPCK.

Polkinghorne, John 2005. *Exploring Reality: The Intertwining of Science and Religion*. New Haven, CT: Yale University Press.

Polkinghorne, John 2011. *Science and Religion in Quest of Truth*. London: SPCK.

Provan, Iain, V. Philips Long & Tremper Longman III 2003. *A Biblical History of Israel*. Louisville, KY: Westminster John Knox Press.

Rogerson, J. W. 1974. *Myth in Old Testament Interpretation*. Berlin: De Gruyter.

Rogerson, J. W. 1976. *The Supernatural in the Old Testament*. Guildford: Lutterworth Press.

Rogerson, J. W. 1977. "The Old Testament View of Nature: Some Preliminary Questions". In *Instruction and Interpretation: Studies in Hebrew Language, Palestinian Archaeology and Biblical Exegesis*, Oudtestamentische Studien, A. S. van der Woude (ed.), 67–84. Leiden: Brill.

Rogerson, J. W. 1983. "The World-View of the Old Testament". In *Beginning Old Testament Study*, John Rogerson (ed.), 55–73. London: SPCK.

Rolston, Holmes III 2001. "Kenosis and Nature". In *The Work of Love: Creation as Kenosis*, John Polkinghorne (ed.), 43–65. Grand Rapids, MN: Eerdmans.

Rolston, Holmes III 2005. "Inevitable Humans: Simon Conway Morris's Evolutionary Paleontology". *Zygon* 40: 221–9.

Ruse, Michael 2001. *Can a Darwinian be a Christian? The Relationship between Science and Religion*. Cambridge: Cambridge University Press.

Ruse, Michael 2010. "Atheism, Naturalism and Science: Three in One?". In *The Cambridge Companion to Science and Religion*, Peter Harrison (ed.), 229–43. Cambridge: Cambridge University Press.

Russell, Robert John 1996. "T = 0: Is it Theologically Significant?". In *Religion and Science: History, Method, Dialogue*, W. Mark Richardson & Wesley J. Wildman (eds), 201–24. New York: Routledge.

Russell, Robert John 2002a. "Eschatology and Physical Cosmology: Preliminary Reflection". In *The Far-Future Universe: Eschatology from a Cosmic Perspective*, George F. R. Ellis (ed.), 266–315. Philadelphia, PA: Templeton Foundation Press.

Russell, Robert John 2002b. "Bodily Resurrection, Eschatology, and Scientific Cosmology". In *Resurrection: Theological and Scientific Assessments*, Ted Peters, Robert John Russell & Michael Welker (eds), 3–30. Grand Rapids, MI: Eerdmans.

Sanders, E. P. 1985. *Jesus and Judaism*. London: SCM.

Sanders, E. P. 1993. *The Historical Figure of Jesus*. London: Penguin.

Schloss, Jeffrey P. 2002. "From Evolution to Eschatology". In *Resurrection: Theological and Scientific Assessments*, Ted Peters, Robert John Russell & Michael Welker (eds), 56–85. Grand Rapids, MI: Eerdmans.

Schroeder, Gerald L. [1990] 1992. *Genesis and the Big Bang: The Discovery of Harmony Between Modern Science and the Bible*. New York: Bantam.

Segal, Robert A. 2011 "What is 'Mythic Reality'?". *Zygon* 46: 588–92.

Sharpe, Kevin & Jonathan Walgate 2003. "The Emergent Order". *Zygon* 38: 411–33.

Southgate, Christopher 2008. *The Groaning of Creation: God, Evolution and the Problem of Evil*. Louisville, KY: Westminster John Knox.

Southgate, Christopher 2011. "Re-reading Genesis, John and Job: A Christian Response to Darwinism". *Zygon* 46: 370–95.

Stoeger, William R. 2010. "God, Physics and the Big Bang". In *The Cambridge Companion to Science and Religion*, Peter Harrison (ed.), 173–89. Cambridge: Cambridge University Press.

Teilhard de Chardin, Pierre 1959. *The Phenomenon of Man*. London: Collins.

Tipler, Frank J. [1994] 1996. *The Physics of Immortality: Modern Cosmology, God and the Resurrection of the Dead*. London: Pan.

Tobin, Thomas H. 1992. "Logos". In *The Anchor Bible Dictionary*, D. N. Freedman (ed.), IV: 348–56. New York: Doubleday.

van Huyssteen, J. Wentzel 1998. *Duet or Duel? Theology and Science in a Postmodern World*. London: SCM.

von Rad, Gerhard 1972. *Wisdom in Israel*. London: SCM.

van Wolde, Ellen 2009. "Why the Verb ברא Does Not Mean 'to Create' in Genesis 1.1-2.4a". *Journal for the Study of the Old Testament* 34: 3–23.

Walton, John H. 2009. *The Lost World of Genesis One: Ancient Cosmology and the Origins Debate*. Downers Grove, IL: IVP.

Walton, John H. 2012. "Human Origins and the Bible". *Zygon* 47: 875–89.

Ward, Keith 1996a. *God, Chance and Necessity*. Oxford: Oneworld.

Ward, Keith 1996b. *Religion and Creation*. Oxford: Clarendon.

Ward, Keith 2008. *The Big Questions in Science and Religion*. West Conshohocken, PA: Templeton Press.

Ward, Keith 2010. *The Word of God? The Bible after Modern Scholarship*. London: SPCK.

Watts, Fraser 2008. "Concepts of Law and Probability in Theology and Science". In *Creation: Law and Probability*, Fraser Watts (ed.), 1–12. Aldershot: Ashgate.

Webster, John 2003. *Holy Scripture: A Dogmatic Sketch*. Cambridge: Cambridge University Press.

Wenham, Gordon J. 1987. *Genesis 1–15: Word Biblical Commentary Volume 1*. Nashville, TN: Thomas Nelson.

Westermann, Claus 1974. *Creation*. Philadelphia, PA: Fortress.

Westermann, Claus 1984. *Genesis 1–11: A Commentary*. London: SPCK.

Whitcomb, John C. & Henry M. Morris 1961. *The Genesis Flood: The Biblical Record and Its Scientific Implications*. Phillipsburg, NJ: Presbyterian & Reformed Publishing Company.

White Jr., Lynn 1967. "The Historical Roots of Our Ecological Crisis". *Science* 155: 1203–7.

Wilkins, John S. 2012. "Could God Create Darwinian Accidents?". *Zygon* 47: 30–42.

Wilkinson, David 2009a. "Reading Genesis 1–3 in the Light of Modern Science". In *Reading Genesis after Darwin*, Stephen C. Barton & David Wilkinson (eds), 127–44. Oxford: Oxford University Press.

Wilkinson, David 2009b. "Worshipping the Creator God: The Doctrine of Creation". In *Darwin, Creation and the Fall: Theological Challenges*, R. J. Berry & T. A. Noble (eds), 15–29. Nottingham: Apollos.

Wilkinson, David 2010. *Christian Eschatology and the Physical Universe*. London: T. & T. Clark.

Willis, W. Waite 2006. "A Theology of Resurrection: Its Meaning for Jesus, Us, and God". In *Resurrection: The Origin and Future of a Biblical Doctrine*, James H. Charlesworth (ed.), 187–217. New York: T. & T. Clark.

Wright, N. T. 1992. *The New Testament and the People of God*. London: SPCK.

Wright, N. T. 1996. *Jesus and the Victory of God*. London: SPCK.

Wyatt, Nick 2005. *The Mythic Mind: Essays on Cosmology and Religion in Ugaritic and Old Testament Literature*. London: Equinox.

Young, Frances 1991. "'Creatio ex Nihilo': A Context for the Emergence of the Christian Doctrine of Creation". *Scottish Journal of Theology* 44: 139–51.

Ziesler, John 1989. *Paul's Letter to the Romans*. London: SCM.

INDEX OF ANCIENT CITATIONS

INDEX